PRAISE FOR
THE PREVIOUS EDITION

"Truly astounding and enlightening. This book is so rich in ideas that before finishing it, one will likely have made plans to read it again."

—*Doug McManaman*

"Hibbs has a resplendent knowledge of, and a chagrined appreciation for, popular culture."

—*Weekly Standard*

"The best way to understand the influence of Nietzsche on popular culture."

—*Boundless Webzine*

SHOWS ABOUT NOTHING

NIHILISM IN POPULAR CULTURE

Thomas S. Hibbs

BAYLOR UNIVERSITY PRESS

Cover Design by Andrew Brozyna, AJB Design, Inc.
Cover Image © iStockPhoto/Ryan Lane

Library of Congress Cataloging-in-Publication Data

Hibbs, Thomas S.
  Shows about nothing : nihilism in popular culture / Thomas S. Hibbs.
-- 2nd rev. and expanded ed.
275 p. cm.
  Includes index.
  ISBN 978-1-60258-378-8 (pbk. : alk. paper)
  1. Nihilism (Philosophy) in motion pictures. 2. Nihilism (Philosophy)
on television. 3. Evil in motion pictures. 4. Culture in motion pictures.
I. Title.
  PN1995.9.N55H53 2011
  791.43'684--dc23

                          2011021756

BAYLOR
UNIVERSITY

Printed in the United States of America on acid-free paper with a
minimum of 30% pcw recycled content.

To my Parents' Children's Children

Lauren, Daniel, and Sara;
Jake, Will, Kendall, and Ben;
Michael and Cecelia

TABLE of CONTENTS

A FRAGMENTARY
PHILOSOPHICAL PREFACE

Frequently Asked Questions about Nihilism and Our Popular Culture

WHAT IS NIHILISM?

The term *nihilism* comes from the Latin word *nihil*, which means "nothing." It is the philosophy or state of life characterized by a lack of meaning or purpose. Nihilism means that there is no basis for distinguishing between good and evil, better and worse, noble and base. It undermines not just traditional religious belief but any normative claims, such as those found in politics concerning the dignity of human persons and the superiority of democracy to other forms of government and in science concerning the pursuit of truth about nature or the superiority of rational investigation to magic and superstition.

Nietzsche sometimes describes nihilism as arising from a two-worlds view of reality, a view that comes both from Platonism and from Christianity, each of which posits an ideal world over against this world and thus evacuates this world of meaning except as an instrument or means of reaching what is really real. But Nietzsche's conception of nihilism cuts more deeply. He associates it with democratic liberalism as well as Enlightenment science.

WHAT ARE THE SOURCES OF NIHILISM
IN LIBERAL DEMOCRACY?

Nietzsche thought that democracy had a leveling effect that was hostile to human excellence and sought to reduce everyone and every aspiration to a least common denominator.

A more politically astute commentator on liberal democracy, the great French political theorist Alexis de Tocqueville, saw liberal democracy as predicated on two principles, liberty and equality, that are not always in harmony. Like Nietzsche, although in less dramatic fashion, he worried about the way egalitarianism might curb liberty. Both principles, unmoored from one another and applied incorrectly and inordinately, can be sources of nihilism. Insofar as freedom comes to be understood in terms of autonomy, it opens the path to nihilism. If free choice is regarded as the highest value, then there is no standard in light of which we can appraise choice. The same can be said of certain forms of equality, not equality of opportunity or equality before the law but equality of opinion. If, in a sort of relativistic manner, every opinion is regarded as equal to every opinion, then there is no basis for distinguishing between better and worse, true and false, noble and base opinions.

WHAT CHARACTERIZES NIHILISTIC STORIES,
OR SHOWS ABOUT NOTHING?

These are stories in which conventional morality is depicted as bankrupt and in which there is no possible recourse beyond convention to, say, nature or God that could be the basis of moral deliberation and the discovery of meaning and purpose. Simply featuring a single character or even a series of characters who embody nihilism is insufficient to label the story itself as nihilistic. The story itself has to rule out the possibility of some basis upon which the audience might see beyond nihilism. For example, Shakespeare's tragedy of *Macbeth* features the lines spoken by the murderous Macbeth near the end of the play, "Life is a tale told by an idiot, full of sound and fury, signifying nothing." Macbeth, the character, is advocating a certain form of nihilism here, but that does not make the play nihilistic, as it shows the defeat of Macbeth and, even more, exhibits his own vice as the source of his nihilistic pronouncement.

ARE THERE TYPES OF STORIES THAT LOOK NIHILISTIC BUT ARE NOT?

Dark and forbidding stories or stories without any hint of a happy ending can seem nihilistic, as can stories that indict conventional morality. But an indictment rests upon the supposition that the audience has access to standards by which it can find conventional society wanting. Only if that possibility is canceled does nihilism arise. Dark stories with unhappy endings are not necessarily nihilistic; indeed, such stories, as in the case of classical tragedy, repose upon the supposition of ongoing human sympathy between audience and character; it also presupposes that the longings for justice, love, reconciliation, and friendship are natural and noble even where those desires are unrealized or frustrated. Nihilism arises only where these desires are treated as pointless and absurd, where they are explicitly or implicitly mocked.

IS AMERICAN CULTURE NIHILISTIC?

No, but it currently contains nihilistic strains. In fact, there is not one culture in America, but multiple, partially overlapping, and often conflicting subcultures. It is increasingly difficult to find any generally shared cultural markers. I am constantly surprised at how quickly not just books but also TV shows and even films disappear from memory as a result of cultural amnesia.

Consider the 2004 release of Mel Gibson's *The Passion of the Christ*. Before it was released, the assumption was that an R-rated religious film, saturated with bloody violence and in Aramaic with subtitles, simply could not fare well at the box office. Once it was released and quickly raced up the charts to become the best-selling R-rated film of all time, there were claims that its success was an indication of the rise of the silent majority of Christians eager for a film that spoke to its core convictions. There is something to that, but any widespread inference about the culture would also have to account for the fact that at the same time *The Passion* was setting box office records, the book sitting comfortably at the top of the fiction chart for book sales was *The Da Vinci Code*, a deconstruction of the central claims of the Gospel. And when *The Passion* finally relinquished its top spot at the box office, Quentin Tarantino's *Kill Bill* bumped it off.

It struck me a decade ago, and still does today, that one surprisingly strong strain in our culture is nihilistic.

ARE THERE ALTERNATIVES TO NIHILISM IN OUR CULTURE? WHAT ABOUT ROMANTICISM?

Romanticism is the most powerful grand myth operative in our popular culture, and it often takes on a religious tone of reverence for nature. Its presence can be seen in films from *E.T.* to *Avatar* and in films as diverse as *Forrest Gump, Dead Poets Society, Twilight: New Moon,* and *The Children of Men.*

Romanticism might be seen as a reaction against the nihilistic tendencies in radical strains of Enlightenment thought, which aims at rendering humans masters and possessors of nature. Construing the external world and even the human body itself as raw material to be manipulated for the sake of whatever ends human beings happen to desire, it sets the human person adrift, no longer at home in a world but in a constant state of conflict with the environment. If there is no natural or divine sense of limits or guidance in our stewardship of nature, then the pursuit of power becomes an untrammeled exercise in tyranny over nature and humanity.

Romanticism invites us to recover our innocence, to seek harmony with nature, and to live by a nobler code than that found in the calculative self-interest of modern economic systems. The problem with romanticism is that it locates human life in the midst of a series of conflicts whose resolution is far from clear. A reaction against the degrading and alienating effects of modern science and modern politics, romanticism embodies a set of oppositions: innocence versus civilization, nature versus technology, child versus adult, feeling versus reason. Thus, romanticism itself can generate nihilism, which arises from the sense that we are hopelessly alienated.

Are there stories that are simultaneously about nothing and something? That is, are there stories that wrestle with but do not succumb to nihilism?

Yes indeed. From *The Ice Storm* and *The Secret Lives of Dentists* to Christopher Nolan's *Batman* movies, film versions of J. K. Rowling's *Harry Potter* books, *The Book of Eli*, and Peter Jackson's film trilogy of Tolkien's *The Lord of the Rings*, popular American books and films address the sources of nihilism and provide imaginative visions that transcend, or at least do not succumb to, nihilism.

DOES NIHILISM ON SCREEN PRODUCE NIHILISM IN HUMAN SOULS? DOES HOLLYWOOD LEAD OR MERELY MIMIC THE CULTURE?

The causal relationship between entertainment and human behavior is highly complex. For example, while some want to indict violent films or video games or rap music as causes of the acts of violent teens, it seems clear that an awful lot must have gone wrong in someone's life for a person to watch, say, *Reservoir Dogs* or *Basketball Diaries* and decide, "I'm going to kill people." Can these forms of media act as contributing causes, among other causes, or in certain cases be the trigger for violence? Certainly. And it doesn't take much effort to see that large doses of toxic images and stories can wreak havoc in the souls of young or old. The chief impact is not overt, large-scale violence of the sort we have witnessed in school killings but the atrophying of the moral imagination.

Often, when Hollywood is attacked for its corrosive effects on the culture, it responds by saying that it is simply reflecting what is out there in the culture already. But this is a dishonest answer, as there is nothing Hollywood prizes more than the idea that it is the source of social reform or that it is the bastion of contemporary creative genius. At its best, Hollywood takes possibilities latent in our culture and makes them explicit by weaving them into a narrative and letting us see those possibilities lived out in human lives and communities.

WHAT IS THE POINT OF WATCHING SHOWS ABOUT NOTHING? CAN WE LEARN FROM THESE SHOWS?

There is little point to watching the most toxic shows, but other shows can illustrate the various sources of nihilism in our culture. Even when nihilistic shows instruct, they cannot, at least directly, do what art or even entertainment should do, which is to nourish the soul and form the moral imagination. Now, shows that acknowledge the possibility of nihilism and display paths by which it might be overcome can indeed nourish the soul.

ACKNOWLEDGMENTS

This book is a revised and greatly expanded version of *Shows about Nothing*, published by Spence Publishing in 1999. I remain indebted to publisher Tom Spence and editor Mitch Muncy for their help in the editing process and for their enthusiastic promotion of the book. The work they did promoting the book resulted in opportunities to write film reviews for *National Review Online* and to dozens of radio interviews, including many NPR shows such as *The Connection* and *On the Media*. Eventually, I began writing regular reviews for *National Review Online* and occasionally for the magazine. I have also written about film for *First Things, Books and Culture*, and *The Chronicle of Higher Education*. Spence Publishing also brought out my *Arts of Darkness: American Noir and the Quest for Redemption* (2008). The present book includes revised material from reviews that have appeared in these journals and magazines.

I began working in this area while I was a faculty member in the Philosophy Department at Boston College, a department that has not lost its soul. In addition to maintaining a serious commitment to Catholic liberal arts education, the department, chaired by Joseph Flanagan, S.J., and then Richard Cobb-Stevens, encouraged faculty to complement their scholarly work in an area of expertise with interdisciplinary research. My own work on Thomas Aquinas, contemporary ethics, and film benefited enormously from this genuinely liberal approach to education.

I began writing on, and teaching, film and philosophy for two reasons, both of which had to do with my experience of teaching undergraduates first at Boston College and now at Baylor University. First, I wanted to find a way to help students make connections between the work they were doing in the classroom reading texts in philosophy, literature, and theology and the world in which they are immersed when they are not in the classroom, a world of image, sound, and technology. In teaching texts and films together, I hoped students would become more reflective about, and more critical of, their favorite shows, films, and music. I also wanted them to see that TV series and films often have implicit philosophical assumptions about human life, about what counts as success or failure, what is to be admired or scorned, what is good or evil. Second, I hoped they would see that reading great texts could provide them with arguments, themes, stories, exemplary characters, and a vocabulary that would equip them to make discerning judgments about cultural products in our time.

When I began, I had some, but a vastly inadequate, sense of how much I would learn from students in the discussion of film and culture. After an initial adjustment from being passive, mentally inert recipients of cultural products to adopting a more reflective stance, students find, sometimes to their great surprise, that they have a great deal to say about these arts. They learn how to articulate what they see and to draw out the philosophical and theological issues latent in films and TV shows. They also learn to develop a language appropriate to the distinctive medium of film and to relate that to other media.

I have discussed nihilism, philosophy, and pop culture with students at Boston College, Baylor University, and dozens of other universities across the United States. The conversations have always been stimulating and enjoyable. Having continued to write about film since *Shows about Nothing* first appeared in 1999, I have often thought about updating the book. When Carey Newman, director of the Baylor University Press, expressed interest in such a project, I planned to add a new preface and a chapter or two to bring things up to date. But when I sat down to reread the original book, I realized I would need to rewrite much of what I'd written and add much more than I initially thought.

I am grateful to Carey Newman for his interest in this project and to Diane Smith and Jenny Hunt for the careful and meticulous work preparing the manuscript. Much initial editing was done by my able graduate assistant, John Spano, who also prepared the index and prodded me with helpful questions along the way.

Although I have revised the text in places to make my thesis clearer, I have not altered the thesis itself. Only in two places have I changed my interpretation of particular shows. Partly on the basis of conversations with William Peter Blatty, author of the book and screenplay of *The Exorcist*, I have altered somewhat my interpretation of *The Exorcist* and its engagement with nihilism. The only judgment that I have retracted is the alignment of *The Simpsons* with *Seinfeld* as a form of comic nihilism.

I have seen fit to subtract some material from the original book, to change the order in which I present some subjects, and to add quite a bit. The biggest change concerns the expanded treatment of shows that engage nihilism without succumbing to it. One of the most common questions asked of me after the release of the book had to do with alternatives to nihilism. Although I never stated that I thought American culture had become exclusively nihilistic, some thought that was my view. In fact, even in the original book, I offered examples of alternatives to nihilism, of which there are an even more significant number today than there were a decade ago. Expanding that portion of the book for this new edition should enable readers to understand nihilism itself better, as they now have numerous examples of shows that overcome nihilism.

The initial book received a good deal of critical attention, with reviews appearing in, among other magazines, *The American Enterprise*, *The Weekly Standard*, *Reason*, and *Society*. As I mentioned, the book was also the occasion of many radio interviews. In the course of those radio shows and after dozens of lectures on college campuses on the topic of popular culture, certain questions recur. Instead of writing a standard book introduction, I have included in the preface brief responses to the most significant questions.

1

NIHILISM, AMERICAN STYLE

In the introductory voice-over to Woody Allen's film *You Will Meet a Tall Dark Stranger* (2010), the narrator quotes Macbeth's lines: "Life is a tale told by an idiot, full of sound and fury, signifying nothing." In an interview with *Commonweal* just after the release of the film *Whatever Works* (2009) and not long before *Tall Dark Stranger*, Allen confesses to feeling "impotent against the overwhelming bleakness of the universe." He states, "Everybody knows how awful the world is and what a terrible situation it is and each person distorts it in a certain way that enables him to get through." Asked about the plot of *Crimes and Misdemeanors*, Allen's only truly successful serious film, in which the main character, a murderer, is surprised to discover that his conscience really does not bother him and that he has been able to move forward with his life, Allen states that there are people who

> commit terrible crimes and they have wonderful lives, wonderful, happy lives, with families and children, and they have done unspeakably terrible things. There is no justice, there is no rational structure to it. That is just the way it is, and each person figures out some way to cope. . . . Some people cope better than others. I was with Billy Graham once, and he said that even if it turned out in the end that there is no God and the universe is empty, he would still have had a better life than me. I understand

that. If you can delude yourself by believing that there is some kind of Santa Claus out there who is going to bail you out in the end, then it will help you get through. Even if you are proven wrong in the end, you would have had a better life.[1]

This may or may not be helpful as a commentary on his films; as a piece of amateur philosophy, it is sheer rubbish. There is no evidence that Billy Graham is actively deceiving himself or that he could maintain his hope and joy if he tried to embrace the Christian faith or any other by playing cognitive tricks on himself. Indeed, that is a bizarre, one is tempted to say incredible, model of how beliefs are formed. What might be more accurate is to say that the only way Woody Allen could imagine himself becoming a Christian would be for him actively to deceive himself. But what sort of belief would that be? There can be distraction or diversion, and for Allen, art seems to serve this episodic function, but once and for as long as nihilism takes hold, there is no remedy.

When the artist becomes a theorist, both off and on screen, of the meaninglessness of existence, the balm of art loses its power to assuage our fears and alleviate our malaise. When the film insists on telling you directly and repeatedly that life is pointless, that illusion is necessary, and illusions are to be valued insofar as they suit you, then the illusion is unmasked and no longer works as an illusion. The problem with the therapeutic bluntness is that whatever works does not work.

Always tempted by nihilism, Allen's early work was almost exclusively comic. If in the earlier films relationships are almost always doomed, marital love unreachable, and the purpose of individual lives unknown, there is nonetheless an accent upon the felt gesture of sympathy across the divide of the broken, impossible relationship. Ordinary human sympathy tempers the nihilism and affirms the viewer's desire for human connection and friendship. Only recently, and in films in which he does not appear as a character, has Allen seemed willing to allow his nihilistic theories to dominate his art. It is not surprising that the quality of his art has suffered considerably. Even in *Crimes and Misdemeanors*, the character espousing nihilism without regrets is but one character in a larger drama, and he speaks at a peculiar moment in his own life, the moment when he has the sudden realization that his world has not collapsed because of his heinous deeds. We might wonder whether his account of his own freedom from the qualms of conscience is not self-justifying or whether he will be able to sustain his equanimity, especially given that the lies about the murder of his adulterous lover cannot simply be kept in the past, locked away from his ongoing relationship with his wife.

Indeed, the suspicion that meaning is a construct gives rise to the thought of nihilism. As a popular song puts it, "When everything feels like the movies, you bleed just to know you're alive" ("Iris," Goo Goo Dolls). From *The Matrix* to *Inception*, many highly successful contemporary films begin from the assumption that what we have taken to be real is in fact a construct. The quest is to make clear the distinction between fantasy and reality and return to the latter. If the line becomes entirely blurred, then we are lost in a hall of mirrors where images end up reflecting one another. Reality dissolves into a self-referential trap.

Nihilism generates banality, an egalitarian sense of emptiness. But Allen feels compelled to bestow gravity upon nothingness by alluding to great literature. That is true of the opening quotation from *Macbeth* in *You Will Meet a Tall Dark Stranger* and of an allusion to Dostoevsky's *Crime and Punishment* in *Match Point*, a film that replays the central themes of *Crimes and Misdemeanors* in a much less interesting way. Dostoevsky's great novel of rebellion, guilt, and redemption might have had some place in *Crimes and Misdemeanors*, where the question of God is still a real one, but it is wholly without significance in *Match Point*, where there is no great passion, no great guilt, and no question of whether God and the devil are at war in the human heart. Even less appropriate is the passage from *Macbeth* in *Tall Dark Stranger.* The words themselves do not work here, as Allen's film is a rather tame tale of the role of chance in modern life, hardly a tale of sound and fury. Moreover, Allen turns the view of one character in *Macbeth* into the whole story, indeed into the story of all stories. But Shakespeare does not share Macbeth's nihilism; instead, he gives an account of how the murderous intentions "return to plague the inventor." The action of the play represents not the exaltation of nihilism but its defeat and the restoration of moral and political order. Nihilism is the vantage point of the morally depraved, not the normative judgment of the artist.

If art no longer communes with the good, the true, and the beautiful and if it feels duty bound (whence such an obligation in a nihilistic world?) to inform us that its magic is merely illusory, then it loses its capacity to enchant or even pleasantly distract. It loses its claim on us. Citing great works of the past, whose very assumptions the new art has dismissed as so much infantile wishful thinking, cannot improve matters.

Nihilism on screen is not nearly as terrifying as nihilism in real life. The recent suicide of an educated, handsome, witty thirty-five-year-old, Mitchell Heisman, on the steps of Memorial Church in Harvard Yard shocked his family. In his *Boston Globe* article (September 27, 2010), David Abell comments that Heisman's 1,905-page suicide note "included 1,433 footnotes, a 20-page bibliography, and more than 1,700 references to God and 200 references to the German philosopher Friedrich Nietzsche." In the note Heisman wrote, "Every word, every thought, and every emotion come back to one core problem: life is meaningless. . . . The experiment in nihilism is to seek out and expose every illusion and every myth, wherever it may lead, no matter what, even if it kills us."[2]

Serial killers, from Manson and Berkowitz to Ramirez and Dahmer, have often held the national imagination captive, and the killers' wacky theories have become as notorious as the heinous acts they committed. After he was apprehended, Ramirez taunted citizens, the media, and the justice system with the Nietzschean line, "I'm beyond you. I'm beyond good and evil." More recently, from Paducah, Kentucky, and Jonesboro, Arkansas, to Pearl, Mississippi, and Springfield, Oregon, towns known for nothing other than their decent, law-abiding citizens have given birth to children capable of positively demonic deeds. Aside from the rural settings and multiple victims, another common feature of these killings has been the influence of films such as *Natural Born Killers* and *Basketball Diaries*, of fantasy video games, and of the nihilistic lyrics of Marilyn Manson.

Whatever one makes of the causal relationship between the endemic violence of our popular culture and the behavior of those immersed in it, this much is clear. The universal availability of popular culture—through videos, cable television, radio, and the Internet—means that no place can be protected from its corrosive influence. Wherever you are, it can find you.

As Michael Medved, one of our most informed and eloquent critics of contemporary mores, notes, we have no other culture than popular culture, and popular culture is Hollywood, especially television. In *Hollywood vs. America: Popular Culture and the War on Traditional Values*, Medved details Hollywood's strong amoralist bent and argues that the entertainment industry is hostile to mainstream American values. There is little doubt that Hollywood's nihilism has the effect of coarsening our public life, desensitizing us to violence, and making us generally more cynical. In its celebration of the grotesque artistry of destruction, of evil for its own sake, and of untutored, adolescent self-expression, Hollywood promotes a debased, Nietzschean culture and the side of Nietzsche that values unrestrained creativity.

It does not follow from Hollywood's nihilism, however, that the primary target of the entertainment industry is the traditional values espoused by Republicans or the Christian Coalition. Such hostility is incidental, for nihilism cuts much more deeply. As we shall see, it attacks the very foundations of modern politics, whose assumptions both the Left and the Right share. It puts into question democratic ideals such as individual rights and human dignity, the politics of equality and consensus, the pursuit of happiness, and the possibility of progress, even modern science and medicine. These ideals supply the framework for what it means to lead a good human life and the principles for our code of good and evil. If they are exposed as bankrupt, then to move beyond good and evil, to attempt to transcend our conventional moral code, can be seen as liberating, as a perverse affirmation of life and freedom in opposition to a degrading moral system. The pursuit of evil has a certain grandeur to it, or at least it seems cool and hip.

Those of us inclined to be critical of Hollywood would do well to ponder the following questions: Why does our democratic culture breed such demonic characters? And why should American citizens be so captivated by these figures of rebellion both in real life and in fictional accounts? Indeed, American fascination with crime and criminality remains high even as there has been a remarkable decline of serious crime in most large cities. Furthermore, nihilistic premises pervade our popular culture, infiltrating not just horror films and violent movies of the week but also the most successful mainstream sitcom of the last thirty years, *Seinfeld*, a show about the comical consequences of life in a world void of any ultimate significance or fundamental meaning. By its own account, it is a show about nothing. Is there perhaps some as yet unnoticed link between the American experiment and nihilism? Can our contemporary popular culture be seen as drawing out the natural consequences of certain strains of liberal individualism? That is precisely the suggestion we will explore in the present study. The thesis gains some credibility from the fact that thinkers as diverse and as profound as Nietzsche, Tocqueville, T. S. Eliot, and Arendt have detected a subtle link between certain forms of democratic liberalism and nihilism.

As Harvard political philosopher Harvey C. Mansfield observes, Friedrich Nietzsche, the nineteenth-century German philosopher best known for announcing the death of God, is the philosopher of our times. He surfaces with some regularity in popular culture. In the 1991 film *Cape Fear*, an execrable film in the otherwise glorious career of Martin Scorsese, the evil protagonist, played by Robert DeNiro, takes breaks from terrorizing, mutilating, biting, blinding, and raping the locals to visit the library and read *Thus Spake Zarathustra* by Nietzsche. Woody Allen's films offer frequent comic reflections on Nietzschean themes. In the midst of one of his many forays into pop philosophy, Allen has a desperate character, played by himself, rehearse various philosophical analyses of the meaning of life. He mentions Nietzsche's theory of the eternal return but flippantly dismisses it: "It wouldn't be worth it. I'd have to sit through the Ice Capades again." Allen pokes as much fun at nihilistic theories as he does at claims to have discovered the meaning of life.

Both scholars and laypeople see Nietzsche as the philosopher of nihilism—the era, according to Nietzsche, of the ultimate degradation and degeneration of man. Francis Fukuyama caused a stir when he suggested, in *The End of History and the Last Man,* that the nearly worldwide acceptance of democracy means we are now living in a postrevolutionary age, that humanity has no great battles left to fight, and hence that we have reached the end of history. Absent some clearly defined enemy or profound challenge, there is a danger that the tensions and springs of human greatness will dissipate, that human beings will become what Nietzsche called the "last men," who have a calm indifference to all elevated aspirations.[3] Writing as a social critic influenced more by Tocqueville than by Nietzsche, Andrew Delbanco traces three great moments in the American manner of construing the purpose of our lives together: the first, the Puritan moment, was organized around the Christian God; the second, which comes to fruition in Lincoln, focused on the sacred nation itself; and the third, our current era, a period of liberation from all external standards, bestows the highest value on the self. Our era is an era of irony, of detachment from deep and lasting convictions.[4]

NIETZSCHE AND DEMOCRATIC NIHILISM

In *Thus Spake Zarathustra,* the eponymous hero predicts the coming of the last man: "Alas, the time of the most despicable man is coming, he that is no longer able to despise himself. Behold, I show you the last man. What is love? What is creation? What is longing? What is a star? Thus asks the last man and blinks. The earth has become small, and on it hops the last man who makes everything small."[5] The last man is timid, enervated, self-enclosed, and self-satisfied, an industrious economic animal who always finds it in his best interest to go with the flow, to conform to the dictates of common opinion. Yet he does not regard this conformity and passivity as slavish because there is no one person to whom he submits. In following the majority, he does but follow his own will. Zarathustra expatiates, "No shepherd and one herd. Everybody wants the same, everybody is the same: whoever feels different goes voluntarily into a madhouse. . . . One has one's little pleasure for the day and one's little pleasure for the night: but one has a regard for health." When Zarathustra speaks these words to ordinary citizens, instead of being insulted by his images of their shallow and petty souls, they clamor, "Turn us into these last men."

Nietzsche is virulently antidemocratic, for he believes that the politics and science of the Enlightenment preserve what ought to perish and are at war with greatness and singularity. The imperative of the herd, he tells us, is that there should "one day be nothing anymore to be afraid of."[6] The herd's longing for a cessation of struggle, though, is an "anti-biological" pathology: "Life itself is a consequence of war; society is a means to war." Democratic morality is the code of the slave, who finds existence so painful that he needs morality and religion to make life worth living. His morality is essentially one of utility; his religion is one of pity. Nietzsche scorns the modern, liberal notion of progress with its goals of equality for all and the easing of all physical and psychic trials. He contrasts the slavish with the noble: "You want . . . to abolish suffering. And we? It really seems that we would rather have it higher and worse than ever. Well-being as you understand it—that is no goal, that seems to us an end, a state that soon makes man ridiculous and contemptible—that makes his destruction desirable." Only through the "discipline of great suffering" does man, the "as yet undetermined animal," develop.[7]

Not all conform to common opinion, however, especially the opinion concerning the equality of all. In some, there remains the desire for excellence, for transcending the life of the herd. The society of the last man is adept at satisfying nearly all desires for pleasure, but it cannot satiate—indeed, it positively frustrates—the will to excel, to prove oneself superior to others. The part of the soul that seeks excellence, which Plato called the spirited part, displays itself in circumstances of danger and risk and finds little room for exercise in the competition with neighbors over the accumulation of better, newer, and bigger consumer goods.

Spiritedness is distinct from the other passionate part of the soul, the erotic. Our culture also distorts this part of the soul. Classically understood, eros is not reducible to the desire for bodily pleasure, even less to the gratification of the sexual appetite, but encompasses these desires within a longing for beauty and wholeness. By offering citizens an endless array of petty delights, consumer societies eviscerate eros and sap the human soul of its elevating power. As advertisers are well aware, sex sells, and the perpetuation of the myth that we are still repressed Victorians plays nicely into the machinations of the market. Couple this with another myth, that orgasm is the most authentic experience, and we have a recipe for transforming the pursuit of happiness into the pursuit of the perfect climax. Such a serial and horizontal pursuit closes off the transcending and integrating aspiration of eros.

The *pursuit* of happiness has always been problematic. It invites an endless and ultimately unsatisfying search and diverts our attention from the past and the present to the yet-to-be-realized future. Tocqueville detected in this phenomenon the source of the peculiar melancholy and restlessness of the American spirit. Yet Nietzsche notes that some may come to find such a pursuit "ridiculous and contemptible." They must undertake a different sort of pursuit or quest amid stifling democratic mores. Spirited people, for example, sometimes find fulfillment in the world of high finance, in the aspiration for unadulterated capitalist competition. In Tom Wolfe's highly successful novel *The Bonfire of the Vanities* and in its woeful film version, Wall Street brokers vie to become masters of the universe. The amoralism of that way of life and its attractiveness to the spirited soul are also depicted in the movie *Wall Street*, in which Michael Douglas delivers his famously blunt speech in praise of raw greed. Although the unrestrained greed of Wall Street would not achieve the highest rank in Nietzsche's hierarchy of values, it comes closer than does socialism. With its morality of selfless altruism, socialism runs counter to the fundamental principle of "growth": "to have and to want to have more."[8] The basic truth of existence is that "A living thing seeks above all to discharge its strength—life itself its will to power; self-preservation is only one of the indirect and most frequent results."[9] When the desire for self-preservation becomes dominant, we are well on our way to nihilism, to emptying human life of all meaning, of any distinction between higher and lower. Given the bankruptcy of modern politics, of its tidy division of persons into normal and abnormal, the pursuit of evil—at least what society deems evil—can be a sign of health and life.

The lowly, according to Nietzsche, put pressure on the great to conform to the laws of the majority. Since the slavish soul is timid, fearful, and unable to form an opinion of itself without the assistance of others, it resents independence. Nietzsche depicts the war of the slave against the noble soul thus: "What has been deified? The value instincts in the community. What has been slandered? That which set apart the highest men from the lowest, the desires that create clefts."[10] The need of most human beings to believe in a moral universe is proof for Nietzsche that lies and self-deception are essential conditions of human life. Once one acknowledges that untruth is a condition of life, one can transcend traditional codes of good and evil. This recognition is closely allied to Nietzsche's famous teaching on the death of God. He does not mean that a supreme being once existed and now has passed out of existence; rather, the human capacity for creating an absolute moral law is also a capacity for the creation of a divinity as the source and guarantor of the law. Nihilism ensues from the death of God, that is, from the growing sense that no religious or moral code is credible. Yet this "pessimism," Nietzsche holds, is but a "preliminary form of nihilism."[11]

Nihilism itself is "ambiguous" between its active and passive forms: the latter is a mark of "decline and recession," whereas the former is "a sign of increased power."[12] The chaos following the death of God is likely to lead many to despair, to a stagnation of the creative will; for others, it will engender a creative violence greater than that known in any previous age. Thus, Nietzsche foresaw that the twentieth century would be a time of unrivaled violence. Unlike many who blithely advocate individual self-creation, as if it brings about an epoch of harmony and peace, Nietzsche anticipates and readily embraces the destructive consequences of the desire for self-creation. The belief that to create one must first destroy leads Nietzsche to celebrate the antipolitical virtue of creative boldness—antipolitical because it is not subordinate to a common vision of the goods it supposedly defends. The advent of nihilism deprives us of any common vision as it unveils the arbitrariness of all codes of good and evil, and Nietzsche's own project might be seen precisely as the destruction of all previously existing religious and moral codes. The noble soul, which understands its desires as self-justifying, needs no extrinsic justification for such destruction. Nietzsche's great hope is that precisely through the suffering and disorientation of the nihilistic era there will emerge a more profound and higher type of man. He does not believe that the rejection of the slavish distinction of good and evil means that no appraisal of actions or ways of life is possible. He consistently praises the healthy over the sickly soul, ascending over descending patterns of life, and the affirmation over the negation of life.

The two most profound twentieth-century followers of Nietzsche, the German Heidegger and the French Foucault, became, respectively, a notorious Nazi sympathizer and an advocate of the liberating power of sadomasochistic sexuality. Echoing Nietzsche's celebration of extremes, Foucault lauds the "limitless presumption of appetite" and counsels the "transcendence of reason in violence." As Roger Shattuck has shown, the great authority in these matters is the Marquis de Sade, who pronounced a "new Gospel" of *"crime-connaissance"* through creative sexual violence.[13] In Sade's novel *Juliette*, the main character states, "When one has become accustomed to scorn the laws of nature on one point, one cannot find any pleasure unless one transgresses all of them one after another."[14] Crude versions—can there be non-crude versions?—of this principle can be found in the contemporary subgenre of horror film known as torture porn and in the TV series *Nip/Tuck*, a show in which plastic surgery opens up the path to the radical reconstruction of the human body in the spheres of medicine and sexuality. Since prohibitions serve only the negative function of enhancing the exhilaration of transgression, these projects are subject to the law of diminishing returns. An especially rigorous practice of asceticism is required to revive and intensify the experience of pleasure. The practice of the new gospel mimics as it inverts the life of Christ. It exercises asceticism on the body not for the sake of moderating the passions that thwart knowledge and love of others but for the sake of ever more refined manipulation of the bodies of others. In lieu of a forgetfulness of self in love of another, "impersonal egoism"—in the words of Bataille—treats the body as a "vile thing." Anyone who stops at theory and fails to embrace this raw, nihilistic truth in practice is a bourgeois coward.

But there is a tension in Nietzsche between an amoralism that repudiates all objective standards and a distinctively hierarchical kind of thinking that ranks souls on the basis of their vigor, health, power, and creativity. The very distinction between slave and noble morality presupposes a judgment of what is better and worse, higher and lower. Nietzsche simultaneously insists that there is a rank of value and that at the top of that scale resides radical self-creation. By making man the creator, Nietzsche would vindicate the claims of humanity against the Judeo-Christian God. Human creativity will now supplant the transcendent creator of all things ex nihilo. Although the blatant hubris of this project renders it comically implausible, the real difficulty is that the exaltation of man as creator seems to relativize all values, leaving nothing in light of which the "revaluation of all values" might occur.

For Nietzsche, nihilism means "the highest values devalue themselves," that the "aim is lacking," and that "'Why?' finds no answer."[15] The long reign of Christian morality, which is still operative in modern politics and especially in the naive faith of Enlightenment science in objective truth, "was the great antidote against . . . nihilism."[16] The disappearance of these antidotes means, "Man has lost faith in his own value when no infinitely valuable whole works through him."[17] Nonetheless, Nietzsche forges ahead and invites the crisis as a means of purification, of restoring an "order of rank according to strength."[18] We can see here the reemergence of the model of the virile, heroic warrior, whose distinguishing mark is a creative and courageous boldness; it is the antithesis of what Nietzsche took to be the feminine, Christian virtues of humility and sympathy. It is a "measure of strength to what extent we can admit to ourselves, without perishing, the merely apparent character" of the world, the "necessity of lies."[19]

It is not surprising that Nietzsche thought of the nihilistic era as tragic because it would mercilessly lay bare the tremendous tension between, on the one hand, the human aspiration for meaning and purpose and, on the other, the pointlessness of such longings. The virtues that Nietzsche praises—courageous resolve and truthfulness about the nonexistence of all objective ideals—are the virtues of those who heroically and tragically confront the emptiness of human life, and there is something noble and edifying in their struggle. It is, however, difficult to sustain the seriousness of the struggle in the face of its meaninglessness. Pointlessness mocks strenuous effort. If no ennobling affirmation emerges from the era of nihilism, then the struggle itself comes to seem foolish and laughable. The tragic thus degenerates into a comic satire of all things serious and elevated.

The problem with the project of revaluing all traditional values is not only that it entails the destruction of the weak; indeed, it involves a great risk even for the noble soul. However much one might sympathize with Nietzsche's diagnosis of the incredible shrinking modern man, one wonders whether his cure is not worse than the disease. Instead of the affirming way of life that Nietzsche wished to substitute for the negating life of the slave, his apparent exaltation of the will can easily be seen as an essentially negative and empty existence defying standards and overstepping boundaries. The difficulty, then, with inviting nihilism, the "unwelcome guest," into the heart of civilization is that it deprives us of any grounds for retaining the elevating and ennobling aspect of Nietzsche's thought. The heroic confrontation with nihilism may be inspiring for a time, but its long-term result is likely to be the trivialization of all aspiration, the inability to distinguish between higher and lower. Instead of providing a way to overcome nihilism, Nietzsche's remedy seems only to immerse us more fully in it. By exalting the confrontation of the creative will with nothingness, Nietzsche hoped to revive the grandeur of the tragic hero. But the absence of any goal or standard in light of which we might appraise the hero's life as noble opens the possibility of a comic reversal in our perception of the hero, whose longings now seem silly and farcical. Comic nihilism, with which Woody Allen and the Coen brothers so often flirt, comes to fruition on *Seinfeld*.

Another problem with advocating the self-deification of man is his temporality and finitude. The will can only will forward, not backward. All it can do to gain control over what has already happened is to eradicate or alter its influence on the present. This is why destruction is integral to creative activity, as Nietzsche understands it. Although it is difficult for us to will the whole of the future, let alone to try to stand outside time and will the past, present, and future, this is precisely the strategy that Nietzsche advocates in his doctrine of the eternal return: "Let us think this thought in its most terrible form: existence as it is, without meaning or aim, yet recurring inevitably without any finale of nothingness: the eternal recurrence."[20] In spite of its implausibility, the eternal recurrence captures Nietzsche's sense that the remedy for nihilism involves uprooting from one's soul any vestige of resentment toward life and instead affirming the whole of existence.

Whatever might be the deficiencies of Nietzsche's godlike affirmation of the whole, more modest cyclical journeys can foster growth and development or a new and deeper appreciation of one's point of departure. American film has produced a variety of narratives of the return. There are sentimental versions, as in Dorothy's chant "there's no place like home" in *The Wizard of Oz*. And there are morally serious versions, as in Simba's somber and edifying affirmation of his role in the cycle and hierarchy of nature in his return to his kingdom at the end of *The Lion King*. After the death of his father, Simba's passage from childhood to an adult acceptance of his duty is interrupted. Simba gets caught in a world of endless adolescence, whose theme song, "hakuna matata," promises no worries, no responsibility, and no connection to anything other than immediate gratification. There is an instructive irony here. The chief threat to the moral seriousness *The Lion King* persuasively portrays is the sort of shopping-mall mentality that Disney so effectively markets: forgetfulness of the past and the sense that we are no more than our momentary preferences. Consider, by contrast, the pivotal scene in *The Lion King*. Simba's father appears to him, chastises him for neglecting his place, and counsels, "You are more than what you have become." His final command, "Remember," resonates throughout the film.

One of the more nuanced recent variations on the theme of the return is the comedy *Groundhog Day*, which features Bill Murray as a smug, crude, and cynical weatherman sent to cover Groundhog Day festivities in Punxsutawney, Pennsylvania. Murray loathes the town, its people, and their quaint way of life. He cannot wait to leave. But when a snowstorm renders the highway out of town impassable, Murray reluctantly returns to town for the night. To his consternation, he awakens the next morning, and for many mornings thereafter, to find himself repeating Groundhog Day. While Murray remembers each previous day, the others in Punxsutawney do not. Since he is attracted to the station manager, played by Andie MacDowell, who has accompanied him to Punxsutawney, he devotes each day to some new and increasingly extravagant ruse of seduction. None succeed. Desperate to escape, he resorts to numerous methods of suicide—including some that would take the groundhog out with him—only to awaken yet again in the past. In *Groundhog Day*, the cycle is a motif of determinism, illustrative of the way vice turns us in on ourselves, stifling freedom and development. Predictably, Murray eventually learns the difference between love and self-gratification and comes to acknowledge the humanity of others. Only after he undergoes a conversion of character does he awaken in and to the future. The irony is that the cycle is the vehicle for the recovery of the self and the overcoming of alienation from others.

Yet without a deep appreciation for and reaffirmation of the past, the cycle becomes what it is in much contemporary drama: a motif for determinism and entrapment. One risk is that fear, terror, and loathing will give way to jaded amusement.

Nietzsche would, of course, expect such responses from democratic man who, he contends, is capable of only passive nihilism. But it is hard to see this as an inappropriate response to a philosophy that grounds the future of humanity in the privileged acts of will of the philosopher-artist. Rather than pointing the way toward the overcoming of nihilism, Nietzsche's thought would so fully engulf us in nihilism that the very notion of a way out or a way beyond might come to seem unintelligible and laughable. Nihilism thus simultaneously opens and forecloses possibilities.

AMERICAN CULTURE AND THE UNRAVELING
OF THE ENLIGHTENMENT

Before turning to an extended consideration of contemporary popular culture, it may help to have before us a sketch of the development of modern liberalism and of America's place in it. This development can be described in terms of three stages in the understanding of the rights and dignity of the individual. Liberalism first expressed its teaching in the social contract, the mutual recognition of rights bestowed on us by virtue of our nature or of God or both. Eventually, liberalism came to view our dignity as grounded in our capacity for self-legislation, beholden to no external authority. Finally, it acknowledged individualism as aesthetic self-creation. How did it move from the first understanding to the third?[21]

The original liberal project grounded the rights of the individual in assertions about nature, or at least about a common human condition, and placed clear limitations upon the exercise of individual rights. John Locke's *Two Treatises* and Jefferson's Declaration of Independence appeal to nature and nature's God as the basis of our rights: "We hold these truths to be self-evident: that all men are endowed by their creator with certain inalienable rights." Classical liberalism saw the need to give some sort of account of the source of rights and liberties. Another important feature of the classical view is its insistence that rights have corresponding duties; without this assumption, rights could not be the basis of the liberal social contract.

This is the model of American liberalism that dominated the classical period of Hollywood and the early years of television, lasting well into the 1960s. The most successful creator of these sorts of American narratives was undoubtedly Frank Capra, who saw his films as vehicles for the communication of an American civil religion. Of *You Can't Take It with You,* he said that it was an opportunity "to dramatize Love They Neighbor in living drama. What the world's churches were preaching to apathetic congregations, my universal language of film might say more entertainingly to audiences." In *Mr. Deeds Goes to Town* and *Mr. Smith Goes to Washington,* Capra juxtaposes the slick, jaded, and conniving denizens of the big city, and especially of the U.S. Congress, to the straightforward virtue and simple pleasures of the ordinary, unassuming American citizen. These films put on trial the corruptions and flaws of American democracy, but the accuser is not the cynical loner. He is, rather, the embodiment of the virtues and ideals that America was founded upon and to which it remains tied. Even most of the bad guys in these films are treated with a comic touch that enables us to perceive their redeeming qualities. The most severe judgment in these films is bestowed upon the unfeeling capitalism of the usurious Mr. Potter in *It's a Wonderful Life* (1945).

These movies exalt the virtues of old-fashioned American individualism, which really is not individualism at all. Capra often sets an individual, Deeds or Smith, for example, against a group, but the individual himself embodies the ideals that the group is presently falling short of. Capra's films are stories that revive America's founding spirit. In this America, there is no such thing as a completely private life to be disposed of as one wishes. In *It's a Wonderful Life*, George Bailey's attempted suicide is an act of despairing self-absorption. When his guardian angel, Clarence, intervenes to rescue him from the frigid waters, George insists that he and everyone else would have been better off had he never existed. Nearly destroyed by his sense of failure, George Bailey is the closest anyone comes to nihilism in a Capra film. To instruct George, the angel grants him his wish of nonbeing. He learns in painful detail what it means to lack the recognition of neighbors, friends, and family. More positively, he realizes that individualism is a dangerous and destructive illusion, that each life is mysteriously intertwined with many others.

All of these films are comic, even when they include a treatment of serious matters and real evils, and are at least implicitly theological in structure. In fact, these films contain elements of film noir. Mr. Smith undergoes tremendous physical and emotional turmoil as he attempts to fight off not only his external, human opponents, the corrupt members of Congress, but also his internal temptation to despair. George Bailey's angel leads him through the city that would have been had he never existed; he must endure the sight of his town turned into a living hell named Pottersville. If Capra's America is finally an image of paradise, it is always a potential inferno from which art must strive to rescue us.

Related strategies are on display in *Casablanca*, a film in which Humphrey Bogart plays the sort of diffident, detached, tough guy for which he would become famous in a series of classic noir films, beginning with *The Maltese Falcon*. A saloon keeper in Nazi-occupied Casablanca, Rick, who sticks his "neck out for nobody," appears to be motivated exclusively by rational self-interest. But he is a man with a complicated past. By the end of the film, in what is perhaps the most memorable concluding scene in all of American film, love, patriotism, and friendship emerge as the prevailing motives in his life—a scene that mesmerizes and inspires Woody Allen's character in *Play It Again, Sam.*

Just as religions must face the problem of evil in the world, so too must nations face its presence in their land. This test has special significance when the nation is America. The most prescient observer of things American, the nineteenth-century Frenchman Alexis de Tocqueville, called democracy a "providential fact" and America the "image of democracy."[22] As our faith in the American experiment waxes and wanes, so does faith in the experiment of the modern world. Capra's films are defenses of the essential goodness and justifications of the ultimate victory of American democracy. The gravity of evil is never the final world, just as the failure, despair, and isolation of the protagonists are only momentary and apparent. The protagonists embody the American dream and, although they begin at a lowly level, achieve an exalted state, just as do the characters in classical comedies. For Capra also, America is a providential fact.

Both in film and on television, the dramatic justification of the American way of life used to focus on the justice system, especially the courts of law. Tocqueville observed that the court system was so deeply woven into the fabric of American life that children introduce the jury system into their games. That system is an embodiment of the American principle of equality before the law. Of course, there have been egregious violations of that ideal in our history. Even when it appears to work well, its success is always tenuous. In according rights to the accused, it risks protecting the guilty rather than the innocent. By insisting on trial by jury, it puts the fate of the accused in the hands of untutored citizens. One film that addresses this inconsistency is *To Kill a Mockingbird* (1962), based on the best-selling and Pulitzer Prize-winning novel of the same title by Harper Lee (1960). The film is set in Macon, Georgia, in 1932 where a young black man, Tom Robinson, is wrongly accused of raping and beating a white girl. The hero of the story is Atticus Finch, a widowed father of two and the small-town lawyer who defends Tom.

The film is replete with peculiarly American maxims. Atticus explains the term *compromise* to his daughter as an "agreement reached by mutual consent." In so doing, he gives eloquent expression to the principle of the social contract. His summation before the jury invokes Jefferson's great principle of the equality of all citizens. Finch argues that equality has special application to the courts, which are intended to be the "great levelers." But the lessons involve much more than exercises in Enlightenment procedural justice. The title is taken from a story, which Atticus relates to his own children, that his father told him on the day he gave Atticus a gun. Atticus' father would prefer that he shoot only at cans, but since he knew Atticus would eventually get around to shooting birds, his only prohibition was the killing of mockingbirds. It is a sin, Atticus' father tells him, to kill a harmless mockingbird.

Although Atticus is by education and character superior to others in the town, he does not denigrate them but appreciates their differences in character. To see things from a neighbor's point of view, one has to "crawl around in his skin," he tells his daughter. One has to get to know one's neighbors, who are of different races, religions, and economic status. Not an abstract procedure but recognition of our common humanity is the basis of the American regime. The film also teaches lessons in the courageous and restrained facing of violence and willful deception. Atticus and his children are taunted as "nigger lovers"; a drunken Bob Ewell spits on him. Through all this, he remains calm and counsels his children, especially his volatile daughter, Scout, to do the same. In these Hollywood films, courage is not Nietzsche's antipolitical virtue, nor is it depicted as sufficient in itself. It serves the maintenance of social order and the protection of the innocent; to succeed it must be accompanied by a host of other virtues.

Mockingbird celebrates American virtues in the ordinary man. Atticus is as concerned about raising his now motherless children as he is about his own career. In fact, his profession is more like a calling than a career. After he has lost the case, a neighbor comments to his children that some men are "born to do unpleasant jobs." Atticus' virtues, as is generally true of the common man, are most evident in his failures. *Mockingbird*'s affirmation of the American way of life is remarkably restrained, sober, and modest. Atticus is the embodiment of what Walker Percy calls southern stoicism.

Yet even the tragic depiction of America in a film like *Mockingbird* can seem to gloss over American failings. The optimism, rationality, and legitimacy of the liberal Enlightenment project remains open to question. In this context, the quest for evil can be a healthy response to the naive and dehumanizing optimism of Enlightenment liberalism. Such a quest is not new to American popular culture. American films of a previous era, especially in film noir, took the possibility of nihilism seriously and even flirted with presenting the criminal as a heroic counter to a timid and decadent society. Although these productions are markedly different from more recent approaches to nihilism, they do anticipate the recent critique of America, its benevolence, and its system of justice, its belief in equality and dignity, and its aspiration to happiness.

While there is no consensus on precisely what defines film noir, its exemplary instances occur in the post-World War II period, a period of tremendous success, progress, and growth in America.[23] Yet it was also a period of unease, uncertainty, and foreboding. The populist films of that era provide positive visions of American life, but film noir captures the disconcerting and often suppressed sense that something is deeply awry. It is a dark negation intended to counter the bright affirmation of the public culture of the era. Yet it is never a simple negation. Indeed, film noir is both dramatically and artistically complex. Its darkness and shadows, its emphasis on absence over presence, underscore the depth and mystery of the most mundane experiences. Into such a disorienting, threatening, and yet inviting world, noir thrusts its would-be hero, who sets out on a quest to solve a particular mystery. But the quest is equally a search for communication, love, and meaning. At a crucial juncture in his journey, the hero is often joined by a woman, who as often as not ends by deceiving and destroying him. As one critic puts it, noir involves a "double quest: to solve the mystery of the villain and of the woman."[24] The modern city, in which the plot is usually set, is a kind of labyrinth, which provides a "set of conditions producing a*maze*ment" and which is symbolic of "meaning's multiplicity and elusiveness."[25]

The opening scene of *The Killers* (1947) introduces us to ruthless killers who sit in a diner waiting for the man they plan to murder, Ole Anderson, known as the Swede (played by Burt Lancaster). To employees and customers, they speak with frank brutality: "We're killing him for a friend, just to oblige a friend." After the gunmen leave for the Swede's apartment, a customer rushes to warn him. But the Swede shows no interest in escaping his fate, commenting, "Once I did something wrong." He is murdered, and we are left wondering what he did and why he lost his will to live. An insurance investigator, played by Edmund O'Brien, is our guide to the Swede's life story; the rest of the film is mostly a series of flashbacks prompted by the insurance investigator's interviews with acquaintances of the Swede. His is a hard-luck story, the tale of a failed boxer who is led by desperation and love to become involved in a heist. Deceived by a beautiful but crafty woman into believing that the rest of the gang is plotting to exclude him from their profits, he is duped into stealing the heist money, which she then steals from him. The story is not really about the killers, who reappear at the end only to be killed, but about the fragile psyche of the boxer, whom circumstances and unrequited love conspire to destroy.

Film noir does not, then, present us with heroes who stand beyond good and evil but with the seeming impossibility of heroism in a hostile world. It proffers "a disturbing vision . . . that qualifies all hope and suggests a potentially fatal vulnerability."[26] Still, the downfall of the protagonist is not entirely negative. The tragic structure of the would-be hero's quest underscores the gap between his longing for intelligibility, meaning, and love, on the one hand, and his failure to figure things out and achieve salvation, on the other. This longing itself provides the motive force for the drama, for its attempt to "formulate our place in the cultural landscape." Despite its opposition to our simplistic assumptions about shared public meaning, noir does not finally treat that aspiration as foolish or silly but as ennobling. In attempting to speak both of our desire for meaning and of the obstacles to realizing that desire, noir effects a "talking cure" and can be seen as an affirmative "genre of life."[27]

The motif of the flashback, which we have noted in *The Killers*, pervades this genre (the noir classic *D.O.A.* consists entirely of an extended flashback). By insisting on the way the past impinges upon the present, the flashback underscores the contingency of the present and future, the way we are held captive by the past. But this is not a fatal determinism, because it prompts a quest through memory to discover the truth about the past, a truth that is never evident but that may allow us to endure in the present. According to the conventions of society, the quest and the risks it involves are disproportionate. In *The Killers*, the insurance investigator and his boss joke that his solving of the Swede's case, to which he has devoted inordinate time and energy, will end up saving his company a paltry sum of money. Were he not the best in his field, he likely would have been fired. The levity veils the seriousness of the quest.

By putting our conventions into question, film noir opens up the possibility of a more fundamental and more comprehensive inquiry. Its accent on darkness and mystery is an affront to Enlightenment confidence in transparent objectivity and progress. According to the modern conception of progress, we know precisely where we are, where we want to go, and how we are to get there. Film noir recovers the premodern conception of life as an always tenuous quest, wherein we are dependent on veiled clues and the uncertain assistance of others. Although fulfillment is never secure, the erotic longing for wholeness and love remain at the very center of the plot. Autonomy is a debilitating illusion and bold self-assertion, a self-destructive vice. Film noir thus engages, without succumbing to, nihilism.

The erotic element in film noir typically centers on the female lead. Long before the antinomian *Thelma and Louise*, there was *The File on Thelma Jordan* (1949), starring Barbara Stanwyck, the queen of noir. The film opens with a drunk assistant district attorney (played by Wendell Corey) bemoaning his alienation from his family. In walks the seductive Thelma Jordan, who gradually draws him into her life; unbeknown to him, he is a pawn in a plot she has hatched with another man to murder her elderly aunt for her money. Or is he something more than a pawn? The more embroiled she becomes in her own plot and the more the D.A., now her prosecutor in the murder for which she has been arrested, becomes aware of her motives, the more uncertain she seems about where her true allegiance lies. After the D.A. throws the case and she is acquitted, his hopes for their future together are thwarted by the reappearance of her co-conspirator. But the ending is unhappiness for all involved. Thelma is undone not by the law but by the reckless driving of her thug boyfriend, who dies in the crash that leaves her with injuries that soon prove fatal. On her deathbed, she issues a double confession—that she committed the murder and that she loves the D.A., who has already gone before a judge to accuse himself of subverting justice. The unhappy ending of the film is hardly nihilistic; indeed, the multiple confessions rescue the main characters from the nihilistic web of lies and destruction in which they had immersed themselves.

If the first stage of liberalism provides the political and social horizon for the populist Hollywood films of the classical era, the principles of the second stage, an attempt to ground morality and politics in self-legislation, seem to have had little impact on popular culture. According to the chief architect of this position, Immanuel Kant, a democracy is a community of individuals who are simultaneously sovereigns and subjects. No longer is revealed religion, nature, or nature's God an appropriate basis for our self-understanding. Since these are all in some measure extrinsic to the human will, reliance on them is seen to be alienating, an infringement of the dignity of the individual. In Kant's technical language, submission to them puts the individual in a state of "heteronomy," the exact opposite of autonomy. Kant is remarkably optimistic about the agreement that is likely to result from everyone's cultivating one's own autonomy, for he supposes that since each is under his own command, each will acknowledge and respect the dignity of the others in their capacity for self-legislation. It is possible to see a story like *To Kill a Mockingbird* as straddling the first two stages of liberalism. The film makes no reference to God or nature and is replete with lessons about equality and seeing the world from the vantage point of those who are culturally different from us. Yet *Mockingbird* seems to be of two minds about tradition and cultural particularity. On the one hand, in Kantian fashion, it asks us to prescind from the prejudices of blind tradition and to look past the superficial veils of race. On the other hand, the conception of duty that Atticus embodies is infused with the code of honor appropriate to the southern gentleman. From the Kantian perspective, then, *To Kill a Mockingbird* would be a somewhat impure depiction of the politics of autonomy. That assessment may tell us more about the deficiencies of the model of autonomy than about the dramatic flaws of the film.

In popular culture at least, we jump rather quickly from the first stage of liberalism to the third, in which the notion that universal agreement could arise from personal autonomy is seen to be preposterous. Nietzsche believes the third stage of liberalism is a secularized and impoverished version of Christian morality, a tenuous middle ground between the Christian worldview and the unleashing of a more radical conception of freedom. As he puts it, the "terms autonomous and moral are mutually exclusive."[28] In its break with external authority, the second stage of liberalism paves the way for a doctrine of freedom as unfettered self-expression, as the creation of value. The logical conclusion of this doctrine is on display in the prodrug comedy *Trainspotting*, in which the main character describes the decision of his friends to go back on heroin as a fully informed, democratic choice. Astonishingly, what Nietzsche articulated as a fundamentally antipolitical principle has found its way even in Supreme Court jurisprudence. In the 1992 decision *Casey v. Planned Parenthood*, the majority claims, "At the heart of liberty is the right to define one's own concept of existence, of meaning, of the universe, and of the mystery of human life." Now *Casey* was an abortion case, and the poetic praise of autonomy in the decision favored the left-wing promotion of abortion rights. But the same creed supports right-wing libertarianism. In fact, when it comes to the rhetoric of radical autonomy, there is little difference between NOW and NRA.

The ideal of radical autonomy is hardly compatible with civil society, and so there are attempts to limit its scope. But once it takes hold, it treats all resistance as an unwarranted and arbitrary circumscription of its exercise. Although the Supreme Court has resisted the inference, the right of self-creation seems naturally to support the right to physician-assisted suicide, just as the slogan "my body, my choice" is a natural advertising jingle for the cloning industry.

A dream team of contemporary political theorists defends the application of the principle of autonomy to the question of whether and when to end one's life: "Most of us see death . . . as the final act of life's drama . . . and we want that last act to reflect our own convictions." Autonomy is the overriding principle whenever "choices central to personal dignity" are at issue.[29] The language of the court and these liberal political theorists is an unstable mixture of the final two stages of liberalism. The problem is that radical autonomy easily gives way to nihilism because it undercuts faith in any objective or communally shared source of morality. Once cultural nihilism becomes prevalent, no one has the right or the capacity to determine where the lines ought to be drawn. Religion, philosophy, government, the court—all can come to seem arbitrary.

In a trend that continues, popular films (featuring actors like Clint Eastwood and Charles Bronson) began in the 1970s to depict the justice system as complicit in the very evil it purports to oppose. There are echoes of classic noir in these films, which are not necessarily nihilistic, as they presuppose sympathy for innocent victims and a horror at the injustices of criminals and petty bureaucrats. Other popular reality-based films critical of American government (*All the President's Men*) or of law enforcement (*Serpico*) supply us with heroic journalists or rogue cops with integrity. Yet, in the same period, a certain strain of neo-noir film would break from one of the central imperatives of classic noir, the deeply democratic, if antiprogressive, demand that no one wins; in neo-noir stories, from *The Getaway*, *Chinatown*, and *Body Heat* up to *The Usual Suspects*, criminal characters, who get away with their crimes, not only escape the noir trap, but they also ensnare others in traps of their own devising. Thus, in neo-noir, there emerges a sort of aristocracy of evil.

TOCQUEVILLE AND THE NEW SHAPE OF SERVITUDE

In spite of the surprising impact of Nietzsche's antipolitical principles on American thought and culture, Nietzsche himself remains something of an outsider, little understood in the culture he has helped shape. It is unlikely, for instance, that he will ever be given the attention that channels like C-SPAN regularly devote to the nineteenth-century French political theorist Alexis de Tocqueville, author of *Democracy in America.* Yet in his work, we find a startling anticipation of much of what Nietzsche prophesied about the epoch of political equality, especially about how certain forms of liberalism naturally generate nihilism. According to Tocqueville, there are two dominant passions in democracy: the love of liberty and the love of equality, the most powerful of which is the latter. When allied to the longing for physical well-being, the passion for equality leads to a remarkable sameness of condition and to uniformity of opinion, even as it dissipates the soul by immersing it in the pursuit of consumer goods and petty pleasures.

In political discourse, liberalism has become associated with big government, and this might seem antithetical to the account of liberalism as always potentially radically individualist. Liberalism was indeed founded on the principle of limited government, which leaves local communities and intermediate-level institutions free to develop in common their own ways of living together. Tocqueville thought that Americans could resist the twin dangers of centralization and individualism only as long as they participated in democratic life, only as long as they were what the *Federalist Papers* calls an "active and engaged citizenry." But the passion for equality and comfortable living can be at variance with the spirit of liberty. It leads citizens to welcome the intrusion of government into every aspect of daily life to rectify wrongs and to equalize the unequal. The weakening of the ties between the individual and mediating institutions creates a political and existential vacuum.

If citizens abdicate their responsibility for self-government, they are all too willing to permit government to perform a vast array of functions for them. Thus do centralization and individualism reinforce each other. The battle between big-government Democrats and libertarian Republicans fosters the diminution of people and overlooks important social phenomena. Cornel West argues, for instance, that both sides fail to come to terms with or even adequately acknowledge the basic threat to the black community in America, the "nihilistic threat." Neither the "liberal structuralist" focus on government programs nor the "conservative behaviorist" call for individual responsibility addresses the "loss of hope and the absence of meaning."[30] As experienced in the black community, nihilism is not so much a philosophical doctrine as a "lived experience of coping with a life of horrifying meaninglessness, hopelessness, and (most important) lovelessness."

There is, then, a hidden alliance between centralized government and individualism. They are mirror images of one another; each tends to give birth to its opposite. How are we to understand the relationship? According to Tocqueville,

> When the inhabitant of a democratic country compares himself individually with all those about him, he feels with pride that he is the equal of any one of them; but when he comes to survey the totality of his fellows and to place himself in contrast with so huge a body, he is instantly overwhelmed by the sense of his own insignificance and weakness. The same equality that renders him independent of each of his fellow citizens, taken severally, exposes him alone and unprotected to the influence of the greater number.[31]

The impotence of the individual before the whole of society makes possible a hitherto unknown form of tyranny, a "new physiognomy of servitude." The great danger is not, as it was in previous eras, that of the despotism of a single man or even of a class. We witness

> an innumerable multitude of men, all equal and alike, incessantly endeavoring to procure the petty and paltry pleasures with which they glut their lives. Each of them, living apart, is a stranger to the fate of all the rest; his children and his private friends constitute to him the whole of mankind. . . . Above this race of men stands an immense and tutelary power, which takes upon itself alone to secure their gratification and to watch over their fate. That power is absolute, minute, regular, provident, and mild. It would be like the authority of a parent, if . . . its object were to prepare men for manhood; but it seeks, on the contrary, to keep them in perpetual childhood. . . . For their

happiness such a government willingly labors . . . what remains, but to spare them all the care of thinking and all the trouble of living?[32]

What sort of citizens does such a regime produce? Tocqueville does not give them a name, but it would be hard to distinguish them from Nietzsche's last men. According to Tocqueville, these enervated souls suffer from the shrinking of each person's world to a very small circle. Some social conservatives might be surprised to learn that what they call family values and see as an alternative to liberal individualism is nearly indistinguishable from what Tocqueville calls individualism: "a mature and calm feeling, which disposes each member of the community to sever himself from the mass of his fellows and to draw apart with his family and his friends, so that after he has thus formed a little circle of his own, he willingly leaves society at large to itself."[33]

Tocqueville, the most prescient analyst of American democracy, anticipates many of Nietzsche's insights about the subtle link between democratic liberalism and nihilism, even if he rejects Nietzsche's antipolitical corrective. Instead, he advocates ways to temper our passion for equality of condition and physical well-being. More important than institutional structures and constitutional principles are the customs and mores of democratic nations. He thought it was crucial that popular mores invigorate individuals with a sense of the grandeur of life in a democracy and that they present examples of the virtues and sacrifices necessary to keep alive the spirit of liberty. Without being explicitly religious, popular culture should contain a kind of civil religion that teaches us to cherish, love, and care for our common life. It should also draw us out of our concentration on the present and our immersion in the limited circle of family and friends to take a long-term view of our lives and to participate in the political life of the nation.

Both Nietzsche and Tocqueville see the problem as more than a matter of altering the structure of political regimes. The underlying difficulty is one of mores or habits arising from a shift in the understanding of the place of humanity in the universe. We can see this transformation best in the modern idea of scientific and technological progress. For all its undisputed contributions to our understanding of the universe, science often undermines the dignity of the individual so prized by modern political theory. Think of the way Darwin's theory of evolution demotes human beings from their traditional rank in the universe, of the way Freud's theories reduce conscious, rational life to the subconscious and irrational, or of the way contemporary biology explains our apparently free decisions in terms of physical-chemical processes. If there is nothing especially distinctive or noble about human beings, then on what grounds do we celebrate their intrinsic dignity?

Further complicating matters is the stance of Enlightenment science toward the world. Considered the founder of modern philosophy, seventeenth-century French philosopher and scientist René Descartes articulates one of the fundamental goals of the Enlightenment. The end of science, he writes, is to "render us masters and possessors of nature." This ambitious, one might say hubristic, project has given rise to numerous crises, not the least of which is the insoluble question of the place of humanity in nature. To master and control nature would seem to entail our standing above or outside it, even against it. Where do we fit in? Do we have any natural place within the world? And what, if any, are the limitations to our project of mastery? The result of modern science's view of nature as raw material to be disposed of at our discretion is the alienation of humanity from the world.

Here we confront the "dread chasm that has rent the soul of Western man ever since . . . Descartes ripped body lose from mind and turned the very soul into a ghost that haunts its own house."[34] Consider, for example, the Human Genome Project, which has been described as the "grail of human genetics . . . the ultimate answer to the commandment, 'Know thyself.'"[35] In this case, knowledge is equivalent to power. By knowing our origins, we can determine our future. The irony, lost on the scientists, is that in the process "we" will have vanished. If the self is but a genetic code and if the code can be altered at our discretion, then the self is something even less substantial than Descartes' ghostly ego. In his comical lack of self-reflection, the scientist fails to ask the question, Who or what knows the code, and who or what

is deciding how it should be emended? Wouldn't it be an embarrassingly hollow answer, demeaning to the dignity of the scientist, to say
that a code is being known by a code? Scientific indifference to these
issues confirms Nietzsche's suspicion that Enlightenment science will
bring us face to face with our own nothingness. The admonition of
Montaigne and Pascal that whoever strives to be an angel ends up the
beast now seems naive. At least a beast is something.

In jettisoning authority—indeed, the past itself—Enlightenment
progress is supposed to liberate the individual. But progress puts the
individual at the service of large, impersonal, historical forces. Tocqueville worried that the modern emphasis on historical progress
would engender in individuals a sense of helplessness and impotence
born of the suspicion that the actions and thoughts of an individual
are as nothing in comparison with the force of history.

Numerous hidden and powerful forces, then, conspire to render
human life small and insignificant. A state of perpetual childhood,
Tocqueville fears, may result not only from encroaching centralized
power but also from the absence of any clear notion of what it means
to be a mature human being. Their claims to foster personal growth
notwithstanding, contemporary self-help guides exacerbate the problem. Given the absence of any criteria in light of which one might
distinguish between progress and regress, growth and decay, their
language is bankrupt. Indeed, their effect is often to bring about a
kind of paralysis of the will, an inability to make any long-term com-
mitments. The project of creating a self ex nihilo leads to a restless
uncertainty about the future and the frenetic and violent process of
making and unmaking decisions.

The result is a kind of perpetual adolescence, a natural consequence of the disappearance of any clear model of adult life, of what
it might mean to grow or develop from a child into an adult. Too
often, the passage means simply that without external intervention
we can now do as we please. But once we reach a certain age, society
expects us to conform to some of the external trappings of adult life.
The curse is that the fragility of the self precludes bold rebellion and
fosters timid conformity.

The Hollywood of classic films, some of which we have discussed, had clear notions of the differences between childhood and adulthood and of the appropriate paths from the former to the latter. Like the sitcoms of its era, *To Kill a Mockingbird* often succeeds best at depicting the world of children. The entire story is told from the perspective of Scout, who was only six years old at the time of the events. The epigraph to the book is from Charles Lamb: "Lawyers, I suppose, were children once." This is a world that is generally safe for children not because there are no threats to their well-being and not because every child comes from a well-adjusted home with a happily married mother and father: the Finch children are motherless. It is safe because there is a community ordered to the raising of children that is generally agreed on the essential virtues that need to be inculcated in them. This sense of communal responsibility for children also realizes itself in certain predictable vices—snooping, gossip, and unwelcome and imprudent intrusions—that are better articulated in the book than in the movie.

The Enlightenment viewed childhood as an obstacle to be overcome at all costs. Because youth is the time of our greatest dependence on tradition and authority, when others largely do our thinking for us, it is the antithesis of the Enlightenment ideal of autonomy. A chief exponent of this line of thought is Descartes.

> I thought that we were all children before being men, at which time we were necessarily under the control of our appetites and our teachers, and that neither of these influences is wholly consistent, and neither of them, perhaps, always tend to the better. It is therefore impossible that our judgments should be as pure and firm as they would have been had we the use of our reason from the time of our birth and if we had never been under any other control.[36]

Descartes' corrective is to repudiate every opinion he has inherited from others, to destroy the entire edifice of his beliefs and rebuild knowledge upon a firmer foundation. The passage is an early

statement of the goals of liberal enlightenment and scientific progress. One must extirpate the influence of tradition, convention, and
authority from one's reasoning, to act autonomously, to dare to use
one's reason by and for oneself.

ROMANTICISM'S AMBIGUOUS RELATIONSHIP TO NIHILISM

Reacting against the alienating, degrading, and dispiriting consequences of the Enlightenment, nineteenth-century romanticism presented an alternative ideal. It exalted instinct and imagination over
reason, spontaneity and poetry over calculation and science. Wordsworth's famous poem "Ode: Intimations of Immortality" celebrates
the natural harmony of the child with nature and the divine. As
the child becomes initiated into so-called civilized society through
the learning of language and the immersion in the world of utility, he or she becomes alienated. In spite of his adulation of childhood innocence, Wordsworth did not think we could or should
simply return to that original state. The romantic celebration of
the natural innocence of the precivilized child recurs as a model
of goodness in contemporary American popular culture. Part of the
new problem of evil is the problem of goodness, of the absence of
models of virtue and excellence. In movies like *Forrest Gump* and
Rain Man, we discover Hollywood's present-day penchant for equat-
ing goodness with insuperable innocence and perpetual childhood. A
mental disability actually frees one from the corruptions of civilized
adult life. Although *Gump* ambitiously invokes the central motifs of
Capra's populism, its main character is an incorrigible child who is
incapable of suffering the trials characteristic of film noir or of the
Capra classics. Gump's strategy is to circumvent evil and misery,
not to overcome it by going through it. Mark Edmundson calls this
strategy "facile transcendence."[37]

In our culture, romanticism is the principal alternative to nihilism. From *E.T.* to *Avatar*, romanticism supplies a powerful affirmative
myth. Of course, it also embodies a radical critique of conventional
society, indeed, of civilization itself. "We murder to dissect," wrote
the great romantic poet Wordsworth. In *E.T.*, America is a heartless
society given to cold, scientific analysis. Elliottt complains that once

E.T. is dead, the scientists will just "cut him up." The film embodies a standard set of romantic oppositions: innocence versus civilization, nature versus technology, child versus adult, feeling versus reason. Its counter to the corruptions of America's calculative, rationalist adult world is E.T.'s bright, red, pulsating heart shining through his transparent chest. Existing in harmony with nature, E.T. revives drooping flowers and creates no fear in animals. As if to underscore this point, the final scene of the film depicts E.T.'s spaceship vanishing into a rainbow across the evening sky. The problem with the film's underlying romantic mythology is that it never suggests how we might reach this state, how we might mediate between or reconcile reason and feeling, technology and nature, adulthood and childhood.

More recently, James Cameron's blockbuster *Avatar* features a dramatic conflict that rests on romantic divisions between a primitive, basically peaceful, and organic culture, on the one hand, and an advanced, bellicose, and artificial culture, on the other. The much-touted look of the film is, indeed, mesmerizing, but the visuals work largely because Cameron is so effective in constructing an entire world, that of the Na'vi tribe. The very blue inhabitants of Pandora are deeply bound to each other and to a particular place, especially to the sacred tree and the goddess who dwells there. The tree happens to grow on mineral deposits that are valuable to the militaristic capitalists who want to relocate the tribe, by diplomacy or war (preferably the latter), so as to exploit Pandora's natural resources. With its positive portrait of a sacred society, Cameron's film stands as one of the most powerful religious films in recent years. Its conception of the sacred, in keeping with the romantic myth, is entirely immanent, not transcendent.

Indeed, one of the attractions of romanticism is that it counters the reductionist tendencies of the modern world. Romanticism reacts against the elimination of mystery from human life and the reduction of human sexuality to a mere appetite and of love to a contractual arrangement. As Roger Scruton argues, romanticism is a remedy for what ails the modern world—a "morbidly unheroic world" dominated by "cost–benefit calculation," which tempts us to regard our own existence as a "cosmic mistake."[38] The remedy is to "live as if a heroic love were possible, and as if we could renounce life for the sake of it." In the hugely popular teen vampire romance *New Moon*, the female lead, Bella, is in the grip of precisely such a vision. But we have serious reason to wonder how admirable her vision (or Scruton's, for that matter) is. Her love-death passion for the vampire Edward is an escape from the banality of ordinary life: boring high school classes with dull kids and a humdrum family. In Edward's absence, Bella actively cultivates pain because it is a "reminder." One of her friends worries that she is suicidal, but she is not so much in love with easeful death as she is in love with the thrill of the constant risk of death—especially of a dramatic death. As she puts it in her opening voice-over in the first film, "I never really thought about death. . . . Dying for someone else would not be a bad way to go."

It is not difficult to see how romanticism itself could generate nihilism. Existing civilization is utterly debasing and alienating; yet the alternative—a return to childhood innocence or to a pretechnological harmony with nature—is impossible for us. What, then, is left? Perhaps the ennobling, if self-devouring, pursuit of love-death.

THE REVENGE OF THE DARK GOD

Nietzsche traces the origin of nihilism to the death of the Judeo-Christian God, to the vanishing of the supernatural from human life. In fact, Nietzsche believes the seeds of nihilism are latent in the Judeo-Christian story. By opposing this world to the next, passion and instinct to divine law, and denigrating the former in favor of the latter, the Judeo-Christian religion empties this life of significance. It is essentially an antivital principle.

But Nietzsche is hasty here. It is possible to trace the religious roots of nihilism not to the original Judeo-Christian view of God but to a distortion of it in the late medieval and early modern period.[39] A certain conception of divinity, which arose with voluntarism and nominalism in the late medieval era, accentuates God's absolute freedom and power and thus sees him as all-powerful, arbitrary, and capricious. There is no intrinsic, intelligible link between the world and God, between human and divine morality. Nature either becomes mute or it speaks in convoluted and contradictory ways; it is no longer a book in which, with the help of Scripture, we might read the signs and symbols of divine art.

It does not take much imagination to detect similarities between an omnipotent, arbitrary deity and the contemporary antihero who displays his creative power in capricious acts of destruction. This is the dark God whose possible existence Descartes sought to eliminate. Assaulted by doubts, Descartes wanted to find a sure and useful foundation for all knowledge, especially for scientific knowledge. As a means of gaining absolute and unshakable certitude, he proposed to subject all his beliefs to the most stringent standards of proof. Any belief that allows for a degree of doubt must be set aside. For example, sense experience is at times deceptive, so we must discount it entirely. For similar reasons, Descartes questions the existence of all external objects, other persons, and even his own body. Having dismissed all this, he goes on to consider whether he might be deceived even about apparently certain truths like those of mathematics. For the sake of argument, he postulates the existence of "not a God, who is the supreme source of truth, but a certain evil spirit, not less clever and deceitful than powerful, [who] has bent all his efforts to deceive me." Descartes famously thought that he might be able to compete with such a deity or at least that he could carve out a realm of knowledge immune to the tricks of such a being. He states, "I . . . shall prepare my mind so well for all the ruses of this great deceiver that, however powerful and artful he may be, he will never be able to mislead me in anything."[40] This leads to the notorious argument that even if Descartes is being deceived, at least he is sure of this much—that "it is he who is being deceived." Since his being deceived presupposes his thinking and his existence, he is immune to deception about one truth, "I think, therefore I am."

Descartes' victory is Pyrrhic; he wins only at the cost of sacrificing the external world, his body, and other persons. The hollow self that remains anticipates the flimsy sense of self possessed by the last men. According to Nietzsche and many others, Descartes failed to achieve the goal of rational enlightenment: he never conquered the dark God.

The preoccupation with the malignant evil genius is present not only in Descartes, the founder of modern philosophy, but also in Hobbes, the founder of modern political science. His famous state of nature is an amoral universe in which every individual pursues a "restless desire for power after power." This is the war of all against all. The way out of this situation, which is suffused with the fear of violent death, is through a social compact, wherein each individual cedes natural rights to gain peace. The compact vests the right to make and enforce law in a Leviathan, or absolute ruler. Although his legitimacy is grounded in the original act of the consent of the ruled, the Leviathan's unencumbered freedom to determine law and punishment is similar to God's right to rule by his "irresistible power."[41] We owe him obedience not as a "gracious creator" but as an omnipotent ruler.

Descartes thought he could refute the existence of such a being or at least defend himself against his deceptions, whereas Hobbes sought to ground a rational science of politics on such a conception of divinity. Both projects saddle us with a dilemma. Since this God is not necessarily good or just, it is not a God that one could reasonably worship. It is not clear what would satisfy him: perhaps worship, perhaps indifference, perhaps hostility. One possible response is to combat this deity by engaging in a battle of will. We may not be made in the image of a benevolent, provident God, but we can still cultivate the detachment and malevolent humor of the dark God.

As much as the ideal of autonomous self-creation as an *imitatio diaboli* may surface in Hollywood films, it has a very limited presence in the lives of ordinary Americans. Yet the role of autonomy exercises an increasing role in our courts and our public philosophy, especially in our intractable debates over rights and liberties. Once radical autonomy takes hold, it is hard to resist its nihilistic implications. Undoubtedly the funniest and among the most compelling illustrations of this claim can be found in the 1996 prodrug film *Trainspotting*, in which the main character lays bare the nihilism at the root of the modern exaltation of choice. Here is a taste of his argument:

Choose Life. Choose a job. Choose a career. Choose a family. Choose a fucking big television, choose washing machines, cars, compact disc players and electrical tin openers. Choose good health, low cholesterol, and dental insurance. Choose fixed interest mortgage repayments. Choose a starter home. Choose your friends. Choose leisurewear and matching luggage. Choose a three-piece suit on hire purchase in a range of fucking fabrics. Choose DIY and wondering who the fuck you are on Sunday morning. Choose sitting on that couch watching mind-numbing, spirit-crushing game shows, stuffing fucking junk food into your mouth. Choose rotting away at the end of it all, pissing your last in a miserable home, nothing more than an embarrassment to the selfish, fucked up brats you spawned to replace yourselves. Choose your future. Choose life . . . But why would I want to do a thing like that? I chose not to choose life. I chose somethin' else. And the reasons? There are no reasons. Who needs reasons when you've got heroin?

Tocqueville noted that American democracy was about equality and liberty. The danger he saw is that an intemperate pursuit of equality would come to diminish our appreciation of certain forms of liberty. One of the most powerful contemporary sources of nihilism is a kind of soft relativism that applies the notion of equality to the veracity of our opinions, all of which are to be considered equally valid. That fits rather nicely the definition of nihilism as the absence of a basis for distinguishing better from worse or noble from base. Of course, certain conceptions of liberty that exalt the capacity of choosing also court nihilism. If there are no standards in light of which we can appraise choices, then they are all equally meaningful and equally meaningless.

But society, even more than nature, abhors a vacuum. Many worry that our contemporary popular culture is confused, chaotic, and destructive, although they may not call our age nihilistic. It would be wrong, however, to think that the influence of nihilism leads to chaos and anarchy. Nihilism is a kind of limit, which we can approach asymptotically but never reach. Just as for Aristotle there is no such thing as unformed matter, so too there is no utterly shapeless life. The paradox of nihilism is that it generates more determinate and more mechanistic social forms. Thus, the complexity, depth, and flexibility appropriate to human life are lost.

NIHILISM'S OVERCOMING

If the strains of nihilism in contemporary popular culture were the whole story, we would indeed have reached a dead end. Contemporary art is more resourceful, just as human nature is more resilient, than this pessimistic judgment allows, however. Throughout most of the last decade of the twentieth century and the first decade of the twenty-first, Hollywood simply did not depict as admirable ordinary American life in the present. When it did offer heroism, usually in the form of war films such as *Braveheart, Saving Private Ryan,* or *Gladiator,* it found examples from other places or other times. In the last decade, there has even been renewed attention to positive depictions of the lives of ordinary Americans. Some of the shift is traceable to Hollywood's response to real-life heroism of ordinary Americans after the heinous attacks of 9/11. Films such as *Flight 93* and *World Trade Center* present ordinary Americans achieving extraordinary things in the face of catastrophic evil. Other films based on real events, such as *The Pursuit of Happyness* or *The Blind Side*—a surprise nominee for a Best Picture Oscar in 2009—also show ordinary citizens overcoming obstacles and realizing admirable goals.

Moreover, there are, as we will show in later chapters, a number of significant films that engage without succumbing to nihilism. If what we now lack are complex and nuanced depictions of goodness or of the struggle between good and evil in weak and flawed but nonetheless admirable characters, there are a sufficient number of notable examples to point the way. If the mainstream horror film finds itself for the most part degenerating into torture porn or self-parody, it is also witnessing something of a return to suspense and to a supple probing of the mysteries of both goodness and evil in the films of M. Night Shyamalan and an appreciation of the nobility of sacrifice in *Pan's Labyrinth,* directed by Guillermo del Toro, a filmmaker influenced by

William Peter Blatty, author of *The Exorcist*. Christopher Nolan has treated the perilous pursuit of justice in the modern city, inhabited by fearful last men and evildoing superheroes, with remarkable artistic dexterity and moral gravity in his two *Batman* films.

The nihilism at the heart of the suburban family is a staple of the Hollywood film industry. *American Beauty* is perhaps its exemplary statement, but another film from Sam Mendes, *Revolutionary Road*, attempts to expose the historical roots of suburban malaise. A much better handling of early 1960s American culture can be seen in the critically acclaimed AMC series *Mad Men*, which lays bare the futility of the self-made man even as it exhibits greater respect for what actually motives the businessman. Consumerism, fed by the illusions of the advertising industry and paired with the dream of sexual freedom, characterizes American life in these films and TV series. Yet in *The Ice Storm* and *The Secret Lives of Dentists*, the artistry of the film provides viewers with a moral perspective in light of which to judge the hollow lives of the characters who themselves lack a vocabulary to describe the loss that they feel. The films depict nihilism without falling prey to it.

One of the most notable trends in popular Hollywood films in the last decade is the success of fantasy films featuring heroic battles between good and evil. The *Star Wars* prequels, the *Spider-Man* series, the new *Batman* films, the *Lord of the Rings* trilogy, and the film versions of *Harry Potter* have all done extremely well at the box office. The astonishing popularity of J. K. Rowling's *Harry Potter* novels and the films based on them gives evidence of a hunger in Americans, especially the young, for something more than either debased Gothic or facile transcendence. The stories feature a character, Lord Voldemort, who supplies a succinct expression of nihilism: "There is no good or evil. Only power and those too weak to use it." They also supply a counter to nihilism in the form of communal life unified through the practice of a set of virtues, especially the virtue of sacrificial love.

One point is clear from the artistically impressive list of films that wrestle with nihilism while showing a way beyond it: there is no easy way back to Enlightenment ideals. When contemporary art seeks to find a way through the misery and seeming chaos of contemporary life, it does so by reviving the classical, premodern conception of life as a quest. That is true in the religious sphere as well, as is clear from the Denzel Washington vehicle *The Book of Eli*, a film that is a meditation on Psalm 23, which speaks of religious faith not as offering cheap grace or easy transcendence but as enabling one to walk through the valley of darkness. If Rowling's books constitute the most significant popular antidote to nihilism in the world of contemporary popular literature, Peter Jackson's *Lord of the Rings* represents the most compelling film version of nihilism's overcoming, and it does so in a way that appreciates the strengths of romanticism while resisting its vulnerabilities.

2

THE QUEST for EVIL

With the advent of the aesthetics of evil, the allegiance of viewers shifts from victims and societal order to sympathy with the devil. Moral ambiguity and black comedy are not new to the world of American film. Both trends can be found in film noir and in popular Hitchcock movies. What is new is the grotesque brutality that accompanies them. Also unrivaled is the critique of conventional society and the confidence with which demonic characters are celebrated for their courageous and creative transcendence of the categories of good and evil. Since the release of *The Exorcist* (1973), we have been inundated with demonic horror films. Many of these films explore in detail the themes of the aesthetics of evil, the villain-hero who exists beyond good and evil, and the impotence of the American systems of justice and psychiatric medicine. *The Exorcist, Cape Fear,* and *The Silence of the Lambs* contain all these themes, although they do not fit neatly into a single genre. With the possible exception of *Cape Fear,* all achieved a certain measure of critical acclaim; all have gained a wider audience than the typical horror film. Their influence is far-reaching; scenes from these films have become ingrained in the popular cultural memory. Given their heterogeneity, what makes these movies appropriate vehicles for exploring the new problem of evil in popular culture?

In spite of their differences, these films exhibit an underlying similarity in themes and strategies. What are the common themes and strategies? As in *The Exorcist,* so too in *Cape Fear* and *The Silence of the Lambs,* the demonic villain takes center stage as his personality transfixes the audience. By means of didactic speeches and grotesquely offensive acts, all these incarnations of evil mock fundamental features of contemporary American life: (a) the cowardly and merely artificial mores of conventional society, (b) the arbitrary system of American justice, and (c) the intellectual poverty of our standard mechanisms, especially that of behaviorist psychology, for understanding evil. In each case, the evildoer is invulnerable to our morality, our punitive threats, and our attempts at explanation. American society is feeble, shallow, and complicit in the very evil that it supposedly wants to eradicate.

Cultural critics bemoan these attacks on civility and traditional morality, and they may well be right about the corrosive effects upon American culture. But these critics too often misconstrue the target of these films, which they assume to be the segment of American society committed to so-called traditional values. Wittingly or unwittingly, the real target of these movies is Enlightenment politics and science. The utopian, rationalist vision of the Enlightenment, luring us with the promise of eliminating both physical and moral evil, is no longer credible. Contemporary horror films mercilessly unveil the bankruptcy of contemporary psychology, sociology, and law—all Enlightenment disciplines. The roots of nihilism in popular culture are deeper and earlier than the book indicates.

Such critiques are not limited to the horror genre. In the late 1960s and early 1970s, with the demise of the Hollywood Production Code and in the aftermath of political and social turmoil, films saturated with violence and cynicism about conventional society and rife with nihilism began to be produced. Films in this group include *Bonnie and Clyde* (1967), *The Graduate* (1967), *Rosemary's Baby* (1968), *M*A*S*H* (1970), *Deliverance* (1972), *The Getaway* (1972), *Chinatown* (1974), and later, *Taxi Driver* (1976) and *Apocalypse Now* (1979). Consider the plotlines of three of these: *The Graduate, The Getaway,* and *Deliverance.*

THOSE '70S SHOWS

One of the defining films of the late 1960s that sets the stage for the film culture of the early 1970s, Mike Nichols' *The Graduate* is a wonderful send-up of the corruptions of the establishment generation, the venality of the corporate world, and the vacuity of suburbia. It is also an indictment of the educational system. Benjamin (Dustin Hoffman) has been to the best schools, and his life is utterly void of formation or purpose. At the dreadful party held by his parents for his graduation, he escapes to his bedroom while the partygoers listen to a list of his accomplishments from his college yearbook: "captain of the cross-country team, head of the debating club, associate editor of the college newspaper in his junior year, managing editor in his senior year." The best the next generation can offer is "plastics"— a term that signifies much more than its speaker intends—and vague counsel about graduate school. More school, wonders Benjamin, for what? Later during the party, he has a telling exchange with his father.

> Ben: I'm just . . .
>
> Mr. Braddock: . . . worried?
>
> Ben: Well . . .
>
> Mr. Braddock: About what?
>
> Ben: I guess about my future.
>
> Mr. Braddock: What about it?
>
> Ben: I don't know. I want it to be . . .
>
> Mr. Braddock: . . . to be what?
>
> Ben: . . . Different.

An innocent with no strong sense of virtue or vice, bliss or misery, hope or despair, Benjamin falls easy prey for the sensual wiles of Mrs. Robinson (Anne Bancroft), the classic bored housewife. But she is hardly the libertine she might seem. When Benjamin's affections turn to her daughter, Elaine, Mrs. Robinson rapidly embraces the conventional position of power to which her money and status entitle her.

As he lays the purse on Elaine's shelf in her room, Mrs. Robinson enters behind him totally naked, her nudity reflected in the glass which covers her daughter's portrait (foreshadowing the contrasting role that both women will play in his life—one innocent and young, the other older and sexually aggressive).

With the younger Elaine Robinson, he seems able to express himself in a less disjointed fashion, even if what he articulates is merely a sense of loss and entrapment:

> I've had this feeling ever since I graduated. This kind of compulsion that I have to be rude all the time . . . It's like I was playing some kind of game, but the rules don't make any sense to me. They're being made up by all the wrong people. I mean, no one makes them up. They seem to make themselves up.

Benjamin thinks he has found what he is looking for in Elaine. So he spends the rest of the film fending off the threats of her parents and trying to win back Elaine's affection after she learns about his affair with her mother. As if to underscore the notion that he is on a quest, a great deal of the footage in the second half of the film is devoted to Hoffman driving the California coast in his MG. In the final segment, he attempts to find Elaine on her wedding day and save her from a conventional marriage. He is seen driving hurriedly and then running from church to church. The seeming directedness of his action, his eagerness to get from one place to another, to fend off the threats of the establishment and to save the youthful from the clutches of shallow conformity—all this is an illusion. What gives it all away is the final scene.

At last discovering the church where Elaine's wedding is scheduled, he interrupts the ceremony, uses a crucifix to fend off Elaine's parents, and then escapes with Elaine onto a municipal bus filled with the elderly. As they sit isolated on the bus, they initially seem giddy, proud that they have foiled their elders. As that sense subsides, they seem isolated not just from those on the bus but even from one another. They sit silently, staring straight ahead, not even acknowledging each other's presence. The vacant and uneasy expression on Benjamin's face indicates that his only purpose was negative; he has no future, no hope, and no purpose.

Based on Jim Thompson's neo-noir crime drama, *The Getaway*, starring Steve McQueen and Ali McGraw, is a love story and a heist film. It is also a celebration of the way violent criminals get away unscathed and profit from lives of theft and murder. The ending turns the classic noir plot inside out. In classic noir, justice might not be served, but the universal rule is that no one wins. After the heist, which involves fairly predictable complications, Doc and Carol face numerous internal and external obstacles to their attempted escape to freedom. Beyond the question of whether they will be apprehended, there is the question of whether, if they escape, they will be able to live together in peace. After a culminating bloodbath at an El Paso hotel, only Doc and Carol are left alive. Just at the point where the viewer might expect fate to deal them a cruel blow, they experience remarkably good fortune. Emerging from the hotel, they enlist the services of an old man in a decrepit pickup. He is thrilled, invites them in, and sends his truck hurtling through parking lots and over curbs, as he confesses lightheartedly, "I've been in trouble with the law myself." The discrepancy between Doc and Carol's wanton lawlessness and any minor transgression the old man may have committed comes off as light comedy. They offer the old man $30,000 for his truck, and he exclaims jubilantly, "Hope you find what you're looking for. Vaya con Dios. Goddamn!" Decidedly upbeat music plays as Doc and Carol drive toward the Mexican mountains.

The ending of *The Getaway* not only makes light of the traditional happy Hollywood ending but also expresses an aversion to the quasi-tragic endings of classical noir. It might seem that the title itself hints at the ending; however, the film takes instructive liberties with the ending to Jim Thompson's famous noir story, an ending that stressed the continued strife between Doc and Carol. In Thompson's book, composed during the period of classic noir, the title is cruelly ironic, as befits a noir tale. Their only means of escape from America and into Mexico requires that they agree to live permanently in an

upscale, criminal safe house. In exchange for protection from the law
and other criminals, they agree to pay fees for room and board, fees
that slowly diminish the large sum of money stolen from the bank.
The safe house is a sort of socialist police state with everyone under
the watchful eyes of those in power. It is in fact a prison, a place from
which Doc and Carol have no hope of release or escape. The Mexican
safe house is so thoroughly and so ruthlessly guarded that they give
no thought to going elsewhere. Meanwhile, they live in constant suspicion of one another.

> They knew each other too well. They lived by taking what they
> wanted. By getting rid of anyone who got in their way or ceased
> to be useful to them. It was a fixed pattern with them; it *was* them.
> And in the event of a showdown, they would show no more mercy
> toward each other than they had toward so many others.[1]

In contrast to the book, the film embraces nihilism with a happy
face. The film's ending locates Doc and Carol blissfully beyond
good and evil, having escaped from the noir world of crime and law
enforcement and transcended noir's uncompromising insistence on
the incompatibility of crime with love and trust. The movie holds the
destiny of its main characters in suspense until the very end, when it
lapses into soft, comic nihilism.

The film *Deliverance* is about the conflict between civilization
and nature or rather about the way morality and rationality are but
a thin veneer over nature's amorality and irrational display of power.
The film begins with a group of Georgia businessmen, led by Lewis
(Burt Reynolds), deciding to take a trip into the backwoods to ride
the Cahulawassee River, an area about to be taken over by urban
developers, who will bring civilization to the backwoods, eliminating
its beauty and submerging nature's challenge to rational control and
orderly morality. As Lewis lectures his friends,

> they're buildin' a dam across the Cahulawassee River. They're
> gonna flood a whole valley, Bobby, that's why. Dammit, they're
> drownin' the river . . . Just about the last wild, untamed,

unpolluted, unfucked up river in the south. Don't you understand what I'm sayin'? . . . They're gonna stop the river up. There ain't gonna be no more river. There's just gonna be a big, dead lake. . . . You just push a little more power into Atlanta, a little more air-conditioners for your smug little suburb, and you know what's gonna happen? We're gonna rape this whole god-damned landscape. We're gonna rape it.

The image of violent violation is of course borne out in one of the most terrifying, most disgusting, and most famous scenes in the film: the rape of one of the businessmen by toothless denizens of the backwoods. The redneck denizens of the woods have remained in the popular memory as representatives of the primitive South. They are that and more; they are a clue to nature's primordial unity, not a peaceful harmony but a violent conflict. The film thus reverses the popular romantic myth about pristine, innocent nature. Morality reposes upon the ability to make distinctions, to discern and stipulate that this is appropriately separate from that. The genetic disorders and physical imperfections afflicting the locals are all traceable to intermarriage, to incestuous relations that blur distinctions held firm in the civilized world; the same is true of homosexuality in the film. Unpredictable violence and wanton destruction rule in this natural oasis. To survive the river, the men must commit deeds they never would have contemplated in the civilized world, a world that has lied to them about nature and rendered them ill equipped to confront it.

In these three films, nihilism arises from the insight that the ethical codes of civilization are arbitrary, that American society is hollow and corrupt, and that conventional justice is no match for crafty and strong-willed evildoers. If at the outset of the chapter we distinguished between mainstream films featuring nihilism and horror films, we now need to see how the two are intimately connected in *The Exorcist* (1973), the most successful horror film of all time, the film that continues to exercise a decisive influence on the genre nearly forty years after its release, and the film that subsumes within its narrative the questions about meaning characteristic of the generation of the 1960s.

THE QUEST BEGINS: *THE EXORCIST*

The Exorcist, directed by William Friedkin and based on a screen-play by William Peter Blatty, was a revolutionary film, a terrify-ing and dramatically compelling story of demonic possession and of the battle between faith and doubt amid the manifold confusions of the modern age. It features conflicts between primitive nature and sophis-ticated society, between medieval religion and Enlightenment science, between the romantic myth of innocent children and the reality of a young girl exhibiting diabolical behavior. Known more for the film version than for the original book, *The Exorcist* calls to mind images of projectile vomiting and head spinning of Regan, the possessed girl played so effectively by Linda Blair. Those scenes in *The Exorcist* did help spawn the endless one-upmanship among horror filmmakers, a competition in the surface aesthetics of evil to see who could produce, at a faster rate, ever more gruesome scenes of grotesque mutilation. It is important also to note that the scenes occur only sporadically and well over halfway through the film; attention to them has proven a distraction from central dramatic motifs of the story, which have more to do with goodness than evil.

Blatty's book and script have in mind the turbulence of the 1960s and the growing skepticism about religion.[2] Just as in the demonic thriller that preceded it, Ira Levin's *Rosemary's Baby*, so too here God's existence is very much in question. Just a few years earlier, in April 1966, *Time* featured a cover story entitled "Is God Dead?" a copy of which Mia Farrow's character in *Rosemary's Baby* peruses in a doctor's office. To the vanishing of God corresponds erosion in the language concerning evil. In such a context, what sort of quest remains?

How varied, even inverted, the quest can become is evident in Walker Percy's novel *Lancelot*, an extended monologue from an admit-ted murderer, who is now in a psychiatric hospital where he is visited regularly by an old friend, a priest-psychiatrist who has himself lost his faith in God. The main character taunts the lapsed priest about the old quest for God, which he claims is "all washed up." He poses the following set of questions:

Can good come from evil? Have you ever considered the possibility that one might undertake a search not for God but for evil? You people may have been on the wrong track all these years with all that talk about God and signs of his existence. . . . But what if you could show me a *sin*? a purely evil deed, an intolerable deed for which there is no explanation? Now there's a mystery.[3]

Something like this apparently perverse quest for evil is, I think, operative in many of our best horror films. Often derided as mindless entertainment, the genre of the horror film is, in addition to providing the scares and shocks that audiences crave, capable of raising all sorts of interesting questions about the nature of evil, about the unanticipated dangers that attend the human attempt to control and manipulate nature, about Enlightenment science, and even about the existence of God. In the face of a behaviorist account of human action, where freedom is reducible to antecedent influences, psychological or chemical, evil, understood as an act for which an individual is freely responsible, dissolves. Many modern horror films, from *The Exorcist* to *The Silence of the Lambs*, presuppose a kind of behaviorism or at least a reductionist view of evil as susceptible to medicinal or psychiatric explanation and treatment. These films raise the question of whether evil exists. By implication, they also raise a host of other questions (a) concerning human freedom, moral responsibility, and the possibility of goodness and (b) concerning theodicy and providence. Recall the opening query in the passage just quoted from *Lancelot*: "Can good come from evil?" In traditional theology, bringing good out of evil is one of the activities of divine providence. Much of contemporary film, particularly in the horror genre, narrates evil overcoming goodness or evil ceaselessly and mechanically generating evil. The quest here is undermined in advance; characters find themselves trapped in the past by evil deeds performed or endured that haunt them in the present and whose repetition awaits them in the future, a future dictated by past malevolence.

Blatty links questions about evil to questions about cosmology; the problem of evil is both deeply personal and deeply metaphysical.

The implicit metaphysics of Blatty's novels is one in which goodness has priority over evil and in which evil performs providential function. If much of the celebration of evil in our popular culture in the time since the release of *The Exorcist* portrays a cycle of violence and retribution in which evil mechanically and inexorably generates more evil, Blatty's vision sees the possibility of good being brought out of evil through a providential design of which we can manage only glimpses in the interstices of events.

Offering sustained reflection on the supernatural, even the occult, Blatty's fiction, especially in *The Exorcist*, reveals the deep magic of the universe, as C. S. Lewis called it, a magic that the modern world claims to have transcended but which modern horror repeatedly calls back into existence. It is a diabolical magic that ensnares human beings within its malevolent clutches and strives to implicate them in their own destruction. Yet also like Lewis, Blatty discerns the workings of a deeper magic, subversive of ordinary magic and suggestive not of the downward path of dissolution but of an upward path of restoration and transformation.

Blatty has always thought of *The Exorcist* and its related stories as supernatural thrillers rather than horror stories. One critic has classified *The Night Configuration* among the greatest surrealist films of all time, but the film aims at what might be more accurately called supernatural realism. Just as Blatty's characters are typically either believers undergoing a crisis of faith or agnostics who find their anticreeds threatened by evidence for God that they cannot quite dismiss, so too his plots create doubts about the clear lines of demarcation between sanity and insanity, between modern rationalism and primitive myth, and between comedy and tragedy. An admirer of Graham Greene, who described his own stories as existing on the "dangerous edge of things," Blatty deserves to be called a theological writer for a number of reasons. There is, first, his preoccupation with the relationship between religion and science, most obviously with the way the limits of the latter invite us to reconsider the merits of the former. But Blatty is also interested in the analogies between science and religion, with the way the scientific impulse, especially in the field of cosmology, is motivated by the same sort of wonder about the whole as is the religious impulse. This is a Catholic insight, fostered in Blatty as much by his training in Thomism as by his early admiration for Teilhard de Chardin, the model for Lancaster Merrin, the elderly priest in *The Exorcist*. There is, second, his preoccupation with the culture of violence and its logic of endlessly perpetuating vengeance, a culture that, in his novels, finds itself eclipsed or undermined by a different sort of logic, that of sacrificial love. Most notably in *The Exorcist* but also elsewhere, the logic of redemption is expressed in sacramental terms, as grace operates through sensible signs and through the authority of the ordained priest.

Blatty's gift for imaginatively arresting openings is evident in the way *The Exorcist* moves back and forth between an archeological dig in the still-primitive world of northern Iraq and the sophisticated center of world power, Washington, D.C., and Georgetown. The introductory sequence suggests not only a connection between characters in geographically quite distant parts of the world but also a tension between a superstitious premodern world of myth and the sophisticated world of enlightened science and secular politics.

The blurring of the profound and the absurd reaches its zenith in Blatty's self-proclaimed sequel to *The Exorcist*. *The Ninth Configuration*, the leanest of Blatty's books, mixes zany humor with metaphysical speculation. The various psychological tensions in the story—between levity and gravity, between the suppressed past and the uncertain present, between guilt and healing—find explosive release in one of the most macabre bar fight scenes in film history.

The setting is a remote Pacific Northwest castle, a makeshift sanitarium for shell-shocked soldiers from the Vietnam War. Colonel Kane (Stacy Keach in the film), who suffers from nightmares of battle scenes in Nam, is the new doctor sent to treat the inmates, who include an astronaut, Captain Cutshaw, who went insane just before a scheduled space trip. Cynical officials suspect that many of the inmates are feigning madness to avoid military service. Recurring allusions to Hamlet, including an impromptu performance involving dogs as actors, highlight the thesis that, as one character glosses Hamlet, one might feign madness to fend off actual madness.

Blatty's interest in the intersection of science and religion is on full display in this novel. Its postwar setting links madness to fear and violence, to guilt and trauma, and to the surprising reappearance of conscience in the souls of the most bloodthirsty of men. (It helps to recall that the earliest version of this story was called *Twinkle, Twinkle, Killer Kane.*) But this also raises the question of alienation and whether the evolution of species is the best means of understanding human history. As Kane muses at one point, perhaps conscience is a memory of an original state, perhaps we have not evolved and are actually going backward rather than forward and, in the process, becoming increasingly alienated from God—the word, he is quickly reminded, modern psychiatry is forbidden to speak.

There is also the problem of evil in an apparently godless universe, a problem science has had no greater success than religion in resolving. As Cutshaw bluntly puts it, "I believe in the Devil alright. And you know why? Because the prick keeps doing commercials!" About to blast off on a moon mission, Cutshaw was paralyzed by the prospect of entering vast, empty space. A phrase from Pascal captures his psychic dejection: "the silence of these infinite spaces fills me with dread." He could not travel alone into what is "just empty space . . . so cold . . . so far away." If he were to get stuck up there, and if there were no God, then he would be "really, really alone."

The fusion of the metaphysical and the personal, the cosmological and the existential again calls to mind Walker Percy. *Lost in the Cosmos*—the title of a Percy book and a pervasive theme in his fiction—might have made a good subtitle for *The Ninth Configuration.* In this case, the reckoning with chance opens up the possibility of perceiving a deeper and higher order at work. Blatty highlights the striking parallels between twentieth-century science and religion, the mysterious ways paradox operates at the subatomic level, and especially the stupefying way simplicity and chance give rise to marvelously complex orders within orders. As Kane puts it, "For life to have appeared spontaneously on earth, there first had to be in existence a protein molecule of a certain dissymmetrical configuration, the configuration point nine. But according to the laws of probability. . . ."

Another Percy theme, this one from Percy's *Lancelot,* is a commonplace in Blatty's writings: the notion that, if everyone is either nice or sick, there is no longer any such thing as evil or heroic sacrifice. The dramatic depiction of the reality of evil, in the face of various modern attempts at reduction, is at the heart of *The Exorcist,* one of the most terrifying tales of all time. After a sinister opening in Iraq, the story settles into Georgetown, where the actress Chris MacNeil (Ellen Burstyn) is filming a movie. As filming begins, MacNeil's daughter, Regan (Linda Blair), suffers various kinds of strange afflictions and exhibits unnatural powers. As the girl her mother has known gradually recedes from view, a malevolent and grotesque personality announces its presence.

As is often the case in tales of evil, the family is in some sense seen as the source of the affliction. Regan MacNeil is the only child of divorced parents. An early scene on Regan's birthday has the mother failing to contact Regan's father who is away in Europe with another woman. As her anger and frustration swell, she curses Regan's father in words overheard by Regan. The daughter indirectly expresses her anxiety over her absent father by inquiring about her mother's relationship with the director of her movie, Burke Dennings. Chris feebly tries to assuage her worries, but the mood runs counter to her assurances. In fact, the setting for the exchange is Regan's invitation to her mother to join her in playing with her new imaginary friend, Captain Howdy (her father's name is Howard), on the Ouija board. Lacking human affection and communication, Regan conjures up an apparently make-believe friend.

Through the strategy of subtle but cumulative suggestion, we are led slowly into a confrontation with evil. Increasingly strange sounds, emanating from behind Regan's closed bedroom door, repeatedly call her mother (and us) up a staircase, down a hallway, and into her room. With each trip, we mark the growing alienation of Regan from the public world of her fellow humans. We are gradually enveloped by an insidious and inexplicable force. Evil's insidiousness is evident at the cast party held at the MacNeil house early in the movie. Without provocation and without evidence, a drunken Burke Dennings belligerently accuses MacNeil's German servant of being a Nazi. Dennings is later pressed into service to watch over Regan and is found dead at the bottom of those now famous steps, with his head twisted around. The inexplicability of evil is indirectly portrayed in the only scene that shows us MacNeil at work on her movie, in a scene about a student rebellion on the campus of Georgetown University. As Dennings gets things rolling on the set, a producer, played by Blatty, asks, "Is the scene really essential, Burke? Would you just consider it, whether or not we could do without it?" To this question, MacNeil adds one of her own concerning the motives of the student protesters: "Well, why are they tearing the building down?" Dennings answers only Chris' question: "Shall we summon the writer? He's in Paris, I believe." To which Chris responds, "Hiding?" This film within the film subordinates the question about the motives for rebellion and destruction under the question of who is in charge of the script and what his intentions are. This turns our attention to the author of *The Exorcist* and the author of the story of human life, namely, God. The question of whether God speaks in *The Exorcist* is never unequivocally answered.

The strategy of Blatty and Friedkin in the first part of the film is an application of T. S. Eliot's principle that the "religious mind works by exclusion." The film carefully sets up and then punctures the dominant, secular account of evil, notably that proffered by Enlightenment science which reduces evil either to antecedent, external influences such as childhood trauma or to underlying somatic illness. The method meets the audience on its own terms. Because the family of Regan has no religious beliefs, they begin where most Americans begin, by seeking out the psychosomatic roots of the girl's disorder. The doctors methodically attempt, first, to "exhaust the somatic possibilities" and then to trace her illness to a "lesion in the temporal lobe." When neither offers any hope of a cure, the dream team of doctors concedes that exorcism has an "outside chance of a cure" as a kind of "shock treatment." The disorder, one doctor explains in dispassionate and clinical terms, is rooted in conflict and guilt. Since the patient suffers from a "delusion of invasion," the exorcism may work "purely through the force of suggestion."

Abandoning medical science, Chris MacNeil introduces herself to Fr. Karras, a Jesuit psychiatrist from Georgetown University, and then abruptly inquires how one would go about getting an exorcism. An incredulous Karras responds that the first thing Chris would have to do is travel in "a time machine back to the sixteenth century. We simply don't use exorcism now that we know about various psychological disorders—all the things they taught me at Harvard." The scene sets up the battle between medieval Catholicism and modern Enlightenment science with its eschewal of religion as superstition. Although the movie takes seriously the claims of modern science to explain certain kinds of disorder and hence to reduce some evil to psychosomatic illness, it reverses the modern hierarchical relationship of science and religion. At one point, the film alternates between scenes of Fr. Karras saying Mass and the doctors' performing a rather gruesome series of tests on Regan. The Mass is depicted at the moment of consecration, when the bread and wine become the body and blood of Christ. It commemorates Christ's personal sacrificial offering of his body for sinful humankind. In the hospital scenes, Regan, observed from afar by a team of doctors, is injected with dye and inserted into a variety of monitoring devices. The dispassionate and impersonal manner in which her body is subjected to the instruments of medical science is excruciating to watch.

More than any other character, Karras mediates between the audience and the direct confrontation with evil. He is an attractive and sympathetic figure, at once athletic, intelligent, and vulnerable. He suffers the doubts symptomatic of the modern age; his struggle with faith, his perplexity, is ours. Two early scenes in the movie clue us into his trials and the fault lines in his character. In the first, he begs for reassignment to New York, where he might care for his aging mother. He also voices concerns about whether he's fit to continue as a psychologist for priests. He confesses, "I think I've lost my faith." In the second, on one of his trips to New York, his uncle accusingly states, "If you weren't a priest, you'd be a famous psychiatrist and your mother" wouldn't be destitute. As the pressure builds, we are shown a scene of Karras, the former boxer, pummeling a boxing dummy. This foreshadows the final scene of the film, where Karras will once again resort to pugilism as a release of his frustrations. The film accentuates male figures, especially priests and fathers, both by their presence and their absence. Questions about male authority and fidelity and about the nature of masculinity, courage, and violence are never far from the surface of the plot. Nonetheless, the skeptical modern priest will become the sacramental vehicle of the liberation of a soul from the clutches of evil. The significance of Fr. Karras' given name, Damien, is not lost on Fr. Merrin, who explains to Chris MacNeil that Damien was a priest to lepers on the island of Molokai who ended up catching the disease himself. Later, Merrin comments to Karras on what a beautiful name Damien is. Here as there, sacrificial love defeats the cynicism of evil and undoes its mechanical chain of malicious acts.

If Fr. Karras is our way into the action, he is not, at least initially, the principal opponent of the demon. The film begins with Fr. Merrin, a frail, elderly Jesuit and an experienced exorcist, on an archeological dig in Iraq, near the ancient biblical city of Nineveh. When he discovers a small statue of a demon, he begins to tremble and makes plans at once to return to the United States. The opening foreshadows the ultimate explanation of the mysterious events now beginning in Georgetown. It also links the modern skeptical world of contemporary America with the primitive and apparently superstitious world of the Middle East.

When Fr. Merrin enters the house to the screeching sounds of the demon echoing his name through the building, he wants to begin the exorcism at once. Karras asks, "Do you want to hear the background of the case?" Merrin responds, "Why?" When Karras continues and notes that there seem to be three personalities, Merrin responds curtly, "There is only one." The invading spirit seems less interested in Regan, an easy conquest, than in the priests. When Fr. Karras first visits Regan, the demon challenges him by saying, "The sow is mine." When Karras suggests an exorcism, the demon welcomes it as a means of bringing them closer together. Karras asks, "You and Regan?" The demon responds, "No. You and us." The spirit preys upon Karras' weaknesses, his faltering faith, and his guilt over abandoning his mother. Worn down by the rigors of the exorcism and especially by the devil's use of his dead mother's voice to play upon his guilt, Fr. Karras is unable to continue. In the final scene, Fr. Merrin orders an exhausted and nearly defeated Karras to leave the room. When he returns, Karras discovers Merrin dead on the floor and the possessed child chuckling on the bed. He seizes Regan and beats her. When he realizes what he's doing, he stops and shouts, "Take me." As the devil enters him, Karras strains to resist him and then leans toward Regan as if to strangle her. Momentarily regaining control of himself, he hurls himself out the window and down the steps, where he lies limp and dying at the bottom. His closest friend, a Jesuit, arrives, holds Karras' hand, and asks whether he is sorry for his sins. Karras flexes his hand in affirmation.

There is an intimate link of everyday vices and foibles to a cosmic battle between good and evil. Through our manifold weaknesses, we are vulnerable to assault from malevolent spiritual forces. If there is an answer, it is one that points beyond morality narrowly construed to a narrative of redemption, not to what we achieve on our own but to what can be done for us through a divine gift. The key to the battle between the devil and Merrin is that the latter is merely an instrument, admittedly a conscious and willing instrument, of the grace of Christ. This is one reason that the exorcist must adhere so closely to the prescribed ritual. The incarnation of evil in an act of possession is countered by the sensible signs of priestly garments, scriptural prayers, and holy water, all of which reflect the incarnation of God himself in Christ. The sacramental response to evil requires free human cooperation with the divine and the mediation of God's love and mercy through bodily things.

Without the prescribed ritual or some other means of expressing the love of God for the child, what little intelligibility there is to the human cooperation with the divine in the eradication of evil is lost. Indeed, except for the occasional maternal lamentations of Chris MacNeil, no one in the film expresses love for Regan. Even Merrin seems more interested in confronting his old nemesis than in restoring Regan to health. On the question of the purpose of possession, an important exchange occurs in the book, only a severely truncated version of which appears in the movie:

"Then what would be the purpose of possession?" Karras said, frowning. "What's the point?"

"Who can know?" answered Merrin. "Who can really hope to know?" He thought for a moment. And then probingly continued: "Yet I think the demon's target is not the possessed. It's us . . . the observers . . . every person in this house. And I think—I think the point is to make us despair; to reject our own humanity, Damien: to see ourselves as ultimately bestial; as ultimately vile and putrescent; without dignity; ugly; unworthy."

Of course, certain scenes in *The Exorcist* did help to unleash the theatrics of evil in mainstream horror films and to provide fodder for comic spoofs of levitating bodies and head-spinning, vomit-spewing teen girls. Neither the low art of the grotesque nor the trivial pop culture allusions ought to be the final word on *The Exorcist*. In contrast to contemporary horror films in which vivisection is on display from start to finish and serves no moral or even dramatic purpose, the elements of the grotesque emerge in *The Exorcist* only well into the second half of the film and in the context of what is, by that point, clearly a diabolical invasion. Although the film became famous at the time of its release for the trauma it caused audience members, the most traumatic scenes were not those dealing with demonic possession but with an ordinary set of medical procedures, in which the camera captures in an unadorned fashion the use of needles on Regan's body. Moreover, the demon never actually creates; it only mimics, inverts, and mocks. Its apparent artistry is entirely parasitic. Evil is a vacuum in an otherwise good created order. Asked to reveal its name, the demon responds, "I am no one," and begs not to be sent back into the void.

Blatty certainly did not intend to skew our conception of evil toward the singularly dramatic cases of full-scale possession and away from ordinary acts of malice. Merrin explains to Karras that he sees the influence of evil "not in wars and very seldom in extraordinary interventions such as here . . . this girl . . . this poor child. No, I see it most often in the little things, Damien; in the senseless, petty spites; the misunderstandings; the cruel and cutting word that leaps unbidden to the tongue between friends. Between lovers. Enough of these, and we have no need of Satan to manage our wars; these we manage for ourselves . . . for ourselves . . ."

Something of the enduring influence of Blatty's work is evident in a recent interview with contemporary Mexican filmmaker Guillermo del Toro, who exhibited his talents in such horror films as *Cronos* and *Hellboy* and the darkly political *The Devil's Backbone*. Talking with *Sight and Sound* about *Pan's Labyrinth*—a remarkable film that moves between history and fantasy, drama and myth, and thus creates an adult fairy tale imbued with a profound ethical vision—del Toro credits the influence of William Peter Blatty, particularly his *The Ninth Configuration*, for its dramatically convincing portrayal of "redemption through sacrifice and the giving of your blood to save others." As was true in Blatty's work, so too in del Toro's latest: some of the conventions of the horror genre open up the possibility of the recovery of symbols too often trivialized in modern life. What del Toro says about the difference between a maze and a labyrinth helps elucidate Blatty's labyrinthine plots of good and evil. Whereas the maze is a "place where you get lost," the labyrinth is "essentially a place of transit: an ethical and moral transit to an inevitable center." Thus, the tasks of the main character, a young girl named Ofelia, are not simply arbitrary trials from which she will emerge to proceed with her previous life. Instead, they are trials that will test her character and that underscore the fundamentally ethical character of human choice. With its deployment of the classical motif of the labyrinth, *Pan's Labyrinth* invokes various pagan themes, but as is made clear by the conclusion, the film's ethical vision, its forbidding of direct harm against the innocent, is more at home in a Christian than in a pagan universe.

Similar motifs surface in another recent Spanish-language film, *The Orphanage*, produced and presented by Guillermo del Toro but directed by Juan Antonio Bayona, which features a spectacular setting for a ghost story—a large, old house, surrounded by thick woods, and just yards from the coast, where the sea has carved out hidden caves along the strand of an isolated cove. With echoes of *The Sixth Sense* and *The Others*, *The Orphanage* is a crisp and well-executed film, with outstanding performances in the lead roles of mother and son, moments of genuine suspense, and an ending that poses the question of whether—as Donne puts it—death is nothing more than "one short sleep past." As was true of *Pan's Labyrinth*, there is a dramatic intersection of fantasy and history, the dead and the living. Interest-ingly, *The Orphanage* also recalls Blatty's *Ninth Configuration*, specifi-cally in the role played by a religious medal (of St. Anthony) and in the theme of death embraced as a proof of love. "Can I wake up now?" is a question Simon poses to his mother early in the film. That question resonates throughout the entire story, a convincing portrait of souls caught between two lives in the short sleep that is death.

In contrast to the nothingness of evil, there is, in these films, the enduring power of sacrificial love. Here one cannot help but recall Fr. Merrin's explanation that Damien was named after the saint who in the process of ministering to lepers caught the disease himself and died of it. Damien Karras offers himself in place of the girl, tries to resist the demon's attempt to take over his will, and—when he realizes he may do harm to the now cured girl—does the only thing he can do to eliminate that occasion of sin. He hurls himself out the window. Not only is his final act not an act of suicide, it is in fact a triumph, as Blat-ty's description of his final moments at the bottom of the now famous steps indicates. Dyer arrives, kneels beside his friend, and offers him absolution for his sins. As the life drains out of him, he is still aware enough to respond to questions by squeezing Dyer's hand. Then Dyer sees "peace" in his eyes and "joy at the end of the heart's longing." He also sees something not here in this world. Our glimpse of his glimpse of heaven suggests that love is more powerful than evil, indeed than death itself. For all of the demonic magic on display in *The Exorcist*, the book and film are both about a deeper magic than that.

THE AESTHETICS OF EVIL: FROM TERROR TO COMIC BANALITY

The consequences of reducing multiple perspectives to that of the demonic antihero are played out in two popular films from 1991, *Cape Fear* and *The Silence of the Lambs*. These films, especially the former, treat the traditional divisions into good and evil and into victims and assailants as mere conventions. Societal norms of right and wrong are obstacles to self-knowledge, obstacles that render us timid conform-ists. By contrast, anyone who breaks through the conventions and stands beyond good and evil attains a kind of clarity and resolve that most human beings lack. If timidity is allied to conformity, courage evinces itself in creativity, in an artistic violation of the inherited codes of decent, law-abiding people. The political problem of courage—the difficulty of finding a place for that virtue in modern bureaucratic society—gives rise to the antihero, admired for the antipolitical exercise of artistic boldness. Once these tendencies are unleashed, we're well on the way toward having sympathy for the devil.

The problem with this approach is that it undermines the gravity of the quest for evil. The seriousness of evil dissipates and the tone becomes one of satire or black comedy. Its sensationalistic scenes made *The Exorcist* a common target of satire on late-night comedy skits for years after its release; the same is true of the characters played by DeNiro and Hopkins in *Cape* and *Silence*. Where God is no longer a serious player, the devil's rebellion loses its weight and risks becoming comic. The antics of the demonic agent take center stage as the struggle between vice and virtue in the souls of ordinary human beings gradually recedes from view.

All of these elements are operative in the 1991 film *Cape Fear*, starring Robert DeNiro as an ex-con who returns from jail to torment his defense lawyer, played by Nick Nolte, whom he blames for his ending up in jail in the first place. *Cape Fear* is instructive not only because it contains themes germane to this study or because it explicitly links those themes to Nietzsche's philosophy but also because it is a remake of a version produced in 1962.

In the early film, often loosely associated with the genre of film noir, it seems clear at the very beginning who the bad guy is and who the good guys are. Our first sight of Cady, the ex-con, played by Robert Mitchum, is of him entering a courthouse. As he begins to go up the stairs, he passes a woman carrying a stack of books. She drops one and he never even takes notice of her. The relatively minor act of incivility clues us into his character. He has come to town to confront and ultimately terrorize Sam Bowden, a legal councillor, played by Gregory Peck, who had a confrontation with Cady eight years earlier while on a visit to Baltimore. He heard a girl whimpering in an alley, went to lend assistance, and wound up scuffling with Cady. Since Bowden testified against him, Cady holds him responsible for his incarceration. While Peck does not play a hero, he is a respected member of his community, a faithful husband, and a good father. His wife and daughter are also reasonably intelligent, decent persons. There is not a hint of the detached, mocking tone of irony in the depiction of the Bowdens as upstanding American citizens.

The absence of irony doesn't mean that the American system of justice is beyond question, since it cannot provide invincible protection against the likes of Cady. In spite of Bowden's close association with the police, American law is inadequate. The sense of helplessness of law-abiding citizens generates much of the fear in the story. In a pivotal scene, the mother makes the innocent mistake of leaving her daughter alone in the car for a few minutes, while she attends to some errands. As Cady slowly and deliberately approaches the car, the girl panics and escapes into an adjacent building. When she hears footsteps pursuing her, she runs out of the building and into the street where she is struck by a car. She is luckily unhurt, but the encounter reinforces the sense of the proximity of the threat and of his family's vulnerability to it.

Cady's brutality is most explicitly brought out when he takes a woman he's just met to a hotel for sex. Once in the room, the mood turns ominous. The woman lies in the bed facing Cady, who stands at its foot. She reads the harmful intent in his eyes, cowers in fear, and makes a futile attempt to escape. When next we meet her, she is beaten, distraught, ashamed, and so fearful of retaliation that she's unwilling to press charges against him, even when Bowden tells her of the threat to his daughter. Bowden reluctantly looks for help beyond the law, first from a private investigator and then, at the investigator's suggestion, from some thugs who attempt to rough Cady up.

The sense of being caught in a labyrinth, the accent on the limits to law, and the temptation of the victim to embrace evil mechanisms— these are all motifs of film noir. The Bowdens come gradually to the unsettling realization that they cannot rely exclusively on the law, that they will have to exercise ingenuity in their battle with malignant forces. So they decide to take matters into their own hands, initially by attempting to intimidate Cady and then by setting a trap for him. Trapping Cady is the only means of liberating themselves from his entrapment. At this juncture, it is not so clear who is on the side of the law. Situated now somewhere between the law and Cady, the Bowdens put their own character in question and risk being seduced by Cady's nihilism.

Significantly, the climactic scene at Cape Fear occurs on a houseboat outside the city. The return from the manufactured world of the city to the natural world allows for two possible resolutions. The first is the nihilistic discovery that there is no natural basis for the American system of justice; that is, might makes right. The second is the recognition of a natural standard more fundamental than, but finally compatible with, conventional law. The Bowdens' ruse is not a path away from conventional justice but a circuitous route to its confirmation. When Bowden finally has Cady in a position where he could kill him, Bowden exercises restraint and chooses instead to let him rot in prison where he can contemplate his failed attempt at vengeance. The concluding note is thus one of a sober and modest justification of the American system, of the need for the procedures of justice to be complemented by virtues of prudence, loyalty, courage, and restraint in citizens. Indeed, Bowden's entire family exercises courage, but that virtue is allied to a host of others and is never celebrated as an end in itself. By contrast, Cady's unrestrained boldness is but a simulacrum of real courage, and his preying upon innocent women and children reveals him to be unmanly and cowardly.

Almost thirty years later in 1991, Martin Scorsese directed a new version of *Cape Fear.* In giving small parts to Mitchum and Peck, Scorsese clearly has the previous version in mind. He hints at the contrast between the two versions by shifting the two actors' allegiances. Mitchum now plays a detective attempting to catch Cady, while Peck is the sleazy lawyer defending Cady. No character in the later version of the film is admirable. When we first meet Bowden, played by Nick Nolte, he is on the verge of an affair with a coworker. We soon learn that his past infidelities have nearly ruined his marriage. When the latest object of his lust is beaten and raped by Cady, Bowden shows little or no remorse, even after she confesses to him that she ended up with Cady because Bowden stood her up. Bowden's relationship to Cady is not without ambiguity. Fourteen years ago, he defended Cady in a rape case, and because of the brutality of the act, he suppressed a report that the girl was promiscuous. A not so subtle mixture of sensuality and violence underlies the entire Bowden family. The daughter, who has suffered from the indifference and hostility of her parents toward one another, is withdrawn and inarticulate, with pathetically little sense of self. After she gets in trouble at school for smoking marijuana, her father yells at her but confides privately to his wife that it's not such a big deal because it is almost a sacrament in some societies. To which the wife responds, "Yeah, along with incest, necrophilia, and bestiality." Even more than in *The Exorcist*, in *Cape Fear* the disorder in the family anticipates the evil to be wreaked by the invading assailant.

The most striking contrast between the two versions is in the depiction of the Bowden family. What sort of family is this? It is the family produced by liberal individualism and its sexual revolution. Composed of isolated individuals and dominated by their private lusts, this is a family based not on trust and mutual affection but on lies and suspicion. Their interaction is characterized by studied avoidance and accusing silence, broken by explosive verbal assaults and recriminations. The parents have nothing to hand on to the next generation. Their barely suppressed violence is the natural result of their futile attempt to retain traditional marital roles in a nihilistic culture.

The character of the wife, played by Jessica Lange, is especially amoral. She alternates between being horrified at Cady's acts and wishing for further confrontations. After Cady kills their dog, she weeps but quickly recovers to shout, "I'd . . . like to kill him." Just as in the earlier version, so too here the family attempts to set up Cady. As they wait for him, she calmly admits to Sam, "I'd like to know how strong we are or how weak." The only way to do that, she adds, is by going through this. She is well ahead of her husband, at least in her willingness to entertain the need to match violence with violence. Sam, although accustomed to a host of vices, confesses to the private investigator that he doesn't know whether he can "live with killing a man," and the final scene of the movie finds him writhing in horror at the blood on his hands.

In *Cape Fear*, the only example of a common bond between characters occurs when Cady, pretending to be Bowden's daughter's new drama teacher, calls her on the phone to introduce himself and to set up a meeting with her. Both over the phone and face to face, he plays upon her disaffection with her parents, upon her teenage sense of being misunderstood, and upon her burgeoning sense of her own sexuality. Even after she becomes suspicious and realizes who he is, he allays her fears by playing upon her hunger for understanding and affection. Predictably, she sympathizes with him. Where does this leave the audience?

The feelings of sympathy for the victims soon turn to repulsion or worse, to a kind of detached enjoyment at the spectacle of evil. The only positive feeling that one can take away from a film like the Scorsese *Cape Fear* is a macho feeling of achievement at having endured so much terror. Is this not precisely the education that the pseudo-Nietzschean Cady offers? We participate in his exhilarating project of surpassing established limits and overcoming prohibitions. If law and morality no longer educate or reform, they do serve to heighten and intensify the pleasure derived from acts of violence. The explicit and excessive reliance on sensationalist gore in the new version overwhelms the imagination and stupefies the intellect. It exercises a tyranny over the imagination that resembles Cady's control over the bodies of his victims. By contrast, the older version of *Cape Fear* hints at the commissions of violence by presenting them partially or indirectly. The suggestion to the imagination invites the cooperation of the intellect and awakens it to questioning.

Gone is *The Exorcist*'s attention to subtle differences in character and to multiple perspectives on the human condition. These are replaced by a superficial aesthetics of evil, by trying to outdo other films in the depiction of offensive and degrading acts. This competition is subject to the law of diminishing returns. Once a film has deployed nearly all the available means of explicit terror, it is difficult to surpass it.

Whatever depth there is in the recent *Cape Fear* is derivative of its overt philosophical nihilism. Both movies depict Cady as having received something of a legal education in jail, but only the Scorsese version invests him with philosophical significance. We learn from the investigator tailing him that he spent part of a day in a library reading Nietzsche's *Thus Spake Zarathustra*. Both the investigator and Bowden know that Nietzsche said, "God is dead," but they do not comment on the central role of the superman in Zarathustra. Cady fancies himself a Nietzschean superman. After he beats back the attackers hired by Bowden to rough him up, he yells that he can outthink them, outphilosophize them, and outfight them. Quoting an obscure seventeenth-century philosopher, he adds that "God is not above me nor I beneath him." His "mission" in jail was to "become more than human." The criminal justice system has failed miserably in its intent to educate Cady in the social virtues of American society, whatever they might be. In the absence of any clearly defined sense of the virtues to which American life is ordered or of a persuasive vision of the goals of our society, the procedures of the justice system are but thinly veiled instruments of illegitimate coercion. Jail teaches him that power is arbitrary and that whatever deprivation and punishment one is subjected to can be put to good use. So prison made him stronger and less vulnerable, more capable of evil and less susceptible to the pull of a social conscience. He is liberated from the code of good and evil that society, through both covert and overt means, impresses on the memory of its citizens. He is beyond good and evil.

On the surface at least, these are all Nietzschean themes. For him, man is the as yet undetermined animal, an animal that creates its own values and whose future leaders will engage in acts of self-overcoming to bring about a revaluation of all values. Such a project entails, first, seeing through the conventional code of morality operative in one's society and, second, a violent destruction of that code to clear a path for new and more vital ways of life.

At the end of the film, we are left not only with little clarification concerning the distinction between good and evil but also with the question of whether either side has won. This version also ends at Cape Fear, outside the city and back to nature. But the coastal resort is under siege from a torrential storm. Mirroring the tumult in Cady's soul, nature itself is a merciless vortex of destruction. After a seemingly endless series of confrontations with Cady on their boat at Cape Fear, Bowden manages to handcuff Cady to the boat. As it is torn apart by the raging water, his wife and daughter are thrown free. Nearly at the shoreline, Bowden and Cady beat one another with rocks. Finally, the tide pulls Cady into and eventually under the water. As he sinks, Cady laughs and then sings, "I'm bound for the Promised Land." In this final act, which denies any possibility of rectification or justice, Cady affirms his own way of life. His clarity of purpose surpasses that of all the other characters, weighed down as they are in their bourgeois world of petty pleasures, socially acceptable vices, and suppressed violence.

In contrast to the previous version, in the later movie Cady is not the antithesis of society but its liberation from a thin veil of law and order. He is not a coward whose recourse to violence against the innocent and the weak is symptomatic of his wickedness but rather one who sees that, since all are implicated in evil, no one is innocent. He comprehends and transcends the social world of weak souls, who need one another and the force of the law to reinforce their petty view that self-restraint is good and strength is wicked. In Nietzschean language, the basis of this social world is resentment at those who distinguish themselves as individuals, who exhibit a courageous self-affirmation and refuse to conform to the opinions of the majority.

Is Cady, then, an incarnation of Nietzsche's superman, of his anti-Christ? Nietzsche describes his "free spirit" as being educated by "everything evil, terrible and tyrannical in man." He feels "malice against the lures of dependence that lie hidden in honors, or money, or offices." Cady practices the virtue of courage, of heroic individualism, which is the virtue most lacking in the petty vices of modern society. Like Nietzsche, he is obsessed with Christianity. Despite these similarities, Cady is not a neat fit with Nietzsche's superman. Cady promotes making strength out of fear and is motivated by resentment and revenge, the motives not of Nietzsche's superman but of the petty and sickly soul of the slave. His destructive tendencies are ordered to no great re-creation of higher ideals. His crude and uncomprehending recitation of fragments of a philosophy of the superman are precisely what result from a popularization of Nietzsche's teaching, from the confused attempt of the lower type of soul to live out the destiny of the higher type. He is not, then, beyond the bourgeois Christian world but merely its mirror image. Although Nietzsche would certainly find Cady's character wanting, even comical, his criticisms would not be those commonly associated with traditional morality; if Nietzsche's project was to induce a state of chaos in society so as to incite a search for new modes of life, then he could have little objection to Cady, except to say that neither Cady nor Scorsese should be confused with artists of the highest rank.

Cape Fear was not the most important or successful movie of 1991 to address the topic of evil. That year the Oscar for Best Picture went to *The Silence of the Lambs*, as did the awards for best actor and actress. Since the plot was rather flimsy, the best picture award might be seen as a second commendation of Anthony Hopkins, whose portrayal of the cannibal, Hannibal Lecter, is the film's great draw. Closer to Nietzsche in his refined aesthetic sense, Hopkins' Hannibal shares with DeNiro's Cady a penchant for the aesthetics of evil. As in *The Exorcist*, so too here the authority of medical and psychiatric science comes under relentless scrutiny. Since Lecter himself is the most talented psychiatrist we encounter in the film and since he rejects science's ability to interpret him, we are continually confronted with science's shortcomings. *Silence* also brings evil into closer alignment with the judicial system.

The movie begins with Clarice Starling, a trainee for the FBI, played by Jodie Foster, finding herself in the middle of an investigation of a serial murder case. The murderer has been given the nickname Buffalo Bill because he peels off the hides of his victims. Early in the show, Starling's boss sends her to interview Lecter, a highly successful psychiatrist turned cannibalistic murderer, now housed in a psychiatric prison in Baltimore. Starling thinks she is simply there to get information about Lecter, when in fact her boss hopes that, having developed a rapport with Lecter, she will be able to elicit from him a case analysis of Buffalo Bill.

A salient but mysterious clue in the Buffalo Bill murders is the presence of a butterfly in the mouth of the victims. Lecter interprets this as a symbol of the killer's quest for self-transformation. Starling hits upon a likely behaviorist interpretation: the killer is a transvestite. Lecter counters that the killer only thinks he is a transvestite. Underlying the sexual deviance is a deeper longing for a transformation of a different sort. Into what? We are never told. Perhaps into the sort of being Lecter has become? Violence, murder, and sexual perversion are the instruments of artistic self-fashioning, an art exercised with clinical detachment on the bodies of victims.

The character of Lecter takes to its logical term the criminal's understanding of himself as beyond good and evil. He turns evil into high art. His sense of decorum is evident in his assertion that "discourtesy is unspeakably ugly." After Lecter makes his escape, Clarice is confident he won't come after her: "I can't explain it. He would consider that rude." Lecter is learned, even something of a philosopher. He counsels Clarice to return to first principles and to follow the advice of Marcus Aurelius, who stipulated that of each thing you must ask, "Wat is it in itself? . . . What is its nature?" But the sense of refinement exists alongside, or better coincides with, an unspeakable brutality. The point is dramatically brought out in the pivotal scene near the end of the film, when Lecter escapes by viciously murdering two armed police guards. As he completes his task, his face covered with the blood of his victims, he deftly wields an officer's nightstick in the manner of a conductor. His musical accompaniment? Bach's *Goldberg Variations*.

One of the conversations between Starling and Lecter unveils the motives behind her choice of a profession. In exchange for information on the Buffalo Bill case, Lecter demands that Starling answer questions about her own life. After relating her worst childhood memory, the death of her father, Clarice tells how, as an orphan, she was sent to live on a ranch, where she awakened one morning to an inexplicably horrifying sound. Going to investigate, she discovers lambs screaming as they are being slaughtered. She opens the gate for the lambs, but none escape. In a vain attempt to save at least one of them, she grabs a lamb and runs away. She is of course found, and the lamb is killed. As Lecter proceeds with his analysis, she admits that the screaming of the lambs still haunts her dreams. Lecter concludes that she is pursuing the serial killer in the hope of silencing the lambs by saving an innocent victim. The importance of Starling's confession is multiple. It provides us with her motive: to save the innocent. It also implicitly raises the question at the heart of the old problem of evil: what sort of universe allows for the capricious slaying of the innocent? Both Lecter's resistance to psychological explanation and Starling's motives push us to confront the reality of evil and the unanswerable questions it raises. These themes help to explain Lecter's willingness to work with her, even if that choice is by no means a moral judgment. Instead, it reflects his aesthetics; Starling is more authentic, less trapped in the categories of behaviorism, than are the other authorities.

But Clarice's character does not finally provide a viable alternative to either of the two dominant worldviews in the story, that of bureaucratic, behaviorist law enforcement and that of Lecter's aesthetization of evil. She is Lecter's student, a supposition reinforced by the similarity between his name and the Latin word *lector*, which literally means "reader" but has connotations of one who instructs by lecturing. His name also calls to mind the term "lecher" (in French, the word *lechier* means "to lick"). While he has a sense of decorum, his instruction of Clarice is akin to a sexual possession of her. The crucial clue about Buffalo Bill, the one that leads Clarice directly to him, is that, in Hannibal's words, he "covets." What do we covet? What we see every day. The clue leads Clarice back to the town of the first victim, since the killer must have begun by coveting what he saw in the neighborhood where he lived. From the start, Lecter covets Clarice. In their first encounter, he silently gazes upon her, looking her up and down. A *lector* or reader is someone who interprets by looking or gazing. His psychoanalysis of the deepest secrets of her life is also a kind of covetousness, arising out of a desire to gaze upon, and exploit for his own pleasure, the precious secrets of her psyche. Clarice agrees to Lecter's demand of a quid pro quo and thus willingly submits to his use of her life for his own pleasure in order to gain what she wants from him. Whatever may be its practical efficacy, her consenting to his game subordinates her own vision of the world to his.

Precisely because it is combined with such a sense of decorum and erudition, Lecter's evil is more frightening and more baffling than that of a typical depraved serial killer. Lecter's aesthetization of evil is in part a protest against the standard analyses of evil in his own profession. He refuses to conform to any behaviorist mold. In the first meeting with Starling, she feebly attempts to capitalize on his initial willingness to talk by suggesting that he fill out a questionnaire she's brought along. Lecter balks, "A census taker once tried to test me. I ate his liver with some fava beans and a fine Chianti." He refuses to degrade himself by becoming an instrument; he retains what Nietzsche calls the "pathos of distance" separating the high from the mediocre. In the world of behaviorist psychology, where everything can be explained by case studies and statistics, by tracing deviance to some causal root in the patient's history, there is no freedom and no evil. His successful attempt at eluding the neat categories of psychiatry is a twisted assertion of the reality of freedom, of evil, and of his superiority to those around him. What behaviorism omits is what Nietzsche calls the "basic fact" of the human condition, the "human will, . . . which needs a goal—and it will rather will nothingness than not will." The willing of destruction, of annihilation, as an end in itself is a possible response to the attempt to eliminate inequality, distinction, and freedom from human life.

Given the modern scientific understanding of human behavior in terms of natural laws, there can be no freedom and no evil, because everything is determined by chemical reactions and evil arises solely from a miscalculation of the appropriate way of satisfying genetically determined inclinations. This is the philosophy of progress and Enlightenment; anyone who demurs is labeled irrational and sent for medical treatment. If one actually tries to live consciously in accord with Enlightenment dicta, the result is a paralyzing hyperconsciousness, psychic inertia. (The classic statement of this is Dostoevsky's *Notes from the Underground*.) Precisely what is supposed to lead to the rational satisfaction of all our longings deprives our deliberations of meaning and our actions of any roots in our freedom. Having seen the presuppositions and consequences of Enlightenment theory, who could go on as before? Indeed, who could act at all? If this is right, then there is the possibility of immersing oneself in evil precisely as a means of asserting one's freedom and dignity. This is Lecter's path.

Lecter's cannibalism is the antithesis of civilization, which always includes a code protecting the innocent and a code concerning hospitality to strangers. In ancient societies, it was a mark of humanity to see oneself in the position of the stranger, in a position of weakness and dependence. Hannibal's cannibalism, his incorporating others into himself like food, is a most emphatic denial of the otherness and independence of persons. It is an affront not only to ancient codes of hospitality but also and more pointedly to our code of inalienable human rights and individual dignity. He feeds on other humans (making exceptions not for the innocent but for those he deems "interesting") the way we feed on lower animals. Once again, the body is a vile thing, a putrid object. This is universally true, whether in the FBI laboratory analyses of the corpses or in Buffalo Bill's collection of human hides or, most dramatically, in Hannibal's cannibalism. Modern psychology is perfectly free to analyze him as suffering from an acute narcissistic personality disorder, just as he is free to dismiss that analysis as an attempt to explain his evil away rather than to account for it. Indeed, since there is a comical disproportion between the purported cause and the effect, Lecter will certainly have the last laugh and the last happy meal.

Equality and dignity, the founding principles of Enlightenment politics, are precisely the source of the problem in the behaviorist world of the American criminal justice system. In that world, we are all case studies, reducible to the influences of nature and nurture on us. Everything is predetermined by our past; the future is already a closed book. The only way to excel, to exhibit one's individuality in such a world—a world that has so debased its moral language that goodness is equated with normalcy, that is, with routinized conformity—is to violate the conventions in ways that transcend the standard categories deployed to explain and hence control the abnormal. Lecter exploits the tensions between our hyperbolic rhetoric of individual choice and self-expression, on the one hand, and our sense of increasing homogenization and uniformity, on the other.

These are the mutually reinforcing oppositions that Tocqueville thought would foster the debasement of humanity. Equality of condition renders human beings increasingly alike, yet we continue to boast of diversity and freedom. We have already noted Supreme Court justices, turned poet-philosophers, proclaiming the "right to define one's own concept of existence, of meaning, of the universe, and of the mystery of human life." For most Americans, this right is exercised by a kind of studied indifference to ultimate questions. If a radical conception of the right to self-creation were pursued boldly, the consequences could be terrifying. The desire for unfettered freedom, for complete autonomy, turns everything else, persons as well as things, into a means for the realization of one's personally crafted goals. For some, doing it "my way," to borrow Sinatra's trademark tune, means a preference for Starbuck's decaf latte; for others, it means kiddie porn. If Nietzsche would find such a project distasteful, he would also find the ordinary citizen's preoccupation with justice and with uncovering the hidden roots of conscience in the criminal a boring diversion from the real work of self-creation. But it is hard to see how the radical individualism presupposed by self-creation would not naturally generate narcissism, solipsism, and a violent disregard for all that is extrinsic to the self.

Given the evanescence of supernatural, natural, and conventional codes of conduct, traditional heroism is no longer possible. The film finally celebrates Lecter as antihero. The entire FBI psychiatric team is dependent upon Hannibal's insight. Surrounded by subhumans, he is superhuman: nearly omniscient, he is able to read the secrets of souls on the basis of the slightest hints; virtually omnipotent, he is endowed not so much with physical strength as with supreme cunning and adroitness. At the end, Lecter calls Clarice from the Bahamas. He congratulates her on capturing Buffalo Bill, asks whether the lambs have quit crying, and ensures that he won't trouble her. As she inquires about his plans, the camera shifts from Lecter to Dr. Frederick Chilton, Lecter's nemesis at the Baltimore psychiatric prison. Lecter tells Clarice he is having an old friend for dinner. His insouciant manner of expressing his anticipation of gustatory delight gives a comical note to the ending. The audience is transported from the world of Clarice, who has sympathy for victims, to that of Lecter, who eats them. There are no grounds for seeing Hannibal as tragic. If we find him comic, do we not have a kind of sympathy for the devil?

Sympathy here no longer means pity, because that emotion has been jettisoned along with traditional morality. Instead, it means that we have shifted our way of seeing the world so that we now see it from the devil's perspective and now share his comic take on the bankruptcy of all moral codes.

The comic trajectory of much of contemporary horror presupposes that we have found something attractive in the malignant hero, something that seduces us into his camp. His theatrics demolish the Enlightenment assumption of the neutral observer. Just as Cady and Lecter implicate their interlocutors in their own "liberating" perversity, so too the crafters of their stories implicate us in their visions. The danger is that our laughter will be but an echo of the cynical, mocking laughter of the invading spirit in *The Exorcist*. Of course, the immediate effect of the laughter is the welcome feeling of being released from terror. But even this sort of laughter cancels the great quest for evil by divesting it of significance.

The problem with these heroes is that they negate much but affirm nothing. We may recall here Mark Edmundson's perceptive study of popular culture, which he describes in terms of a dialectical opposition between Gothic elements and the strategy of facile transcendence. The Gothic celebrates hero-villains and depicts all of life as haunted. The dominant, contemporary "antidote" to the Gothic is what Edmundson calls "facile transcendence." It portrays reality in neat and tidy terms and dismisses sinister evil as the stuff of overactive, adolescent imaginations. As Edmundson hints, our Gothic is itself rather facile. Our would-be antiheroes and "avenging angels" have no depth; they are all surface. While they toy with the gap between appearance and reality, they simply substitute the artistic appearances of terror for the appearances of conventional society. Once we see this, they lose their tragic gravity and become comic figures. If the genre of facile transcendence opts for a simplistic metaphysics of goodness, the genre of the debased Gothic opts for a crude and literal metaphysics of evil. If evil is all there is, there is ultimately nothing.

The question is, Where do we go from here? What's the next step in the dramatic depiction of evil? The most obvious move is simply to continue along the same path and to increase the quantity and quality of offensive and shocking material. But this becomes tiresome or ludicrous, as the attempted manipulation of the audience must resort to ever more preposterous methods. Instead of an intimidating profundity, there is a shallowness to the presentation of evil. Evil becomes, in Hannah Arendt's apt term, banal. What makes up for the lack of depth is increasing aesthetic complexity on the surface of the action. As both artist and audience become less capable of taking evil seriously, the adoption of a comic perspective on evil is quite natural.

TORTURE PORN AND THE LAW OF DIMINISHING RETURNS

More recently, horror has surfaced in the form of what is now called torture porn, examples of which can be found in films such as *Hostel* and *Saw*. Concerning the box office success of *Hostel*, writer and director Eli Roth explained to *Box Office Mojo*, "My whole theory was that if it's scary, the public will really respond to it. People want their horror to be horrific. They don't want it to be safe." Respond? Well, yes, the film does call for a response, and at least Roth did not try to dignify the film by describing it as in the tradition of the suspense practiced by Hitchcock. "Horrific" comes closer, but *Hostel* is not so much scary as it is revoltingly grisly. Commenting on *Hostel's* rise, Paul Dergarabedian, president of box office tracker Exhibitor Relations, gushed, "The track record of horror films tells you maybe Hollywood should just release horror movies to be successful. I can't think of a more consistently performing genre at the box office." Well, not exactly. The summer months saw quite a drop in the popularity of the horror film. (Anyone remember the dismal *Dark Water*? I thought not.) Citing the proliferation of zombie movies and "Asian creepy kid movies," a more perceptive studio executive suggests that we are witnessing a "burning-out of the sub-genres" of the horror film.

And before the burnout of the subgenres, there was the burnout of the horror genre's staple, at least in the '80s and '90s—the slasher flick. The modern genre in horror actually dates all the way back to 1960 with *Psycho* and the British classic *Peeping Tom*. It picked up steam over the next twenty years with *Rosemary's Baby, The Exorcist, The Omen*, and *Halloween*—all quality horror films. Two features of these films proved most influential over the next thirty years. First, there is the motif of the serial killer who just cannot seem to be brought under control or even killed, for that matter. Of course, this dramatic device paves a path to endless sequels, but it also stresses a theme of the modern horror genre that evil is something primordial and incapable of being contained by civilization. Second, there are the surface aesthetics of evil, the attempt of one filmmaker after another to outdo predecessors in the number, complexity, and offensive nature of acts of torture, dismemberment, murder, and so forth. Both of these plotting devices are subject to the law of diminishing returns. Audiences, once traumatized by the artistry of *Rosemary's Baby* or *The Exorcist*, are no longer surprised by such things—or at least no longer terrified. Jaded audiences have come to expect such performances and even find them humorous. This trajectory reaches its conclusion in the *Scream* trilogy and the *Scary Movie* films, wherein the conventions of the movie genre (never drink, never have sex, and never say "I'll be right back") are made explicit and spoofed.

Never one to be outdone by his competitors, Quentin Tarantino released the highly aestheticized *Kill Bill*. Tarantino attained fame with a trailblazing and hyperironic mix of humor and violence in two films, *Reservoir Dogs* (1992) and *Pulp Fiction* (1994). With *Kill Bill*, released in two parts or volumes, Tarantino proves that only he can one-up himself. *Kill Bill* achieves what seemed impossible. It is a more intense and more astonishing fusion of the comedic and the violent, a cornucopia of bloody revenge, an effusion of violence not just as entertainment but as a perverse sacramental feast for the intellect, and a "catharsis of bloodletting" that Martin Scorsese has described as a central function of film in our time. Beyond the intellectual excitement of the torturing of the bodies of pregnant women; beyond the simultaneous affirmation of female empowerment (actress Vivica A. Fox thought it was "great" that the women "were in control of our own little world"); beyond the homage to Japanese anime, samurai movies, and spaghetti westerns; beyond all this and through all this, there is Tarantino's giddy obsession with blood—splattered blood, oozing blood, gushing blood. On this subject, his enthusiasm knows no bounds: "Japanese blood is the prettiest. It's like nice, and it has a scarlet redness about it." Chinese blood is "like Kool-Aid almost."

And American blood is "more syrupy kind of stuff." Of the fight scenes between women, Tarantino gushed, "There's something intrinsically cool . . . something intrinsically more painful about beautiful women being abused that way, all right?"

With its fascination with the aesthetics of violence, its varied soundtrack, and its rapid interspersing of brutal violence and light comic touches, *Kill Bill* resembles *Natural Born Killers* (1994), a film for which Tarantino originally helped write the script but from which he removed himself entirely after a dispute with Oliver Stone. Deprived of Tarantino's macabre playfulness, *NBK* became an incoherent combination of over-the-top violence and heavy-handed Stone moralism about contemporary society. By contrast, *Kill Bill* is thoroughly coherent, perfectly executed, and without a hint of morality.

It is true that *Kill Bill* is organized around a revenge plot which itself is understood as an enactment of the samurai code of retaliation. Indeed, it is precisely the Eastern elements in the film, not just the samurai plot but also the stylistic devices of Japanese anime, that make *Kill Bill* something more and different from its predecessors, *Reservoir Dogs* and *Pulp Fiction*. Uma Thurman plays the Bride, a pregnant woman left for dead at the altar by five members of the Deadly Viper Assassination Squad. The film, which resembles *Pulp Fiction* in its violation of linear time sequence, focuses on the Bride's realization of her plot to seek revenge on the squad, with Fox's Vernita Green as the first to feel her wrath.

The film makes an attempt at developing a logic of samurai revenge. The Bride states early on, "It is mercy I lack, not rationality." Rational revenge involves a willingness to kill "even Buddha himself . . . that's the truth at the heart of battle." But the Bride occasionally stays her ruthlessness; moreover, mutual respect and honor surface in the final battle scene with O-Ren Ishii (Lucy Liu), a member of the Viper Squad and an Asian crime lord. After the Bride eliminates a group of warrior servants of O-Ren, she prepares for direct combat with O-Ren, whose character Liu invests with a magisterial and chilling authority. O-Ren smiles and asks, "You didn't think it was going to be that easy?" The Bride pauses, smirks, and admits, "Well, actually for a minute there I did." To which O-Ren responds, "Silly rabbit," a statement the Bride completes: "Trix are for kids." The ensuing battle, shot mostly in black and white, between the Bride and a horde of warriors contains a countless variety of dismemberments and murders. The Bride now faces O-Ren, who first mocks her as a "silly Caucasian girl" who "likes to play with samurai swords" but, as the fight intensifies, quickly apologizes for such ridicule.

The two women face off in soft snow under moonlight and against the background of a beautifully landscaped plot. This is but one of many stylized, orchestrated sets, the upshot of which is to turn the entire film into a vehicle for the aesthetics of violence. For example, Tarantino deploys a sort of *CSI* effect, wherein bullets are shown in slow motion tearing into bodies; he highlights the end-over-end trajectory of an ax that comes to rest in an opponent's skull; and he is ever attentive to blood, which appears first as oil, then as paint, and finally, in cascades, as discolored rain water.

Tarantino thus turns unremitting violence into a sort of perversely religious spectacle, a liturgy that appeals as much to the intellect as to the imagination. Since the 1980s, filmmakers, especially in the horror genre, have sought to overwhelm the imagination of viewers with a magnification of evil, a fact humorously captured in the self-parodies of the horror genre in the *Scream* trilogy. But Tarantino is doing something more and different from simply competing for the title of most violent director. He is, as he recently said, in the business of making viewers aware of precisely how the films work on them. Following *Kill Bill*'s art and action—from humor to excruciating vivisection back to humor—forces viewers to "turn on a dime" and switch emotions. *Kill Bill* is so stylized and so ironic that viewers cannot help but be aware of how the film is working on them.

Now Tarantino is to be credited with forcing on his viewers a cognitive awareness of his film's liturgy of blood. The question is whether the surface irony is sufficient to justify the willing suspension of moral judgment, not moral judgments about the film's hypothetical causal effects on the behavior of already deranged adolescents but the indispensably moral element we bring to any work of art.

While Tarantino seems inclined to offer highly aestheticized versions of torture porn, with real movie stars and technically more sophisticated depictions of bloodletting, other producers take a different approach. For a creative take on the fusion of violent sexuality and sexualized violence that permeates so much of our popular culture, the FX series *Nip/Tuck* was, at least in its initial season, something truly novel. With its only slightly covert allusions to a link between pornography and vivisection, the show features a team of plastic surgeons, Sean McNamara (Dylan Walsh) and Christian Troy (Julian McMahon). With its explicit sexual content, including partial nudity and a penchant for threesomes, its depiction of the blood and guts of plastic surgery, and its violent confrontations between characters, *Nip/Tuck* approaches territory usually reserved for pay cable channels. Woven into its soap opera plotlines is the suggestion of a hidden link between sexual license and the technological project of remaking the human body in light of individual wishes; indeed, the show depicts a deep connection between both of these and raw violence. The show's creator, Ryan Murphy, calls it a "modern day horror story with the plastic surgeons as dueling Dr. Frankensteins."

In its early years, *Nip/Tuck* was the most popular cable-based series among viewers aged 18 to 49; one episode of the series set an FX record with 5.2 million viewers. While the actors see the show as "way over the top" or as "shock TV," Ryan Murphy offers a defense of the realism of the series. He observes, for example, that the medical cases, which range from the surgical removal of an obese woman from her bed to breast implants for a man who wants to sympathize with his wife's breast cancer, are based on actual cases.

Early on, the show set up a stark contrast between Christian as the serial seducer of women and Sean as the family man with wife, Julia, and son, Matt. But in fairly predictable ways, the two have come to resemble each other. Unless they were to become lovers themselves—something not beyond the realm of possibility on a show that knows no limits—it is difficult to imagine two men sharing more than they have. In one episode, they share a prostitute. Beyond that dalliance and their medical practice, they have shared Sean's wife and his son. Christian, it turns out, is the biological father of the son Sean has raised.

In the most dramatically compelling plotline of the first few seasons, the entire world of Miami plastic surgery finds itself in constant fear of the Carver. Reminiscent of the John Doe character from *Se7en*, the Carver assaults and disfigures his victims, making them a sort of public commercial for the moral judgment of the ugliness of our obsession with physical appearance. After a number of attacks, the Carver attacks Christian, who at one point becomes a suspect.

Murphy goes so far as to equate the Carver's butchering attacks with the violence of plastic surgery itself. Of course, on an obvious level, that's a blatant falsehood; those who are attacked by the Carver seek out plastic surgeons to remove their scars and restore their appearance. But on another level, the show dramatically displays what happens once we lose all sense of natural limitations with respect to the body. The surgeons offer not only minor restoration, not just a nip here and a tuck there, but radical reconstructive surgery. The answers to the question "What is it you don't like about yourself?" are potentially unlimited. Their practice embodies the limitless possibility and unrestrained ambition of modern medicine, by whose hands the body itself becomes raw material to be remade in light of whatever self-improvement fantasies the patient harbors. The same logic infiltrates sexual activity.

On *Nip/Tuck*, advanced Western civilization provides no defense against the ravages of nature, which is certainly a Hobbesian state of war. But the world of sadomasochistic sexuality and science without boundaries goes beyond anything in Hobbes. The best philosophical account of this world is to be found in the writings of Sade. (On Sade, see the perceptive study by Roger Shattuck, *Forbidden Knowledge*.) Like Hobbes, Sade insists that we "come into the world as enemies" and live in a state of "perpetual and reciprocal warfare." The bridge from Hobbes' radical defense of a mundane conclusion on behalf of political order to sexual sadomasochism as a way of life is a romantic celebration of excess and transgression. Happiness, according to Sade, is "by way of pain." Pleasure is fleeting and illusory; pain is real and reliable. The key faculty here is imagination, which plays a crucial role in the quality of desire and the degree of its satisfaction. The overstepping of boundaries "inflames" the imagination; hence, those who would make progress in enlightenment must strive to bend the imagination "toward the inconceivable." Of course, the parasitic project of defying limits or laws is itself subject to the law of diminishing returns, as is equally evident in Sade's tedious, turgid prose and in *Nip/Tuck*'s plotlines.

Often intertwined with sexual passion, violence is everywhere in this show. The crudest and most explicit violence is evident in the show's unflinching depiction of surgery and the *CSI*-style close-ups that wallow in bloody gore. But this is symptom rather than cause. Violence permeates human relationships, even nonsexual ones. The best one can do in the world of *Nip/Tuck* is to turn violence against violence in an endless battle of irreconcilable desire.

3

THE NEGATIVE ZONE

Suburban Familial Malaise in *American Beauty*, *Revolutionary Road*, and *Mad Men*

We turn now from nihilism manifest in the civilization-defying artistry of demonic superheroes to the nihilism of ordinary life. The more common manifestation of the nihilism of ordinary life is in the quasi-tragic dramas about the malaise of the suburban family. Perhaps the most prominent depiction of the American dream turned nightmare, of the family as trap, is Sam Mendes' *American Beauty*, Oscar winner for Best Picture in 1999. The main character is Lester Burnham (Kevin Spacey), who, in a retrospective voice-over early in the film, introduces himself to the audience by announcing that within a year he will be dead. But, as he confesses, "he's dead already."

A sort of lackey for the advertising industry, disrespected by his wife and his daughter, Lester will soon be shocked from his living death by the body of Angela Hayes (Mena Suvari), his teenage daughter's cheerleading friend. Awakened by her beauty as he watches her cheer during a high school basketball game, Lester begins to undergo a transformation of sorts. He soon joins up with Ricky, the drug-dealing son of his new neighbors. Hanging out with Ricky and pursuing Angela, Lester recovers his youth, at least until the moment he realizes he is about to corrupt the innocent. Just before and in the moment of his death, the film bestows upon him a vision of transcendence, an escape from the twin nihilisms of consumerism and perpetual adolescence, only to remove him from the scene.

American Beauty is a deeply frustrating film, entertaining and prurient, ambitious and pretentious. It has a sense of what is needed to overcome the trap of the suburban family: the ability to see something more than the superficial beauty—glitz, really—in the images of American happiness hawked by the advertising industry; the possibility of seeing life as a whole, not just as a series of satisfied desires that rapidly give way to discontent; and the possibility of a life rooted in affirmation rather than in restless negation of fleeting pleasures. By killing him at the moment of his conversion, the film lets Lester (and us) off too easily. By killing him, the film avoids the difficult questions: How could someone with Lester's history and habits live in harmony with that vision? How could the vision be embodied in a specific way of life, here and now in America? Or to put it more concretely, how could Lester begin to repair things with his daughter and his wife? The only character who manages to live the vision is Ricky, but his mobility and freedom presuppose an affluence made possible by what the filmmakers apparently think is the only acceptable form of capitalism, drug dealing.

It is instructive that Lester works for the advertising industry; with his superficially perfect wife and his delicately manicured lawn, he has bought into a specific version of the American dream. Concerning the power of advertising in our highly technological world, Jacques Ellul proposes,

> Interested people have to be introduced into a world that is to be theirs and in which the object presented (often furtively) becomes indispensable. . . . Advertising, with an explosion of astonishing, seductive, amusing and interrogative images, fascinates future consumers, who by means of it can enter into a world of dreams that might be a little crazy but is still desirable and appealing.[1]

Other cultural commentators, such as René Girard, focus on the role of "mimetic desire" in the formation of our deepest longings. The desire to possess what our neighbor already has or aspires to have, a desire identified in Scripture as covetousness, is simultaneously an idolatry of other and self. In the modern world, with our boasts of individualism, we are perhaps even blinder than in the past to the role of mimetic desire. Unconscious mimetic desire is intimately connected to envy and can easily turn to hatred of and violence toward the other.

Particularly shocking to our sensibilities is the recognition that mimetic desire and its attendant vices of idolatry, envy, and animosity have infiltrated our families, which we expect to be a harmonious refuge from the competitions of the economically driven social world. In such a context, the family can be nothing more than a trap from which one cannot fully escape and where one experiences the devastating gap between what might have been and what is, between the fictional promise of the American dream and the nightmare of one's actual family. That is the very situation of Lester Burnham in *American Beauty*. The family becomes a sort of semiotic hell wherein the signs of what the family should have been linger in the absence of their realization. The family is no longer a community of persons, ensouled bodies, united in affection for one another and for a shared sense of the good, however unarticulated. Instead, it is a sum of individuals, each of whom regards his or her body and personal space as property that can be offered to another through a contractual arrangement or a violent alienation. In such a context, children are, at best, insoluble conundrums and, at worst, hostile threats. In the face of such lethal knowledge, a knowledge that lays bare the deception of the cultural cover story about marriage, mercy vanishes and, with it, any hope for transcendence.

The nihilism threatening the suburban family is on display in a large variety of contemporary films and TV series. In addition to his *American Beauty*, Sam Mendes has directed *Revolutionary Road*, which reprises themes from *Beauty* but, in its early 1960s setting, tries to get at the origins of suburban familial malaise. More noteworthy as a cultural phenomenon is Matthew Weiner's critically acclaimed AMC series *Mad Men*, set in the same period as *Road* and featuring advertising executives. These stories lay bare the illusions of individualism and of the self-made man. The family context, however much it might be seen as something from which liberation is desirable, exercises an indelible influence, for good and for ill, on the major characters. It undercuts the impulse, or at least the successful realization of the impulse, to construct a life beholden to no past and responsible to no future except that envisioned by the isolated individual. Domestic hostility mirrors the competition in the sphere outside the home, and the sins of the parents are visited upon the children, who suffer various kinds of deprivation, including loss of life, as the home becomes a kind of Hobbesian state of nature, a covert and sometimes overt war of all against all.

Now, in these stories, viewers are invited, as the tag line from *American Beauty* has it, to "look closer," to see what most of the characters, at least most of the time, do not see. Beneath the surface of things, *American Beauty* suggests, there is a hidden reality that is brimming with life and beauty. Floating baggies and dead birds prompt this insight in one of the characters, who seeks to capture the moment on film. The suggestion is that American nihilism results from a flight from death. Not nearly as profoundly or pretentiously, depending on one's judgment of *American Beauty*, *Revolutionary Road* and *Mad Men* attempt to get viewers to see what the characters do not. In the first case, it is the source of the malaise, and in the second, it is the full complex set of human motivations in what appear to be bluntly nihilistic, self-made entrepreneurs. The gap between what characters see and what viewers see opens the possibility for filmmakers to comment on the lives depicted. Thus, a story featuring nihilistic characters need not be nihilistic, as the artist can find ways to comment on the characters, their deeds, and their limited self-understanding. Two contemporary films about suburban families, *The Ice Storm* and *The Secret Lives of Dentists*, work in precisely this way; they give us symbols or metaphors to aid us in the interpretation of the lives depicted, lives that involve the contravention of the natural order.

HOPELESS EMPTINESS IN SUBURBIA: *REVOLUTIONARY ROAD*

Sam Mendes' film *Revolutionary Road* reprises themes from his celebrated *American Beauty* and reunites the stars of *Titanic*, Leonardo DiCaprio and Kate Winslet. Based on a Richard Yates novel, the film depicts the suburban malaise experienced by a young couple (Frank and April Wheeler). April (Winslet) is a stay-at-home mother of two, while Frank (DiCaprio) commutes into the city to work at the same company for which his father labored anonymously throughout his adult life. With its focus on suburban alienation, *Road* calls to mind *American Beauty*. While the Oscar-winning film starring Kevin Spacey holds out the possibility of transcending the twin and interconnected nihilisms of suburban consumerism and endless adolescence, *Road* moves its characters inexorably toward an insuperable experience of nihilism, the recognition of which prompts a malevolent and vertiginous madness. The flaw of *Road* is that its account of the life histories and social context of the main characters is so slender that it cannot explain how the social context exercises its totalitarian pull and stifles all human aspiration. In an interview, Mendes explains the key insight of the film:

> It deals with this idea, that I think a lot of people . . . have felt—which is that you somehow find yourself living a life you hadn't quite expected and certainly one that you didn't really want to live. You find yourself compromising the ideals and the dreams you had when you were younger.[2]

That is a pretty vague thesis, one exemplified in the vast majority of lives lived anywhere and at any time; it would, for example, be an apt description of lead characters as diverse as George Bailey in *It's a Wonderful Life* and Kevin Spacey in *American Beauty*. Featuring a young couple coming of age in the late 1950s in New York City and suburban Connecticut, *Road* has a specific time and place in mind. Its reconstruction of that world is impressive, as is its establishment of a mood of aimless longing and subliminal violence. The film is considerably less convincing on the source of the malaise. As we shall see later in this chapter, a more detailed and gripping account of dislocation can be found in the critically acclaimed AMC series *Mad Men*, which is set in the early 1960s in New York, at roughly the same time and place as *Revolutionary Road*.

The dramatic problem for Mendes' *Revolutionary Road* is twofold. The first is that it is hard to characterize the youthful dreams of this couple as anything more than residual adolescent fantasy, aspirations so disconnected from reality as to be absurd. Frank moans at one point, "I want to feel, really feel." Meanwhile, April moves from fantasizing about another life to making plans for the family to move to Paris. She promises Frank that if they move to Paris, she will work and he will be "free to figure out what he wants." Frank, already having reservations about the move, uses April's unexpected pregnancy as an excuse to call off the relocation. From this point, April falls prey to resentment, anger, and near madness. The dilemma (scorched souls in Connecticut versus self-realized individuals in Paris) is not credible. And this points up a second problem with the movie. It is never clear what the source of the malaise is. The film is at its best in the climactic and emotionally violent confrontation between Frank and April, where the framing of the characters, the soundtrack, and the physical chemistry (one is tempted to call it an antichemistry) between husband and wife offer a chilling picture not just of marital discord but also of lives spinning out of all rational control. It passes credibility to suppose that the sources of the psychic vertigo are a tiresome job, a nice house in Connecticut, and some dinners with superficial friends. Is suburban anomie a sufficient explanation for the depth of self-absorption exhibited by the characters in *Road*, narcissism so great that it involves the denial that anyone else can make any claim on one's life? What sort of antecedent culture would make the promise of suburban bliss tempting in the first place? Or again, what sort of cultural deprivation makes the alternative, the only alternative that the characters are capable of conceiving, so shallow and unimaginative? Mendes has little to say about these matters.[3]

In a crucial scene in the film, the Weavers share their sense of alienation in a conversation with John Givings (Michael Shannon), the mentally imbalanced adult son of their realtor, Helen Givings (Kathy Bates). The son is an intellectually brilliant man whose perceptiveness and honesty are socially disruptive; he insists on providing blunt assessments of the cowardly and self-deceptive lives of those around him. When Frank refers to the hopeless emptiness of American life, John credits him with a deep insight about the hopelessness. Many folks, he says, see the "emptiness but very few the sheer hopelessness of it all." That is, of course, a pretty good working description of nihilism—not only the emptiness of one's present circumstance but the absence of any prospect of future purpose. The film illustrates the way the apprehension of the loss of hope engenders a sense of entrapment, fear, and the violent lashing out against others and oneself. But its sources remain murky. The characters lack a language, other than certain abstractions that might be garnered from a superficial acquaintance with existentialism, to describe their plight. They are deprived of a framework or narrative within which they might come to understand the ways their lives have gone astray. In this film, the only alternative to the sort of mindless routine purportedly caused by capitalism is an airy romantic aspiration for fulfillment. Because the characters' dreams never transcend the realm of adolescent fantasy and because they never express genuine affection for one another, much less for their children, the film cannot reasonably be *seen*, as Mendes describes it, as a "great romantic tragedy."

Nor does the artistry of the film (in contrast, say, to a film like *The Ice Storm*) provide viewers with a perspective from which to understand where and why things have gone astray. The characters are old before their time, already sophisticated, jaded, and growing increasingly incapable of any real imagination, feeling, or emotion. Fantasy takes the place of imagination with dreadful consequences. As Wendell Berry writes,

> Fantasy is of the solitary self, and it cannot lead us away from ourselves. It is by imagination that we cross over the differences between ourselves and other beings and thus learn compassion, forbearance, mercy, forgiveness, sympathy, and love. . . . In sex, as in other things, we have liberated fantasy but killed imagination, and so have sealed ourselves in selfishness and loneliness.[4]

Aside from a growing sense of discontent and an occasional, fleeting glimpse of the pain their acts have caused others, the Weavers possess neither the vocabulary nor the moral imagination to see themselves or others as they are; what knowledge they do possess is death dealing rather than redeeming. It calls to mind T. S. Eliot's line from "Gerontion": "after such knowledge, what forgiveness?" Their knowledge precludes the possibility of knowing how or even why to forgive. "The question," Berry urges, "is not why we have so much divorce but why we are so unforgiving."[5] Void of any sense of connection to anything larger or more significant than their fleeting desires, the characters see no possibility of going forward, of overcoming the curses of the past or the vacancy of the present. Lost in their own private fantasies, the Weavers are unable to imagine a different world, one in which their aspirations might be primarily fulfilled in the self-giving of husband and wife to one another and in the raising of children.

The most that one can say about the characters in *Road* is that they have suffered some sort of deprivation, a lack of sense of time, place, and purpose. Their rootlessness renders them susceptible to the blandishments of fleeting fantasy. But what is the source? Berry argues that a complex set of forces in modern life tends to wipe out local communal life, leaving individuals isolated and powerless in the face of large impersonal forces. The proper mediating role of the community is lost, and individuals, liberated from local traditions and communal expectations, are increasingly subject to the whims of national bureaucracies and international markets. One of the problems with the "family values" espoused by conservatives is that they often leave the nuclear family to itself, isolated amid an increasingly hostile economic and social order. Family values are compatible with what Tocqueville identified as one of the great threats of modern politics: individualism. Tocqueville contrasted egoism, which elevates the satisfaction of one's own desires above all else, with individualism, which is a "mature and calm feeling" that disposes each person to "draw apart with his family and friends" and "willingly leave society to itself." The consequence of this sort of individualism, according to Berry, is the loss of the sense of marriage as anything other than a contract between two isolated individuals. As he puts it, "If you depreciate the sanctity and solemnity of marriage, not just as a bond between two people but as a bond between those two people and their forbears, their children, and their neighbors, then you have prepared the way for an epidemic of divorce, child neglect, community ruin, and loneliness."[6]

The result for children is especially horrific. Something of this horror is on display at the ending of *Revolutionary Road*, an ending whose significance has been little noted by critics. The film is indeed a tragedy not, as Mendes states, for the Weavers but rather for the children of this couple—a point explicitly made by the blunt John Givings, the mentally imbalanced son of the realtor. As he grows increasingly frustrated with the Weavers' lies about their lives, he blurts out that he feels sorriest for the baby growing in April's womb. The filmmaker's choice to render the children nothing more than occasional props in the film nicely reflects the self-absorbed mentality of the main characters. Pregnancy is the great evil in the film, the enemy to be defeated, not because the parents do not have the resources to raise the children or because pregnancy arises from incest or rape but simply because the presence of children punctures the world of perpetual adolescent fantasy to which the main characters are devoted. The family moved to suburbia because of the first pregnancy and then, as April explains, they had a second child to prove the first was "not a mistake." It is not surprising, then, that the culminating act in the film should be a self-inflicted abortion. Rooted in a narcissism that sees others as threats even as it destroys the self, the monstrous turning of a mother against the life that is growing within her very body bespeaks a malevolence for which suburban disaffection is hardly an adequate explanation.

Road was released in 2008, just a year after what some commentators called the year of the pro-life film. The pregnant female leads in *Bella*, *Waitress*, *Knocked Up*, and *Juno* choose life over death, and the results are happy rather than tragic. But unlike the pro-choice propaganda film *Cider House Rules* (1999), none of these films is ideologically driven and none argues directly that laws protecting abortion ought to be repealed. But the portrayal of abortion in *Road* resembles much more a European film from 2007, Cristian Mungiu's *4 Months, 3 Weeks, and 2 Days*, winner of the Palme D'Or at Cannes. Set in the oppressive days of the Ceaușescu regime in late 1980s Romania, *4 Months*, a story of two women seeking an illegal abortion, effectively captures a certain mood of anomie and hopelessness. But this unadorned film seeks to exhibit the disorder that the characters themselves cannot articulate. The surprising thing about the film is not just, as critics have noted, its direct and harrowing depiction of abortion but its willingness to see abortion itself as a capital example of human degradation.

The film focuses on Gabita (Laura Vasiliu) and Otilia (Anamaria Marinca) as they secure an illegal abortion for Gabita. Over the course of the film, Gabita does next to nothing. Yet her passivity is actively manipulative; she persuades Otilia to arrange all the details and then lies to the abortionist, Bebe (Vlad Ivanov), about Otilia, saying that she is her sister. Once in the hotel room where the abortion is to take place, Otilia is the one forced to pay Bebe by providing something other than money. This is a society of vampires and parasites, bent on possessing souls, controlling wills, and destroying lives.

With its pervasive emotional emptiness and human desolation, *4 Months* reflects the deprivations of human life under a brutal, bureaucratic regime. Given this context, it would be easy to see the sinister and hidden manner in which abortion must be procured as yet another repressed liberty in a totalitarian regime. Yet *4 Months* manages to sustain the possibility that abortion itself reflects and contributes to the degradation of human life as symbolic of the barrenness of human interaction.

Abortion is more than mere metaphor, however. One pro-choice film critic calls *4 Months* the "most persuasive anti-abortion argument in any form I've ever heard, seen, or read."[7] In certain respects, this is a strange conclusion to reach: the filmmakers did not intend a pro-life film. Indeed, the production notes highlight the negative effects of the Romanian Communist ban on abortion in the late 1960s: illegal abortions killed nearly half a million women. The notes go on to report on the post-Communist boom in abortions, and the filmmakers proclaim the widespread popularity of abortion as a "method of contraception" in contemporary Romania.

Filmmakers have been willing to depict abortion as something ugly, even as a necessary evil in the face of tragic circumstances. Despite an increasingly explicit film culture, in which it is permissible—indeed, in certain genres, mandatory—to show every manner of torture and physical brutality, the direct portrayal of an aborted

fetus is rare. The way this film depicts the consequences of the abortion packs a chilling emotional wallop. At four months, three weeks,
and two days, a fetus is unmistakably human—small but human. Rec-
ognizing this fact, Gabita begs Otilia to "bury" rather than simply
discard the dead baby.

One of the chief deprivations in a totalitarian police state is
imaginative and linguistic. The verbal communication in the film
is always terse, often brittle, and typically narrowly pragmatic; the
film does not even have a soundtrack. The characters lack a vocabulary to describe their condition; indeed, they are for the most part void
of longing to understand or to communicate. The silence itself, the
physical revulsion in the face of an unspeakable act, has an artistic,
emotional, and deeply moral impact. By giving a face to the voiceless
victim of abortion, this film bespeaks the horror of an unspeakable
act, the way in which the sins of the parents are visited upon children,
in some cases even before they are born.

OUT OF THE PAST: *MAD MEN*'S THE SELF-MADE MAN

A setting similar to that of *Road* can be found in the critically acclaimed
AMC TV series *Mad Men*, which focuses on the life of Don Draper, a
married father of two with a comfortable house in the suburbs and a
successful career in Manhattan at Sterling Cooper, a Madison Avenue
advertising company. The series links advertising—its cultivation of
images of accomplishment and happiness—to the modern American
dream. The simultaneously alluring and deceptive role of images is
nicely captured in the show's paradoxical tag line from its inaugural
season, "Where the Truth Lies." This is the era of the Kennedy-Nixon
election campaign for president, a campaign in which the telegenic
Kennedy profited enormously from his more attractive appearance
during a televised presidential debate. Advertising itself has begun to
play an important role in politics. In the fabric of daily American life,
it is becoming pervasive. Draper is a master of matching image to text
in such a way that ordinary citizens are persuaded that they need what
is on offer. Draper's career would seem both to presuppose and to
foster a notion of the citizen as bourgeois consumer: the sort of individual who when thinking of himself thinks of the opinions of others

and, when thinking of others, thinks only of himself and his interests. But there is more to Don Draper than a caricature of the ad man so often on display in Hollywood stories about American businessmen.

Perhaps the greatest artistic achievement of the series is its convincing portrait of Draper's complex humanity; in this, it is a far better depiction of soul-starved consumerism in the early 1960s than that found in, say, Sam Mendes' *Revolutionary Road.* Having invited viewers to see the vacancy beneath the surface of success, *Mad Men* points up the residual humanity of Draper, his sense of entrapment, and his longing for escape. For all of his efforts to live in one direction, he cannot entirely suppress his past. It is this very complexity that both haunts him, rendering him incapable of living his life entirely in one direction, and makes him such a superb salesman.

Draper's masterful, if not entirely successful, ability to partition segments of his life is made possible not just by the mobility of a capitalist economy but also by the separation of home from work, of wife from husband. Of course, during this postwar period, women were entering the workforce at a high rate. For most of the women in *Mad Men,* secretarial work involves serving men and occasionally savoring some of the freedom accorded their bosses. But even here the real goal for most is to land a man so that they can get married and move out of the city and into a comfortable suburban house. Once there, dissatisfaction and restlessness ensue. The gorgeous Betty Draper, Don's wife, exemplifies the lonely plight of the suburban housewife. A former model, who calls to mind Grace Kelly, she is at one point in the series courted to be the public face of an advertising campaign for Coca-Cola. But the corporation offering her the opportunity is mainly interested in luring her husband away from his current job. When he declines their offer, they drop her. Not wanting to admit her disappointment, she claims to her husband that she has no interest in the position, that she is content as a homemaker. Resignation, it seems, is her lot. But there is an irony here. Were she to have succeeded in escaping the daily routine of the home and secured gainful employment, she would still have been a pawn, an advertising image, desired for nothing more than the way her physical beauty would help to sell soft drinks.

Draper's life illustrates the illusion of choice, novelty, and control in the capitalist world of advertising. It also illustrates the obstacles to human friendship not only between man and woman, husband and wife, but even between free and allegedly equal men. One of the problems with living life in one direction, with no regard for the past, is that everything and everyone rapidly becomes disposable. Draper is a mature member of the team; in fact, during the first season, he is made a partner. One of the senior partners, Roger Sterling (John Slattery), has cultivated and supported Draper, who regards the older man with some degree of affection. Whatever degree of friendship may have existed between them is jeopardized by a dinner at the Drapers' home in which Don suspects, rightly, that Sterling has been ogling his wife. Draper cannot but see his future self in the declining Sterling, whose chasing of much younger women Draper regards as distasteful. Meanwhile, Draper views—again with good reason—the younger members of the advertising team, particularly Peter Campbell, as potential threats to him. As Draper frankly and darkly admits at one point, we live and die alone.

Draper is a complex character, capable of coldly facing the abyss of meaninglessness and of exhibiting vulnerability, residual humanity, and longing for family and love. At just about the time when the show is set, *Life* magazine ran a famous cover story on beatniks, with a picture of them listening to Miles Davis and a text announcing, "The Only Rebellion Around."[8] In one of the funniest episodes, Draper shows up the beatnik rebellion as superficial. Invited by Midge, a rebellious artist, to a party with her artist friends, Draper tries marijuana for the first time. As Miles Davis plays in the background, Draper comments that he feels like Dorothy: "everything just turned to color." After the beatniks self-righteously rail against Draper as an instrument of a system that perpetrates the big lie, he calmly responds, "There is no big lie and there is no system. The universe is indifferent." Frightened by his blunt comment, one of the beatniks complains, "Man, why did you have to say that?" Much more than the posturing beatniks, Draper readily confronts the abyss.

A telling scene that suggests how image and reality have become inverted occurs at a party Draper attends with one of his lovers,

Midge. He takes a photo of Midge with her other male lover, a sort of New York beatnik; looking at the picture, he tells her, "You two are in love. I spend my time constructing images of love and I know it when I see it." Of course, he did not know until he saw it as an image. Looking at the real thing, he was blind.

The most dramatic way the prominence of constructed images is played out in the series has to do with Draper himself, whose very identity is fraudulent. During the first season, clues are planted to indicate that Draper is not who he says he is. These include an encounter with a man who claims to be his brother. He is in fact Don's half-brother, or rather, he is the half-brother of Dick Whitman, who stole the identity of Don Draper. Initially dismissive, Draper eventually admits who he is and tries to bribe his brother never to contact him again. The son of a prostitute who died while giving birth to him, Don was raised by parents with no affection for him. While fighting in the Korean War, Draper stole the identity of a fellow soldier killed alongside him in battle. Having escaped from the past and stolen the name of another, Draper cannot afford to look back. As he tells his brother, he is living his life "in one direction"—forward, not backward.

In the scene in which Draper is finally able to come clean and tell another person about his childhood, it is significant that the person to whom he confesses is a newly cultivated lover, Rachel, owner of her own business. Having made the confession, his impulse is not to reconcile with his past but rather to escape again into a newly constructed future. He invites Rachel to drop everything and move away with him. He tells her, "Let's start over, like Adam and Eve." That's a rich line. Such a fictional notion of self-creation, of starting anew from scratch, supplies an illusory sense of transcendence of past and present.

One of Draper's most awe-inspiring moments occurs after the catastrophic crash of a plane from American Airlines. Since Don manages the American Airlines account, the task of his team is to help the airline come up with an ad to address the massive loss of life and restore confidence in fliers. After his team exhausts itself producing one failed idea after another to help American address the tragedy, Draper emerges from his office to announce triumphantly, "The crash never happened. There is no American history; there is only the frontier." Don is confident that the past can be obliterated.

But Draper is haunted by his past, the lingering presence of which baffles him and often reduces him to silence. Indeed, Draper's wordless moments are the most telling, the moments when the master of language is rendered speechless, as he is both at the beginning and end of this episode. In the opening, Don is alone in his kitchen, late at night, warming milk for his pregnant wife. He begins daydreaming about his own birth and imagines both the death of his own mother in the act of giving birth to him and his being given in adoption to another set of parents, with a mother who could not conceive and a father who abuses her and eventually him. The episode ends with Don and Betty responding to their daughter's question about the day of her birth. Don starts to tell the story but then abruptly stops, caught up in some private emotion, and Betty continues the tale.

In another episode, Don's perusal of photos provokes memories of his childhood, a past he has tried desperately to forget and suppress. It is this very complexity that both haunts him, rendering him incapable of living his life entirely in one direction, and makes him such a superb salesman. For he grasps that it is not just novelty and freedom that people want but also the idea of returning, of recovery of the past. In one episode, Draper pitches a campaign for Kodak's new slide projector, which Kodak has dubbed "The Wheel." Deploying the projector, Draper darkens the room and projects a series of images of happy families, including his own. He comments,

> This is not a spaceship; it's a time machine. It goes backwards and forwards, and it takes us to a place where we ache to go again. It's not called "The Wheel." It's called "The Carousel." It lets us travel around and around and back home again.

This advertising pitch not only persuades the executives from Kodak, but it also manages to produce teary eyes in Draper's hardcore Sterling Cooper colleagues. Such an approach to the past is not to be confused with tradition, the living memory of the dead, the treasuring of ancient ideals, and the cultivation of gratitude for what

previous generations have bestowed on us. Instead, it is mere nostal-
gia, a vague aspiration to return to what once was, or at least to an
image we now have of what was. Such banal sentimentality is a powerful advertising tool. The magnetic lure of such communal images
undercuts our proud individualism and our naive assumptions about
free choice. We are not the autonomous fashioners of our own futures
precisely because, as René Girard says,

> The true guide of human beings is not abstract reason but ritual.
> The countless repetitions shape little by little the institutions
> that later men and women will think they invented *ex nihilo* [out
> of nothing]. Actually, it is religion that invented human culture.[9]

Critics of the series see it as a straightforward celebration, a
romantic affirmation, of a lost, patriarchal society in which masters
of the universe had the freedom to achieve and enjoy greatness in
a free economy. But that interpretation does not penetrate beneath
the elegant and attractive surface of the drama—an image for unreflective viewers. Although not heavy handed, the series brings out
the bigotry and sexism of the period even as it underscores the hol-
lowness of a life lived for nothing more than meeting or exceeding
social expectations. Even more importantly, the show exhibits the
complex contradictions and enduring human motivations of the self-
made man.

At one point, a coworker tells Don, "You have everything, and so
much of it." Don, who thinks mostly about what he lacks, is surprised
at this comment. Don embodies the restlessness of the American
soul that we examined in chapter 1. Tocqueville provides an astute
description.

> A native of the United States clings to this world's goods as if
> he were certain never to die; and he is so hasty in grasping at all
> within his reach that one would suppose he was constantly afraid
> of not living long enough to enjoy them. He clutches everything,
> he holds nothing fast, but soon loosens his grasp to pursue fresh
> gratifications. . . . Death at length overtakes him, but it is before

he is weary of his bootless chase of that complete felicity which forever escapes him.

Of course, for Tocqueville, that is only part of the picture of American life and its restless entrepreneurial spirit. The other part of American life, the part that tempers the potential vices of commerce with the virtues of association and the countervailing forces of the home and family, is missing from the world of *Mad Men*, as Harry Stein points out in "What *Mad Men* Gets Wrong."[10] It gives no attention at all to the decent, family-oriented, patriotic men and women who were likely living in the same neighborhood as the Drapers. In that respect, the series might be seen as playing off the same unconvincing, reductionist views of capitalism and suburban anomie as those operative in Sam Mendes' film *Revolutionary Road*, a film set in roughly the same time and place as *Mad Men*. But Matthew Weiner's *Mad Men* is much more complex and interesting than anything Mendes has done regarding this topic.

Consider, for example, divorce—the personal catastrophe Don faces. Despite Don's confession of the truth about his past, or perhaps because of it, Betty has her mind set on divorce. In a meeting with a lawyer, she learns just how difficult that will be if Don opposes it: "New York state doesn't want you to get divorced." Clearly, the implication here is that divorce laws across America—with the exception of Nevada, where Betty is headed—are irrational and oppressive. Betty's pursuit of divorce also clearly anticipates the greater freedom of no-fault divorce that would come in future years. Yet the show also makes it possible to see the roots of the divorce culture in the rampant infidelity of spouses, in the absence of cultural, ethical, and religious habits that would place marriage and children above the wayward desires of individual adults. The liberated future would foment precisely those passions that make a divorce culture inevitable.

Consider also Don Draper's self-made entrepreneurial identity, an identity that fuses the personal and the professional. Even as divorce looms in his personal life, on the professional front Don faces catastrophe. At the very outset, he learns that he will be losing his best account, Conrad Hilton, because Sterling Cooper, already purchased by a British company, is being sold again. That sale will mean a huge loss of independence for Draper and his colleagues. When senior partner Bert Cooper speaks of going with the flow and waiting things out until retirement, Draper challenges him to try to put together a team to buy the company back. Don is insistent: "I want to work, I want to build something." Here Don's genuine passion for work is presented as admirable, a sign that he wants to live for more than comfort and ease.

Realizing that buying the company will not be possible, they hatch a different plot: to persuade the local British overlord of the company, whose job is also in jeopardy, to fire them and join them in stealing current accounts and setting up a new company. But this will require that Don adopt a quite different attitude toward his coworkers, beginning with the other senior partner, Roger Sterling, and moving on to his younger colleagues Peggy Olson and Pete Campbell. No longer able to ignore them or command their allegiance, Don has to convince them that he values them as individuals and colleagues, that he sees human relations as something more than mere tools of his own advancement—an accusation Roger levels against him. Don does just that, and in a way that convinces us he is not merely acting but acknowledging something he has never before admitted about his dependence on others.

The episode brings out the degree of that dependence in a remarkable series of flashbacks to Don's childhood, to his witnessing his father's struggles to overcome poverty and gain independence from those who would curtail his ability to succeed. In a final flashback, Don recalls his father's senseless death. On *Mad Men*, the flashback is more than a gimmick. It underscores the gap between Don's self-knowledge and what he is willing to disclose to others, even what he is willing to acknowledge to himself. Don's flight from his past is decisively shaped by that very past. Draper wants desperately to live in one direction only, that of the future. Instead, he is, like Fitzgerald's Gatsby, "borne back ceaselessly into the past."

Despite its complexities, *Mad Men* romanticizes both the white, male power structure of business executives in late 1950s Manhattan and the sexual license enjoyed by these masters of the universe. The consequences of that world are not on full display in *Mad Men*.

Wendell Berry lays bare those consequences, even as he criticizes conservatives and liberals. He castigates conservatives for their simultaneous and contradictory promotion of restraint in the area of sexual morality and of laissez-faire economics. That economy brutalizes both nature, treating it as raw material out of which to create "products," and persons, treating them as consumers whose freedom is realized in market preferences. Conversely, liberals who often disdain capitalism but who decry as fascist any conception of right ordering of sexuality end up tacitly advocating the same conception of the person and of choice as that operative in capitalism: the private preferences of individuals. Liberal politics and conservative economics conspire to turn the "body" itself into a sort of "product, made delectably consumable."[11] The consequence for our understanding of sex is predictable. What is left is a "dispirited description of the working of a sort of anatomical machinery—and this is a sexuality that is neither erotic nor social nor sacramental but rather a cold-blooded, abstract procedure."[12] Here we return to a theme already touched upon—the conflation of imagination and fantasy, a conflation that permeates much of our popular culture, even that part of it that wants to indict the conflation. Of course, such a confusion of imagination and fantasy is precisely the goal of the advertising industry, as *Mad Men* dramatically illustrates. The question is whether we can have art that provides an alternative to mere fantasy. The characters in the dramas we have considered suffer from the atrophy of their moral imaginations; the makers of these dramas at some level recognize this, but they do not provide an alternative. Moreover, as much as these artworks may want to indict the society that produced the individuals in their stories, they do not provide a vantage point from which such a judgment can be intelligibly made.

NATURE'S REVENGE

The Secret Lives of Dentists tries to do just that. It focuses on the invasion of destructive forces into a family, but the culprit here is clearly identified as a failure of spousal love and fidelity. David (Campbell Scott) and Dana (Hope David) Hurst are married dentists with three young children, the youngest of whom has developed a habit of slapping adults. After seeing his wife embracing another man, David suspects she is having an affair. Much of the film focuses on the interior life (or lack thereof) of David, whose dark side is prodded by an imaginary presence. Slater, Dennis Leary playing himself in all his obnoxious and humorous glory, is a patient of David; when his newly implanted filling falls out, he taunts David in a public setting. Haunted by that encounter, David receives regular appearances from an imaginary Slater in scenes reminiscent of both Humphrey Bogart in Woody Allen's *Play It Again, Sam* and Brad Pitt in *Fight Club*. Unfortunately, the writing for Leary's part is not nearly as effective as the writing for Bogie or Pitt. He does serve the purpose of fostering in the otherwise passive David thoughts of confrontation and vengeance. Unlike Leary's character, the film itself does not lay the blame for marital collapse solely at the feet of the mother; the film makes it clear that infidelity does not occur rapidly. This is a marriage that has gone hollow from neglect, just in the way teeth begin to rot.

The most instructive and most dramatically compelling themes in *Dentists* have to do with sexual fantasy and a normative order of nature. We are accustomed to the prominence given in Hollywood films to sexual fantasies, especially those of middle-aged men such as Lester Burnham in *American Beauty*. In this case, the fantasies of the male character are not provoked by his desire for a lithe young beauty but by suspicion of his wife's infidelity. Envy gives rise to lurid fantasy as he is haunted by a series of increasingly perverse images of his wife in sexual congress with a variety of persons. The subtext of violence, both in the husband's thoughts of vengeance and in the youngest daughter's outbursts of slapping, evinces an intimate connection between infidelity and violence.

Indeed, the film points repeatedly to the existence of a normative natural order that, once violated, will inevitably find a way to reassert itself. David is at various points a sort of dispassionate chronicler of the way things naturally decay: leaves disintegrating in a pond and food rotting in a refrigerator. The focus on teeth takes us a bit closer to marital decay, as it hints at the way decay operates secretly for long periods of time only to be revealed dramatically when it is nearly past cure. It also underscores the need for care and cultivation. In the film's final, culminating scenes, the family is gripped with a particularly virulent bout of influenza, a virus that is clearly intended as a physical manifestation of the moral sickness afflicting the entire family. The abating of the illness leaves us with multiple, unresolved ambiguities. Has the evil been purged? Will the parents reconcile? Can they move forward? Or are there grounds for pessimism that would illustrate the limitations to the analogy between physical sickness and moral evil? Can human evil, that is, moral evil, be purged in the way an illness can? Or does it require something other and more costly than the application of appropriate medicine? Something akin to conversion? In our age of advanced science, we have clear ideas about physicians for this or that bodily ailment, but who is the physician of the soul? Can art in any way serve this purpose? *Dentists* raises these questions.

Ang Lee's *The Ice Storm* illustrates even more persuasively than *Dentists* the rot that results from untrammeled sexual desire and adultery. The film focuses on two families in the posh suburb of New Canaan, Connecticut, in November 1973. New Canaan is a real town, but the name bears a symbolic significance for the film, as it likely had for the founders of the town itself. Canaan is of course the promised land, the land flowing with milk and honey, promised to those who, through a time of trial, had proven their fidelity. The promised land of early 1970s America is a place of wealth with the resources to fulfill every imaginable desire. It is also a place from which happiness and joy have fled. The film captures affluent, suburban family life in the wake of the sexual revolution. The characters in *The Ice Storm* lack passion and self-knowledge; their despair is so deep they fail to recognize it. It is essentially the story of two families, with the father of one and the mother of the other engaged in an affair. After one of their midafternoon adulterous liaisons, Ben lies next to Janey and rambles on about personal problems. Obviously put off, Janey curtly states, "You're boring me. . . . I have a husband." Ben, played by Kevin Kline, is married to Elena, with whom he has two teenage children, Paul and Wendy. Janey, played by Sigourney Weaver, is married to Jim, with whom she has two sons, Mikey and Sandy. The two families socialize regularly and live within walking distance of one another. Although they are oblivious to it, they lead terrifyingly ordinary lives, void of communication, love, longing, or hope. Despite their wealth or perhaps because of it, Elena and Wendy, mother and daughter, both shoplift. The brothers, Mikey and Sandy, are socially awkward. The younger one, Sandy, is an introverted pyromaniac, launching explosives from the family's deck. When their father returns home from a business trip to Houston and exclaims, "Hey guys, I'm back," Mikey nonchalantly asks, "You were gone?"

Very little actually happens in the film, but its very stillness brings home the emptiness of the lives led by the characters. *The Ice Storm* depicts in an unadorned style the living death of its characters. While the film immerses the audience in a nihilistic world, it also provides viewers with an awareness, a perspective, that the denizens of that world lack. We are led to see and feel the horror of this way of life. But the mechanism by which we achieve a certain distance from the world of the characters and a perspective that they lack is not that of comic detachment or ironic freedom. The principal artistic device is that of natural sounds and images. To produce its benumbing and instructive effects, *The Ice Storm* makes manifold use of ice.

On the crucial evening in *The Ice Storm*, Paul is at a party in New York City, both sets of parents attend a "key party" where the wives' selection of keys from a bowl determines who will escort them home, Wendy visits Sandy, and Mikey wanders through the frozen woods and streets. As the events of the evening unfold, the ice envelops and covers everything—roads, trees, windows, and walking paths. The evening will witness Ben's drunken and embarrassingly public attempt to retain Janey as his lover, Elena and Jim's artless act of car-seat copulation (a feeble attempt to revenge themselves on their unfaithful spouses), Wendy's seduction of the disturbed and barely pubescent Sandy, and finally, Mikey's death by electrocution from a downed power line. When Ben finds Mikey sprawled out on the side of the road, he takes his body home, where Elena and Jim have just arrived, where his former lover Janey is already in bed, and where his daughter Wendy and Sandy have just emerged from bed. With the exception of Paul, the two families are now reunited in the face of an actual death. Still incapable of comprehending their situation or of expressing profound feeling, they exchange looks of fear and grief, even some tears and hugs, but few, if any, words.

Only Paul, the son of Elena and Ben, who attends a boarding school in the city, shows any sign of transcending the world of New Canaan. Although he is not presented as a remarkably deep or unusual teenager, he has a healthy crush on a classmate, played by Katie Holmes (whom he refuses to molest when she collapses in his arms at a party). He also reads Dostoevsky and comic book stories about the Fantastic Four, whose predicament frames the entire story. The film opens and ends with Paul returning on a commuter train from his evening in New York. The first memorable sounds we hear are of the train crackling along the icy track. As he sits silently reading, a voice-over, identifiably the voice of Paul himself, describes a typical challenge faced by the Fantastic Four, when a nihilist turns the son of one of the heroes into a live atom bomb. What makes these superheroes different is that they are all family, and that means "the more power you have, the more you have the capacity to do damage without knowing it." After we have seen that lesson amply and numbingly illustrated during the film, we return to Paul and the Fantastic Four at the end. Paul's voice explains the role of the "negative zone" in the comic series. It is an inversion of our expectations, where "things don't work out," and which "tempts us to go all the way in."

The restrained aesthetic of *The Ice Storm* captures the paralysis of life in the "negative zone," the subtle, cumulative, perhaps largely unintentional destruction wrought by ordinary acts of evil. The paradox is that, while the characters are isolated from each other, trapped in themselves, their lives are inextricably bound up with one another's lives. Individualism depletes rather than enriches the self. The pursuit of pleasure is self-defeating; instead of liberating passion, we are left with merely mechanical acts of sexual congress. The implicit suggestion is that a natural order in the relations between husband and wife has been abandoned, the result of which is that they see one another as threats to each other's autonomy. The natural order is one in which the union of husband and wife in mind and heart, soul and body, would be nurtured and cultivated by acts of genuine love for the other. *Dentists* and *Storm* do not, however, offer anything more than negative hints at what that order might look like.

4

NORMAL NIHILISM as COMIC
Seinfeld, Trainspotting, and *Pulp Fiction*

In *The Plain Sense of Things*, James Edwards argues that nihilism is now our normal condition: "we are all now nihilists," leading "lives constituted by self-devaluing values."[1] Our cultural pathology is a "hangover from our religious and philosophical history." It is not just that we have yet to find the truth but that the notion of truth itself is now thoroughly problematic. The guiding image for where we are now is the "regional shopping mall," where living becomes a matter of lifestyle choices for "rootless consumers." The most obvious danger is the "triumph of the normal," where normal is understood as a life of accumulation and entertainment. An opposite danger is that of pursuing "novelty for its own sake," arising from a restlessness that always wants to be anywhere but here.[2] Edwards thinks we can avert these two dangers by fostering social practices that cultivate the perception and imaginative appreciation of our forms of life. These are not absolute, unrevisable truths but contingently constitutive features of who we are. Even in this contingency, there is a degree of necessity because who we are is never simply a matter of preference or choice. The ineluctability of our starting points and of the horizon of our options constrains without eliminating our freedom. But we still need sacraments, epiphanies that crystallize our experience of the world from our contingent perspective. For guidance, we can turn to poets like Wallace Stevens who train our imagination to ponder the "plain sense of things."[3]

If one were to object that Edwards' hopeful note is groundless, his response would be, "Precisely." If nihilism means anything, it is that there is no basis—religious, philosophical, or political—for confirming the truth of any position whatsoever; there is only the shifting ground of our history and experience. We will simply have to judge whether his remedy suits our history and our experience. If it does, we can implement the strategies he suggests and see what sort of life emerges. But if one looks at the way nihilism plays itself out in our popular culture, Edwards' suggestions seem naive. Even at the level of philosophy, Edwards' position is an odd mix; he accepts Nietzsche's radical analysis of our times but wants to forestall the devastating consequences Nietzsche thinks flow from it. Edwards gives us conservative nihilism. As a cultural analyst, he gets much right, especially concerning the dangers of our situation. But his own recommendations sound remarkably academic and theoretical, abstracted from the conditions he wishes to help shape.

If there is no possibility of either the classically tragic or the classically comic, the next stage is normal nihilism. Nihilism is no longer wrestled with, heroically embraced, or subsumed within some larger narrative. Instead, it becomes an unspoken assumption. What is peculiar about the late twentieth century is the way meaninglessness has indeed become both a prevailing, if unremarked, supposition and a fertile source of comedy. We have seen ordinary or normal nihilism operate in a series of films about the family, from *American Beauty* and *Revolutionary Road* to *The Ice Storm* and *The Secret Lives of Dentists*. But these films could not be called comic. We have seen anticipations of the comic turn in the treatment of nihilism in *The Silence of the Lambs* and *Natural Born Killers*.

The comic treatment of evil reaches a kind of crescendo in films such as *Trainspotting*, which applies the popular belief in autonomy to the gleeful embrace of a "true and sincere" and freely chosen drug habit, and *Pulp Fiction*, Tarantino's masterful reflection on the ordinariness of criminality. These films break down the opposition between conventional society and the rebellious criminal. The casual ordinariness of criminal life strikes a relaxed comic tone; evil has "neither depth nor any demonic dimension." So it seems that there is no great mystery to be pondered; the search for evil is over. Just how ordinary nihilism can become is evident from the sitcom *Seinfeld*. As we learn in one episode, *Seinfeld* is a show about "absolutely nothing." Of course, it is not all that novel for the plots of sitcoms to focus on the seemingly insignificant events of daily life. What is quite novel and remarkably creative is the depth and complexity of *Seinfeld's* insight into the comical consequences of life in a world devoid of any ultimate meaning or fundamental purpose. This is the basis of *Seinfeld's* comic nihilism.

Seinfeld is important not just because it suits our genealogy of evil in a nihilistic culture. As Michael Medved has noted, popular culture in contemporary America—that is, Hollywood culture—is mediated more through television than through film. If we are right to see in *Seinfeld* a form of comic nihilism, then its presence on prime-time television is quite telling.

In completing the devolution of nihilism in our popular culture, *Seinfeld* echoes themes from *Trainspotting* and *Pulp Fiction*. The vignette structure of *Pulp Fiction* is similar to that of a situation comedy. It is instructive that Jerry Seinfeld sees similarities between *Pulp Fiction* and his own show: "I thought *Pulp Fiction* was very much in the tone of a lot of things we do. Some of that coffee-shop stuff between John Travolta and Sam Jackson—I thought, that's like a me-and-George scene." Tarantino is himself an avowed *Seinfeld* fan. His comment that *Pulp Fiction's* characters are a "cross between criminals and actors and children playing roles" might also serve as an apt description of *Seinfeld's* major characters, who have such a fragile sense of self that they are incapable of living any determinate form of life. Their unformed, childlike characters render them capable of slipping in and out of various roles, even the role of the criminal. In another similarity to *Pulp Fiction, Seinfeld* (more than any sitcom in history) makes ample, even excessive, use of comic coincidence, in this case an antiprovident coincidence that undermines rather than satisfies the desires of characters.

On the surface, *Pulp Fiction* moves us a step closer to the normalization of evil and comic book violence. Like *Killers*, it glamorizes gangster life and derives much of its humor from the casual, conventional depiction of that way of life. Roger Shattuck insists that the normalization of evil in *Pulp Fiction* "neutralizes it—absorbs it into ordinary life, broken by a few thrills and laughs, and desensitizes us to evil." Shattuck rightly rejects the argument that the film mocks the "industry's crass exploitation of violence"; rather, it is "complicit with the violence it depicts." But Shattuck, as we shall see at the end of this chapter, overlooks a novel feature of the film: the suggestion that someone seemingly at home in its world may awaken to the possibility of an entirely different way of life and thus embark upon a quest, this time not for evil but for goodness. *Pulp Fiction* suggests a way of transcending nihilism.

BEYOND THE DYSFUNCTIONAL FAMILY: *SEINFELD*

In linking *Seinfeld* to nihilism, I do not mean to reduce its remarkable success (Jay McInerney has called it the best comedy ever) to an implicit philosophical supposition. Like its successful predecessors, such as *The Honeymooners* and *I Love Lucy*, *Seinfeld* has well-defined characters with great comic range and extraordinary chemistry. Kramer and Elaine provide the sort of physical slapstick humor that was a staple in shows like *The Dick Van Dyke Show* and *I Love Lucy*. Few comedies have had better dialogue, particularly when it comes to sexuality. At a time when untalented entertainers go for the cheap laugh, *Seinfeld* excels at the art of suggestion through indirect locution.

As much as *Seinfeld* may have in common with previous comedies, its underlying nihilism entails a number of departures from its predecessors. Whereas the family supplied the dramatic and moral structure to the plot for earlier comedies, *Seinfeld* focuses almost exclusively on the lives of single individuals, for whom family life seems improbable, if not impossible. As the embodiment of American virtues, the family had provided a framework for that most serious of American pursuits, the pursuit of happiness. These comedies were often didactic, sometimes blatantly so; they provided brief lessons on virtues such as thrift, fairness, compromise, honesty, and hard work. These are not heroic virtues but rather those of the ordinary citizen, peculiarly American virtues whose lineage can be traced all the way back to Ben Franklin's *Autobiography*. Even where these sitcoms are not explicitly didactic, they still exude the confidence of the American spirit, its optimism and buoyancy, its belief in the fundamental reasonableness and justice of democracy, American style.

For these comedies, family life presents an endless array of comic situations, situations that remind us of our limitations, even of the limits of authority figures like teachers and parents. Of course, the foibles of authority figures are not the final word, and the necessity for such figures is never really put in question. The sort of limitations revealed in this genre do not produce radical individualism; on the contrary, they serve to remind us of our need for one another, of our common predicament, possibilities and hopes, and vision of the good life. The main characters are flawed and imperfect persons, often muddling through, but they have enough clarity about their goals to distinguish what is important from what is not. The early sitcoms remind the audience of these things and invite their participation in our common American destiny. Laughter arises from shared vision and feeling. How different is this sort of laughter from the detached and mocking laughter in contemporary depictions of dysfunctional family life?

For all their peculiarly American features, previous sitcoms have a basically classical comic structure. Most episodes of *I Love Lucy* revolve around some loony plan of Lucy's, which puts her in a seemingly insoluble situation. As viewers wonder how she will ever get out of the mess, their feelings of concern mix with an anticipation of the dilemma's resolution. Of course, viewers' expectations are never thwarted, disaster is always averted, Lucy hugs Ricky, and all is right with the world. The typical comedy presupposes sympathy on the part of the audience for the characters. We laugh with Lucy, not at her.

Seinfeld marks a decisive break from nearly all the conventions of the classic American comedy. Perhaps the easiest way to bring out the differences is to focus on *Seinfeld*'s dethroning of the family. *Cheers* anticipates *Seinfeld* in this. The families that do appear—Carla's, Frasier and Lilith, and especially Cliff and his mother—play none of the normalizing roles of families in previous sitcoms. They anticipate the dysfunctional families of 1990s sitcoms. Yet an important theme in *Cheers* was the relationship between Sam and Diane, and at some level, the issue was always whether they would get married. Although there was much fodder for comedy in their impossible relationship, the tone was not finally comic, but that of the sorrowful sense of a possibility lost. Who can forget the maudlin final parting between Sam and Diane, with Sam alone in the bar whispering, "Have a good life"? Instead of banishing the family completely, *Cheers* replaces it with the bar, the place where everybody knows your name. *Cheers* is much too sentimental a comedy to fully dethrone the family.

Seinfeld is never sentimental. Outside a small coterie of acquaintances, Jerry's world is one where very few persons know your name—and you wish that many of those who do know it did not. On one occasion, Kramer nearly ruins Jerry's life by pasting named pictures of all the residents of their apartment building at its entrance. In another episode, Elaine's suggestion to the chief adviser of David Dinkins' mayoral campaign, that everyone in the city should wear a name tag so New York would be just like a small town, loses Dinkins the election. The family is cast in a similar light. Jerry's and George's parents represent a kind of conventionalized lunacy. There is barely a residue of the Sam and Diane relationship in Jerry and Elaine, and it is never really treated seriously. More characteristic is the episode in which they attempt to add sexual activity to their comfortable friendship.

In a world where the family is displaced, children can only be seen as aliens. They are something worse than that on *Beavis and Butt-Head* and *South Park*. On *Seinfeld*, children are rarely seen, and ambivalence about their very existence is hilariously played out in the "vasectomy" episode. To attract women who are sure they do not want kids, nearly all the men decide to have vasectomies. Inevitably, the women change their minds. In an era of technological sexuality, cold calculation replaces romance and passion. In the episode in which Elaine's favorite contraceptive device, the sponge, goes off the market, she initiates a complicated screening process, interviewing potential candidates to determine whether they are "sponge-worthy."

The dethroning of the family does not involve a radical critique of the family or any sense that we could live wholly independent of connections of blood. This is a bit surprising given that the location of the show is New York City, the twentieth-century mecca for angst-ridden artists and rebels against bourgeois values. But rebellion presupposes a standard in light of which present power structures can be found wanting—or at least the presence of something that merits opposition. The advent of nihilism deprives the rebel both of worthwhile enemies and of a claim to moral superiority. The aspiration to radicalism becomes just as silly as the convention it seeks to undermine. Elaine occasionally adopts politically correct positions, but she either cannot sustain her commitment or looks utterly ridiculous.

The distinctiveness of *Seinfeld's* comic nihilism is evident from a comparison with its chief contender for 1990s sitcom supremacy, *The Simpsons.* Neither show offers a moralistic defense or a rebellious critique of the family. The trivial aspirations of the family render it not so much above criticism as comically beneath it. *The Simpsons* illustrates what Tocqueville called the "naturalness" of the democratic family in the absence of the old hierarchical relations between parents, especially the father, and children. Familiarity, it turns out, simultaneously breeds affection and contempt. For the most part, Homer is one of the kids, who address him as they do their friends. When Marge thinks she may be pregnant again, Bart cheers his father, "Homer, you're a machine!" Nearly every episode contains a scene where Bart's acerbic wit provokes Homer into clutching his son's throat and yelling, "Why, you little . . . !" Homer embodies the return to a primitive, nearly subhuman state of nature. He is ruled by his appetites and inclinations, his desire for food, beer, sex, and get-rich schemes. He is capable of detached, malevolent humor at the expense of others; indeed, he often relishes these experiences with his son, Bart. In one episode, after being caught driving drunk, he is forced to attend driver's reform school and watch a gory video of accidents caused by drunk drivers. While others faint or throw up, Homer giggles: "It's funny because I don't know him." Yet he is also capable of affection and sympathy. Throughout, he is barely rational; in the face of the most powerful human experiences, he is typically inarticulate, responding to frustration with his trade-mark "D'oh!" or to grief or joy with a spontaneous moan.

Like the television screen around which the Simpsons gather to watch the violent cartoon *The Itchy and Scratchy Show*, the animated characters on *The Simpsons* are all surface. What one critic says about *Seinfeld's* characters can be easily generalized: "They only play at self-knowledge; any real consciousness of who they are . . . would be like the cartoon moment when Bugs Bunny looks down and realizes he's walking on air." Yet, on *The Simpsons*, irony and cruelty give way to a sympathetic affirmation of the family. In one episode, Homer becomes a restaurant critic and begins writing devastating critiques of the work of local chefs. At a community fair, the chefs conspire to rid themselves of the odious food critic. They poison a giant éclair, confident that Homer will be unable to resist eating it. As Bart overhears their plot, he first laughs, "Hah, they're going to kill Homer." Then a moment later, he yells, "Oh, no. They're going to kill Homer," and runs off to foil the plot.

Although it lacks the overt moralism of many classic American sitcoms, *The Simpsons* regularly finds a way to encompass our cynicism about contemporary institutions—from big government and big business to local schools and police departments—while still affirming family life and local communities.

On *The Simpsons*, father rarely knows best, but the family endures as an anchor to our sense of identity and as the object of our deepest affections. A similar case could be made for another Fox sitcom, *Malcolm in the Middle*, which features the enduring love and affection of the parents of five boys in the midst of the comic insanity of contemporary family life. Such shows offer comic realism about who we are, and we are thankfully still more than ironic spectators, sexual narcissists, or natural born killers. We may be ridiculous and often decadent, but we are not entirely depraved or incapable of true fidelity.

The older tradition of American sitcoms is often rightly criticized for its excessive sentimentality and its sanitized view of family life. The ease with which moral dilemmas were resolved and suffering overcome presupposed an artificial world, void of destructive sin and habitual vice. In spite of both artificiality and superficiality, these comedies were often quite effective at capturing the language and humor of children. Indeed, the shows embodied a clear distinction between the world of children and that of adults and never doubted the task of initiating the inhabitants of the former into the latter. But this distinction is now lost in American society and its television shows. In place of the realms of childhood and adulthood, there is the hybrid of perpetual adolescence. The goal is to have all the privileges of adult life with the lack of responsibility characteristic of childhood. The Puritan work ethic, which was still central to shows like *I Love Lucy* or even *The Brady Bunch*, is completely absent from *Seinfeld*.

Along with the demise of the family, *Seinfeld* exhibits skepticism about the pursuit of happiness. Early sitcoms depicted the family as the horizon of the pursuit of happiness and as the embodiment of the American dream. Over the years, sitcoms have seen an abridgment of ambition with respect to happiness and the American dream. *Seinfeld* represents the disappearance of this overarching pursuit as a major theme. Clearly, there are anticipations of this in highly successful shows like *M*A*S*H*, which during its last years focused on the frustrations of the American aspiration for happiness and on the hypocrisy in the American claim to embody the best life available. Alan Alda's character, Hawkeye, became especially acerbic toward his country. But in its serious, almost tragic, depiction of the costs of war and in its consciously critical stance toward American life, *M*A*S*H* ranges over a number of genres and is therefore no longer merely a comedy. The abdication of pure comedy is an inevitable result of the attempt to treat serious issues seriously. It reflects the more somber, less confident tone of the post-1960s, post-Vietnam, post-Watergate America, a nation much more devoted to self-scrutiny and more afflicted by self-doubt than the nation of the 1950s.

Like much of end-of-the-century America, *Seinfeld* transcends such seriousness; unlike sitcoms from *M*A*S*H* through *Ellen*, it never gives in to the temptation to take itself seriously, and in this respect, it returns us to pure comedy. Jerry Seinfeld traces his inspiration to the skits of Abbott and Costello, a form of comedy void of any interest in moral instruction or social critique. If *Seinfeld* returns to that original model of American comedy, it does so in unprecedented ways. Whereas the older pure comedies avoided serious issues at all costs and thus tended toward innocuous slapstick, the scope of *Seinfeld*'s humor is unlimited. All the grave topics, whose treatment turned other comedies tragic or at least melodramatic, are but additional subjects of comic insight for *Seinfeld*. The unlimited scope of *Seinfeld*'s humor is both a presupposition and a consequence of its nihilism.

The formerly revered American dream is now fragmented and makes its presence felt more in the form of occasionally deceptive nightmares. Characters are episodically gripped by a passion to find a kind of completion to their lives, to have it all, but this is nothing more than a fleeting and irrational passion, one among many possible temporary obsessions to which we are liable. This is the ironic flip side to the pointlessness of life, an irony out of which *Seinfeld* has gotten much mileage. In a world without meaning, anything can become a source of absolute significance or, more accurately, maniacal obsession, at least for a time. Irrational obsession is a dominant theme of *Seinfeld*. Kramer's whole life is consumed by a series of unrelated obsessions: driving a fire truck, hitting golf balls on the beach, or opening a restaurant where customers make their own pizza. Recall the show where Elaine develops an attachment to an unattractive and bizarre man precisely because he cannot remember her name.

The arbitrariness at the root of contemporary relationships and the obsessions that they breed are rich sources of comedy. The breakup is inevitable and is usually occasioned by something trivial, whether it be Elaine's indignation at a boyfriend's failure to write an exclamation point at the end of a message containing dramatic news, Jerry's work as a comic not being respected by his date (a cashier), or his attraction to a voluptuous woman being ruined by her manlike hands.

In a world where arbitrary, individual preferences rule, relationships can be nothing more than games, more or less sophisticated, more or less humorous. In one episode, Elaine is distraught that Kramer extended her regards to a guy she had recently dropped. When Elaine complains that Kramer's "unauthorized 'hi'" has lost her the "upper hand," Jerry comments that "it's like a game of tag." In another episode, Elaine falls for a professional mover who does not play games. Jerry says, "No games. What's the point of dating without games? How do you know if you're winning or losing?" The prominence of adolescent power struggles makes lying an indispensable art, an art for which George has "the gift." As he advises Jerry in one of the many "must-lie" situations on the show, "It's not a lie if you believe it."

THE DEATH OF MAN—AND WOMAN, TOO

In its subtle analysis of relationships, *Seinfeld* discerns something like Nietzsche's will to power. For Nietzsche, the idea of an objective moral ideal is an illusion, a human construct. What is actually at the root of all our conscious life, underlying our division of actions into good and evil, is an unconscious and amoral force, the will to power. He prophesied the coming of a new age of humanity, embodied in the superman, who would emerge richer, stronger, more varied, from having lived through the transforming era of nihilism. Inspired by his deeply aristocratic sense of rank, Nietzsche's superman is an artist who harnesses the chaotic will to power to create new and nobler values. *Seinfeld*'s will to power knows no such grand aspiration. The preoccupation with power evinces the precarious, indeed illusory, character of freedom. Assertions of independence and control inevitably generate a reversal and lead to groveling submission. All the major characters at some point find themselves beholden to the manipulative and devious Newman, whose very name is spoken in a tone of utmost disdain. The Superman of Jerry and George is the comic book figure, whose statue sits on Jerry's bookshelf. They admire him not for his altruistic motives or sense of mission, the things that made him an American icon, but for his power. Their refashioned comic book hero is thus also beyond good and evil, dangerously close to a combination of Superman and Bizarro Superman. Being closer to Nietzsche's last men than to his superman, they do not detect the danger. In spite of their voracious appetite for conversation, they are unable even to formulate their dilemma.

The amoral tone of much of the show's humor does not mean there are no longer any rules. And the rules that continue to function in such a world are essentially comic. As usual, *Seinfeld* has seen this and put it to good use. Some rules have to do with the conventions of power, as in Elaine's game of tag with her former mate or Susan's insistence on the rule that couples tell one another everything. Other rules save us from embarrassment: when asked to comment about the appearance of an ugly baby, one must lie. Sometimes it is difficult to determine precisely what the rule is. How many dates after a sexual encounter must one endure before breaking up with a partner? Lots of traditional moral rules are flouted, and even where they have some force, as in obligatory attendance at funerals, nothing more then external conformity makes sense. Elaine spends her time at one funeral expressing her dissatisfaction with her attire. Most of the rules concern apparently trivial matters, such as George's claim that "airport pick-up is a binding social contract" or Kramer's insistence on the inviolable status of the rules constituting the etiquette of golf—"A rule's a rule and, let's face it, without rules there's chaos." The seemingly insignificant takes on a nonnegotiable status.

One may protest a rule, but it is not really possible to evade it. After apparently having been caught picking his nose, Jerry denies culpability and then complains, "What's wrong with picking? Is it one of the Ten Commandments? Did God say, 'Thou shalt not pick'?" In another episode, Jerry's protests against the obligatory day-after thank you earn him a rebuke from Kramer: "If you don't want to be part of society, why don't you get in your car and move to the East Side?" Kramer learns the hard way about the status of such rules when AIDS walkers vilify and beat him for refusing to wear his AIDS ribbon.

Instead of the nihilistic era eliminating rules, initiating a lapse into a kind of anarchy, there is a medley of rules with no clear relationship to one another. There is something capricious and comical in the continuing hold that rules have on us; they operate like taboos, making little or no sense but nonetheless exercising an irresistible psychological pressure. *Seinfeld*'s insight into the odd ways rules now function in our lives is a remarkable bit of comic genius. Nothing illustrates better the Pyrrhic victory of radical individualism. We have successfully thrown off the encumbrances of authority and tradition only to find ourselves subject to new, more devious, and more intractable forms of tyranny. Classical liberalism thought that the most just form of government was one that recognized the natural and inalienable rights of human beings to self-determination. There was a kind of naive faith in the ability of untutored individuals to choose for the best, to act on the basis of their long-term interests. The belief was that the only rules to emerge from such a system would be rules reasonably consented to by a reflective majority or by their duly elected representatives. But the advent of democratic nihilism renders dubious the assumption of a link between autonomous individual choice and reason and between the fleeting desires of the self and the self's long-term interests.

One episode in particular illuminates the absurd consequences of making an absolute out of choice, the result of which is the trivialization of all objects of choice. After watching the opening of a film in which the main character finds herself in a coma, Kramer decides he needs a living will to ensure he will die with dignity. Contemplating the weighty choice of a proxy, he considers appointing Jerry, who assures him, "Believe me. If given the legal opportunity, I will kill you." He settles on Elaine, who accompanies him to the lawyer's office to consider various hypothetical situations for the ending of his life. For one situation—"You're eating but machines do everything else"— Elaine counsels, "I'd stick," and Kramer agrees: "Yeah. I could still go to the coffee shop." The problem is that the impetuous Kramer failed to watch the rest of the movie before setting off in search of the living will. When he returns to the video, he discovers that the woman comes out of the coma, and he informs Jerry, "I've changed my mind about the whole coma thing. . . . I'm up for it."

As one's vagrant inclinations change from moment to moment, so too does one's thinking about the big questions. The precariousness of one's present choices divests the ultimate issues of all significance. When one's life plan is subject to the unpredictable tyranny of chance events or evanescent passion, the hollow assertion of a dignity based on autonomy becomes fodder for the comedian. It is hard to find a better description of nihilism or of how the type of liberalism that rests upon the inviolable right of each individual to construct his or her own vision of reality naturally generates nihilism.

Seinfeld fulfills the prophetic pronouncements of philosophers from Nietzsche to Foucault about the imminent death of man, the vanishing of the determinate self. In so doing, *Seinfeld* provides its own spin on Nietzsche's doctrine of eternal recurrence. As we have noted, each character's sense of self is subject to a seemingly endless series of changes, and yet each remains unchanged. One of the show's writers has confessed that there is only one rule in the composition of the show: the characters must never learn from their experiences; they must forever be what they intrinsically and eternally are. Self-proclaimed postmodern writers often treat the aspiration for transcendence, for permanence or wholeness, as misguided; they cast off being for the sake of becoming. *Seinfeld* depicts the consequences of such a project. There is nothing but banal repetition and the experience of eternal recurrence as unending frustration.

Each character on *Seinfeld* has his or her individual limits, but these are not moral limits; they are more like the limits of one's personality or lifestyle. This is most pointedly illustrated in the episode where Jerry and George are suspected of being gay. They spend the entire episode vociferously denying the accusation and vigorously defending their heterosexuality. Yet after each denial, they feel compelled to add, "not that there's anything wrong with that." Like other conventions once thought to reflect a natural order, heterosexuality has become an inexplicable remnant from the past. Instead of the body as ensouled, as the locus for the reception and expression of meaning and intimacy, the body is now a neutral and mute collection of organs and parts. The parts can be manipulated to produce pleasure. In one episode, Elaine attributes her failure to persuade a homosexual to change "teams" to her limited access to the male "equipment." When George's mother surprises him and interrupts his self-stimulation, she objects to his treating his body like an "amusement park." The fixation on the body does not unveil any deeper significance; it blinds the characters to the complementarity of the sexes. *Seinfeld* matter-of-factly confirms Renton's revolutionary prophecy from *Trainspotting* that we're heterosexual by default, that in one thousand years there will be no men and no women: "It's all about aesthetics and fuck all to do with morality." All of this confirms Tocqueville's worry that, in spite of our bold proclamations of individualism, the result of our insatiable pursuit of equality is homogeneity. The lead writer for *Ally McBeal*, another important show from the time of *Seinfeld*, David Kelley, remarks, "I cringe when people ask me how I write women characters. The truth is, I just write them the way I write men. I don't distinguish."

Other episodes of *Seinfeld* illustrate the preeminence of lifestyle over morality. For example, Jerry pushes the limits of possibility in his attempt to execute the "roommate switch" to trade his relationship with his present girlfriend for one with her roommate. On George's advice, he suggests a ménage à trois, presuming one woman will be offended and the other intrigued. The strategy backfires when the proposal is accepted. But Jerry cannot go through with it, because "I'm not an orgy guy." He would have to get orgy clothes, buy special oils, and so forth. When George attempts to extricate himself from a relationship with a woman who has a male roommate, he deploys the same ménage à trois strategy, thinking it will disgust her. When the woman turns to her roommate and excitedly informs him that George is "into" the ménage, we are left with the image of George's face in a silent, contorted scream reminiscent of the figure in Edvard Munch's painting *The Scream.*

COMIC ANTIPROVIDENCE

The comparison with Munch's painting might seem inapposite because that image is designed to induce in us a feeling of horror, not laughter. But the way Munch's image of horror has now made it into popular culture in the form of posters, coffee mugs, place mats, and even blow-up dolls is an instructive confirmation of the nearly universal undermining of the grave by the light, the reversal of the tragic into the comic. We may not yet be used to thinking of the pointlessness of life as funny; we are more accustomed to the dreary, depressing angst of artists. *Seinfeld* keeps us laughing, and hence, we fail to see its underlying nihilism. That we find it funny evinces the absence of sympathy, the disconnection, between audience and character. This is the same sort of disconnection that the characters on *Seinfeld* exhibit toward one another. We laugh as much at these characters as with them.

Some fans thought the death of George's fiancée, Susan, who poisoned herself while licking envelopes for wedding invitations, was callous. It may not have been the most creative moment in the show, but nothing in the manner of the termination of that relationship was incongruous with the dominant kind of humor in the show. Her death was untimely only in the sense that it took so long for it to happen. The famous "Junior Mint" episode is also rife with callous humor. It closes with Kramer and Jerry observing surgery from a booth above the operating table. Kramer, who has brought candy to increase his enjoyment of the performance, drops a Junior Mint right into the incision. Before agreeing to accompany Kramer to the hospital, Jerry hems and haws. Finally, he relents, "All right. Let's go watch them slice the fat bastard up." Seinfeld himself has called that line a turning point in the series.

The end of George's ménage à trois episode and Susan's death are but two examples of *Seinfeld*'s art of the unhappy but comical ending. There is often something fitting in the way chance events conspire to undermine the hopes or aspirations of one or more of the characters or, as in the case of Susan's death, in the way one person's tragedy is another's comedy. *Seinfeld* skillfully introduces and balances a number of seemingly unrelated plotlines and then brings them together at the end. The coincidence of events means that we can discern in life something more than mere unrelated chance, even if it does not lead us to apprehend some underlying principle of order in the way comedies of an earlier era do. Not only the endings of particular episodes but also other sorts of partings or separations are treated comically. Compare the melodramatic ending of the relationship between Sam and Diane on *Cheers* with the nonchalant ending of Jerry's engagement, where both blurt out "I hate you" and then casually wish each other well. Lots of shows, for example, *ER*, highlight the frustration of human affection, the way the circumstances of our times thwart the very possibility of love. But to maintain a straight face, let alone a stiff upper lip, in the face of meaninglessness is difficult. Nihilism mocks such gravity. If there is nothing beyond me in light of which I might understand myself and appraise my actions and goals, then how is any particular course of action more worthy of choice than any other? If meaninglessness is the ultimate framework, then what is the point of striving at all? What is all the fuss about? If *ER* comes close to tragedy in its poignant depiction of the inescapable futility of the search, *Ally McBeal*'s penchant for the absurd, for portraying the pursuit of love as a kind of farce, tends toward the comic. But Ally cannot quite relinquish the quest. In a maudlin and mildly self-deceiving tone, she muses at the end of the inaugural episode that she really does not want to be content. That would mean the end of the quest, which she prefers to the catch because the "more lost you are, the more you have to look forward to." The implication? She must "be happy and just not know it."

The abdication of the quest, or at least of any real possibility for its fulfillment, is both a cause and a consequence of the deprivation of the self. *Seinfeld*'s world is populated by Nietzsche's last men, who, when faced with the great questions and ultimate issues of life, blink and giggle. In a world with no ultimate sense of good and evil or of shared purpose, taking a moral stance is inevitably construed as striking a pose. The point is hilariously played out in the show about abortion, where Jerry first instigates a near riot at Poppie's restaurant by bringing up the matter and then nips in the bud Elaine's affection for a man by inquiring where he stands on the issue. The shrill and indignant tone of the verbal battle at Poppie's captures the character of public debate in a nihilistic world, or rather of the impossibility of having a public debate about fundamental issues. In the same episode, Kramer enlists Poppie's support for his idea of a pizza shop where customers make their own pizza. The cooperative venture is quickly doomed by a debate over whether individuals should be given the right to choose whatever topping they wish. Poppie objects and insists, "On this topic there can be no debate." The argument shifts to the controversial question of when a pizza becomes a pizza: when you first put your hands into the dough or not until it comes out of the oven? On the surface, the exchange mocks both sides in the abortion debate, but the underlying motif is that of morality as farce. There is no higher or lower. Pizza, abortion—it's all the same.

The classic American sitcom presupposed both an order of higher and lower and a shared vision of America as providing the best framework for the pursuit of a good human life. As I noted earlier, in spite of the notable absence of explicit attention to religious themes, the original television sitcoms embodied a civic religion, and their ability to bring events to a happy ending was a kind of justification of American democracy. In this genre, the happy ending is usually brought about through an unanticipated event. Whereas in the classic tragedy an almost cosmic necessity leads to the downfall of the hero, in a comedy, chance or coincidence is the key to the culmination of the action. Tragedy, in Aristotle's definitive formulation, achieves its emotional effect by inducing in the audience feelings of pity and fear for the fallen hero. If comedy arouses those feelings at all, it does so somewhere near the beginning of the action, when it leads the characters into apparent harm. But the lighthearted tone of comedy invites the audience to see through the apparent injury and to anticipate its resolution.

Through a chance event, apparent evils and seeming dilemmas are averted. Since a chance event interrupts the flow of the action, it might seem to render the drama incoherent or implausible. Yet because it brings about a happy ending and usually leads the major characters to put any enmity aside and reconcile themselves to one another and to a fate that is better than their behavior merits, the power behind the coincidence is benevolent. The role of chance in comedy engenders in the audience a spirit of wonder and gratitude: wonder because the benevolent orchestration of human events surpasses our immediate comprehension and gratitude because our destiny surpasses our merits.

Given this account of chance or coincidence in traditional comedy, it might seem that *Seinfeld* is not as novel as I have proposed because it is replete with coincidences. Indeed, it makes use of coincidence as a structuring principle much more than any other comedy of which I am aware. What are we to make of the prominent role of coincidence in *Seinfeld*? One possibility is that *Seinfeld* deploys coincidence as mere coincidence, not as opening up the possibility of perceiving some higher order of intelligibility. Many episodes do indeed leave us with simply a series of coincidences. When these coincidences seem to serve a harmonious end, the goodness or order they bring about is not that of a higher or comprehensive sort. In one episode, Jerry regrets having arranged for Elaine to move into the apartment above him, a move that would curb his independence and unduly complicate his sex life. When he learns that someone else has offered $5,000 up front for the rent-controlled apartment and that Elaine is in no position to make a counteroffer, he rejoices. Then he waxes philosophical and confides to George that he used to think that the universe was just a series of unrelated occurrences; he now realizes that there is "reason and purpose to everything." For Jerry, order in the universe is indistinguishable from chance, conspiring to satisfy his preferences.

In most episodes, however, chance events seem ordered to a malevolent end. Instead of coincidence operating as a sign of a benign providential order beyond our comprehension, it functions as a kind of antiprovidence. Even when the conclusion is "fortunate," it does not bring all the parties to a better state. In fact, this is true of the episode just cited, where Jerry's luck coincides with Elaine's loss of the apartment. The good luck of some is purchased at the cost of misery for others. The most humorous illustration of this principle is in the episodes focusing on Kramer's attempt to find himself by traveling to California. Kramer's bad luck, which begins with his car breaking down on the freeway, reaches its nadir when he is charged with being the "smog killer" after the woman he had been dating is found murdered with a piece of paper on her person bearing Kramer's name. At first, things look bad for Kramer. Luckily, so to speak, there is another murder while he is in jail. As Jerry, George, and Kramer jump up and down joyfully chanting that the smog killer has struck again, a family, palpably in mourning, passes them and enters the police station. Even after all this, Kramer considers staying in California. To Jerry's incredulity at his plans and objection that nothing good has happened since he arrived in L.A., Kramer responds, "I met a girl." Jerry again objects, "Kramer, she was murdered!" And Kramer answers, "I wasn't looking for a long-term relationship."

There is explicit evidence of this line of thinking in a number of episodes. Recall, for example, the show about the pilot Jerry and George have submitted to NBC. At one point, the pilot's acceptance looks highly likely, yet George is increasingly paranoid about a discoloration on his lips. Of course, everyone he bumps into, including an Arab cab driver, comments on the discoloration and suggests he get it checked out. Confident that his demise is near, George complains to Jerry: "God will never let me enjoy success." Jerry queries, "I thought you didn't believe in God," to which George responds, "For the bad things I do." In another episode, already mentioned, Jerry all-knowingly informs Elaine that the only reason she is pursuing a certain man is that he cannot remember her name. Shaken from self-oblivion, she states, "That's sick." Jerry dispassionately explains, "It's God's plan. He doesn't really want anyone to get together."

Although much of *Seinfeld* testifies to the death of God, it also lends credence to the view that God is alive and well but indistinguishable from the devil. This is precisely the sort of God that would account for the social world of *Seinfeld*, a world constructed around a set of arbitrary and unavoidable rules. *Seinfeld*'s God is a capricious, whimsical, detached, and perhaps malevolent deity. *Seinfeld*'s God is identical to the hypothetical being that Descartes seeks to vanquish. Recall that this is "not a God, who is the supreme source of truth, but a certain evil spirit, not less clever and deceitful than powerful, [who] has bent all his efforts to deceive me." This is not a God with whom we could enter into a social contract, let alone a biblical covenant. It is not even a God that we should reasonably fear; for, although he is all powerful and has our fate in his hands, he is so unpredictable that our animosity or indifference is just as likely or unlikely to be efficacious as is our devoted obeisance.

This supreme being replaces not only the just and merciful God of the Judeo-Christian tradition but also the intermediate, complacent all-American God. *Seinfeld* has seen through the modern American dream of blissful, uninterrupted leisure. Instead, leisure is tedious and the human condition is, as Pascal observed centuries ago, characterized by "boredom, inconstancy, and anxiety." *Seinfeld*'s comic nihilism divests Pascal's sobering insight of its tragic implications. Human life is a kind of game orchestrated by an indifferent or malevolent supreme being, whose desires we cannot assuage and whose power we cannot finally resist. We are not, however, entirely without recourse. We may not be made in the image and likeness of a good and rational

God, but we can still imitate the divine by cultivating a comic detachment from the spectacle of human life.

PROMETHEUS AS ONAN

For most of the characters on *Seinfeld*, the prominence and function of coincidence serve to point toward the inevitability of their ultimate misery, of their being tricked yet again by Descartes' evil genius. Yet Jerry has a peculiar knack for avoiding such misery, especially in sexual relationships, where he is capable of an unrivaled detachment and indifference. Since happiness with others is not possible, it can be achieved only through a kind of comfortable isolation from others. If George has the gift of lying, Jerry has the gift of innate superficiality.

Given the nihilistic culture he inhabits, Jerry's detachment is both prudent and a source of free entertainment. He boasts to George that the uproar over abortion in Poppie's restaurant was pretty much all his fault. Of course, Jerry's comic take on nihilism requires a kind of stoical distance. It also requires luck. Jerry has both. Like the other characters, he can succumb to little obsessions or passions, most notably when he learns that Elaine never had an orgasm while they were dating. Yet generally speaking, his detachment is greater than that of any other character. Fortune also shines on him: he is, as Kramer calls him, "even Steven." He relishes the way everything balances out for him while the fortunes of his friends are dashed.

Jerry comes closer than anyone else on the show to achieving perpetual adolescence, except of course when his career as a professional comedian is at issue. He does care about his success as a comedian, success that he cannot achieve without the assistance of others. His professional life has complications and frustrations—whether these be in the form of an inept agent or a harassing audience—that his personal life lacks. When it comes to work, Jerry must emerge from the adolescent self-absorption that is a central motif of *Seinfeld*. The aspiration for adulthood is a residual social and psychic artifact, capable of resurfacing almost at any time and catching one unawares. The famous episode where Jerry and George decide to get married begins with the two of them in the coffee shop lamenting their immaturity. "We're like children. . . . We're not men. . . . We come up with all these reasons to break up with women. We're pathetic. . . . It would be nice to care about someone." They make a deal to pursue serious relationships. As George enthusiastically runs off to convince Susan that he's ready to make a commitment, Jerry is saved from such a disastrous course of action by some timely advice from Kramer. When Jerry relates their conversation and resolution to Kramer, he knowingly responds, "So, you asked yourself—isn't there something more to life? Let me clue you into something. There isn't." Kramer proceeds in rich detail to demonstrate his thesis that marriage is a "man-made prison." Bolstered by Kramer's advice, Jerry breaks up with Melanie because she "eats her peas one at a time."

If marriage is hell and relationships are traps, then being alone would seem to be an ideal. In one episode, Jerry comments that a walking date is good because there's not a lot of "face-to-face" contact. Elaine adds, "It's the next best thing to being alone." Isolation involves an abridgment of one's sexual ambitions, or at least of one's sense of sexual conquest, but it by no means entails the elimination of sexual satisfaction. In many respects, autoerotic activity is superior to sexual congress with another because it involves none of the complications attendant upon the latter. The experience of pure sex, of having sex as one wants it, without all the unwelcome human elements that accompany interaction with others, is the impossible dream of *Seinfeld*. Recall the show where Jerry and Elaine, disappointed at their lack of prospects in things genital, hit upon the idea that they could satisfy their needs through one another. Anticipating complications, they introduce certain rules of conduct, for example, staying over is optional and no calling the day after sex. That the experiment is obviously doomed from the outset confirms C. S. Lewis' insight that "lust is more abstract than logic."

The famous "master of your domain" episode underscores the essential role of masturbation in the world of *Seinfeld*. The contest to see who can go the longest without masturbating (won, surprisingly, by George) is provoked by George's relating how his mother had unexpectedly come home to find him, as she puts it, treating his body like an "amusement park." So shocked is she by her discovery that she falls and injures herself. When George visits her in the hospital, she remarks, "Too bad you can't do that for a living. . . . You could sell out Madison Square Garden. Thousands of people would come to watch you. You could be a big star."

SEINFELD'S SEMIOTIC HELL

The America of *Seinfeld* is, as America always has been, the land of endless possibility, the only country founded on the natural right to the pursuit of happiness. But there are no frontiers left to conquer, just fleeting appetites and residual desire for fulfillment. Still, we cannot seem to shake off the language of our history, the language of individual rights, of human dignity, of equality, and of success and happiness. We are trapped in a semiotic hell, of which there is no clear diagnosis and from which there can be no escape. The situation would be tragic were we capable of sustained gravity and were it not so absurd.

In addition to being one of the most humorous examples of a show without a plot, the episode entitled "The Parking Garage" is a splendid metaphor for the vision of human life as a world of apparent signs, symbols, and guideposts leading nowhere. On a trip to a Jersey mall, where Kramer has purchased an air conditioner and Elaine some tropical fish, the gang misplaces the car in the mall's parking garage. Unable to reach any consensus on where they came in, they trade guesses on which color, number, or level the car is located. All the signs begin to merge. Grasping their existential dilemma, George comments, "We're like rats in some experiment." The indifference of others to their plight is evident in Elaine's repeated failures to enlist anyone's assistance in finding their car. After appealing to their sense of compassion—one passerby frankly admits to her that he would not get any satisfaction out of helping them—she adopts a different strategy: "I can understand your not caring about us, we're human, but what about the fish?" The problem is that animal rights activists do not hang out at malls in New Jersey.

After they all become separated, Elaine, Jerry, and George are reunited and fortuitously find the car. Their good luck is but momentary because Kramer, the driver, is not with them. By the time he arrives, Elaine's fish have died. Fittingly, the exhausted crew suffers a final humiliation when the car will not start. We have here of course yet another example of the unhappy but humorous ending. What we can now say about that structure is that it reflects the comic anti-providence of a world governed by a malevolent deity.

The sense of being trapped in a semiotic hell is made explicit in the much-hyped final episode. When Jerry and George receive word that their five-year-old pilot has been picked up by NBC, they suppose that their dreams have been realized and begin to plan their move to California. NBC then calls to offer Jerry and his friends use of a network private jet to travel wherever they want. Soon after they leave on a flight for Paris, the plane is forced to make an emergency landing when Kramer tries to clear water from his ear and ends up crashing into the control panels in the cockpit. During what they think will be a short stay in a small Massachusetts town, they witness a carjacking. As they make sarcastic remarks about the fat driver's misfortune, Kramer captures the moment on video. Soon a policeman arrives and arrests them for having violated a newly enacted Good Samaritan law. The prosecutor makes character the key issue and marshals some eighteen witnesses—a reunion of the most colorful characters to have appeared in the series—to demonstrate a "pattern of antisocial behavior." He promises that they will pay this time. After the jury returns a guilty verdict, the judge scolds them for behavior that "has rocked the very foundations" of society. The ending confirms Newman's prophecy from the opening of the episode; when Jerry refuses to let him tag along to Paris, he warns Jerry that his "day of reckoning is coming," that his "play world" will be shattered and the "smug smile" wiped off his face.

The excessive attention lavished on the show and its stars in the weeks leading up to the last episode calls to mind Geoffrey O'Brien's remark: "Where it might once have been asked if *Seinfeld* was a commentary on society, the question now should probably be whether society has not been reconfigured as a milieu for commenting on *Seinfeld*."[4] Of course, that wry observation speaks volumes about our society, as does *Seinfeld* itself. Amid the mindless adulation before and after the finale, some critics issued jeremiads against the show's celebration of baby boomer self-absorption. This is true but superficial, reflecting the shallow moralism of boomer pundits. Others saw the last episode as a moral judgment on the characters.

Neither the detractors nor the boosters are on the mark. There is, as we have noted, a heavy dose of moralism in the episode, perhaps too much to be taken seriously. One problem is that Newman, the most diabolical person in the series, remains free. Moreover, it is not clear that conventional society or the justice system is much better off than are the characters on trial. Finally, it is simply not the case that up until now they have gotten away with their petty indulgences in the seven deadly sins. The thwarting of their attempt to escape their New York lives and capture the American dream in California is but the final confirmation that there is no way out for them. Whenever they think they are escaping, they run into themselves. Their lives in prison are essentially the same as they were outside. Jerry's biggest adjustment is the alteration of his cereal-eating habits, while Elaine is anxious about having to wear an orange uniform. They have simply traded the coffee shop for the prison. To Jerry's observation that the second button on George's shirt is in the wrong place, George responds, "Haven't we had this conversation before?" They are destined to eternal recurrence.

DARE TO SAY YES: *TRAINSPOTTING*

Eternal recurrence is an apt description of the life of drug use. The typical portrayal of drug addiction is as a sad and self-destructive entrapment that deprives the addict of hope and happiness. *Trainspotting* hilariously turns that assumption inside out. Set in Scotland with indigenous actors, the film nonetheless plays off of a highly influential American vision of the good life, a vision that has been exported to every corner of the globe. At the beginning of the movie, the main character, Renton, speaks in praise of drug use as a way of life. He cleverly and derisively turns on its head every parent's, schoolteacher's, and politician's slogan about a drug-free America. Admitting that you could "choose your future . . . you could choose life," he counters, "Why would I choose to do a thing like that?" Playing upon our nearly bankrupt language of choice, he mocks, "I chose not to choose life."

Posing to himself the next likely question, about the reasons for his choice, he responds, "There are no reasons. Who needs reasons when you've got heroin?" The outside world thinks heroin is all about "misery, despair, and death and all that shit, but what they forget is the pleasure of it." As Renton sees it, the law-abiding world of drug-free society is itself all about pleasure; it just pursues its petty pleasures by more complicated means and in less satisfying ways. An ordinary life of conformity is caught up in all sorts of distracting worries about things like paying bills and making human relationships work. But a "true and sincere drug habit" clarifies things. It gives simplicity and unity to one's life: the only worry is about scoring. Given conventional society's fixation on sexual pleasure, Renton's claim on behalf of heroin is impressive: if you take the best orgasm you have ever had and multiply its pleasure by a thousand, you still have not reached the experience of heroin. By contrast, conventional pleasure is tepid and always adulterated by consciousness of past regrets and future duties or projects.

Like *Killers*, the film indulges in the aesthetics of evil and black comedy. The film alternates so often and so quickly between horror and comedy that it becomes hard to separate them. Most of the scenes in which we approach the horror of drug addiction have a decidedly comic edge to them. In one disgusting scene, Renton takes a drug in the form of a suppository and in his desperate need to relieve his bowels forgets about the pill. We are then treated to fantastic images of him diving head first into a toilet, billed as the filthiest in Scotland, and swimming through a sort of reservoir. Pill in hand, he emerges triumphantly from the toilet. Near the end of the movie, he attends a funeral for a friend and learns that the fellow was so high he failed to clean up after his cat, contracted a disease from ingesting cat feces, and died. The cat? He's fine.

Only one scene in the film captures the numbing terror of drug life. In the home where most of the drug use occurs, a child of one of the addicts crawls aimlessly and unobtrusively from room to room. When the party is interrupted by the piercing screams of the mother as she discovers the child's dead and discolored face, Renton observes with foreboding that this time things will not get better. But as the mother's wailing subsides, she requests a hit, which Renton supplies, but only after giving himself one. The image of the dead child lasts but a moment, and the matter is never mentioned again. Renton is wrong: things do get better, or at least return to their typical state. In the repetitive, circular world of drugs, there is no novelty, no possibility of progress or regress, no ultimate hope or despair.

The film continues the reversal of the relationship between evil and law-abiding society that we have already noted in other films, although there is not as sharp a contrast between the two as there was in *Cape Fear* or *Silence*. Renton is only moderately interested in offending and not at all inclined to terrorize civil society. He meets society more on its own terms: the pursuit of pleasure. Like the rest of us, he wants to be left alone to live his life as he sees fit. The "principal drawback" to a life of addiction is putting up with the endless moralizing from straight friends and family members, who berate Renton about polluting his body and wasting his life. As his subversive deployment of our democratic language of choice and consent indicates, we are already beyond good and evil. Mocking the language of Enlightenment rationality, he describes the decision of his group to go back on drugs as a fully informed, democratic choice. Autonomy gives way to aesthetic self-creation.

The evil of Renton distinguishes itself from the morality of conventional society by its forthright honesty and its blatant exercise of a will to pleasure. Conventional society is banal by contrast. Yet the evil of Renton is itself banal by comparison with that of the invading spirit in *The Exorcist*, Hannibal Lecter in *The Silence of the Lambs*, or John Doe in *Se7en*. There is nothing superhuman or especially diabolical about Renton. His alternation between the terrifying and the absurd is somewhat reminiscent of Arendt's depiction of Eichmann. If Eichmann turns our language of duty against our basic intuitions about human dignity, Renton performs the same reversal with our language of free choice and informed consent. In other respects, however, Renton's banality is quite different from that of Eichmann, whose banality is the result of his unflagging conformity to the dictates of conventional society. Renton is no totalitarian, though he does indiscriminately treat everyone as an instrument for the maximization of his own pleasure. He is, moreover, never unintentionally or unconsciously funny in the way Eichmann was. Renton's sense of irony, a source of much of the film's dark humor, evinces at least a certain level of psychic complexity, whereas Eichmann was all surface. What little depth Renton may possess is a result of his dynamic affirmation of the eternal recurrence of drug life and the utter poverty of the purported goodness of drug-free society.

In the film's final segments, Renton and his buddies plan and successfully pull off a deal to buy drugs cheap and sell them for profit. After Renton takes off with all the money, he admits (to us) that he has no good reason for taking the money except that most of the guys would have done the same thing to him if given the opportunity. The film ends with a monologue: "The truth is I'm bad but I'm going to change. . . . I'm going straight and choosing life. . . . I'm going to be just like you: the job, the family, the fucking big television, the washing machine, the car, good health, low cholesterol, dental insurance, mortgage . . . looking ahead, the day you die." His knowing and inviting smile as he looks directly at us in the final scene implies that we get the joke, that he is already one of us or, more pointedly, that we are already one with him. If we admire his resolve and his clarity, then we are tempted to share his view of the essential sameness of drug and straight culture, or rather of the inferiority of straight to drug culture. Renton's affirmation of the cyclical character of drug life is opposed to the linear structure of Enlightenment progress, whose chief contemporary embodiment is the life of endless accumulation coupled with the futile and degrading attempt to fend off death.

Once again, conventional society is indicted for its hypocrisy and cowardice. Insofar as we agree with the indictment and adopt Renton's posture of ironic distance from society, we prove ourselves at least momentarily as daring as he. The problem for most of us is that we will return to our lives of paying bills and lowering our cholesterol. If we can find no higher goals than those of endless accumulation, and if our heroism peaks at daring to say no to drugs, our life looks pointless and comically hollow. One of Arendt's ways of describing nihilism is as a state where life is an end itself, where nothing higher than the mere continuation of existence assumes public significance.

In its detached, ironic take on nihilism, in its accentuation of pleasure over terror, and in its concentration on the cyclical character of a nihilistic world, *Trainspotting* confirms many of our theses about evil and nihilism. First, although the film is obviously a satire of capitalist-consumer culture, its indictment cuts deeper, mocking the very foundations of liberal modernity. It puts in question our moderate and thoroughly conventional understanding and practice of ideals like freedom of choice, equality, and consent. The film is a dramatic illustration of the thesis of Nietzsche and Tocqueville that certain forms of democratic liberalism naturally generate nihilism. Second, the advent of nihilism brings not chaos and shapelessness but a mechanical and deterministic narrative structure, a structure that reflects the shrinking of human aspiration and the constraining of human freedom. Third, the ultimate trajectory of the narrative approach to nihilism is in the direction of comic irony and the petty laughter of Nietzsche's last men, for whom the absurdity of human life is a source of bemusement.

Renton leads us to the final stage of nihilism, but his attempted transcendence of consumerist life resists the complete conflation of nihilism and conventional society—a conflation on full display in Tarantino's greatest film, *Pulp Fiction.*

COMIC VIOLENCE, CHANCE, AND THE MIRACULOUS
IN *PULP FICTION*

Pulp Fiction consists of a series of interrelated short stories, of which the principal concerns a gangster duo, Vincent (John Travolta) and Jules (Samuel Jackson). Although a number of pivotal events occur in the series of overlapping narratives, what happens is no more important than what the characters say about what happens. The primacy of dialogue is evident in a number of scenes. In the opening, a husband and wife team of robbers decide to rob the restaurant where they are presently eating, but only after they discuss the drawbacks of stealing from banks and liquor stores. The last option is beginning to present serious communication problems because of the predominance of foreign liquor store owners. As the husband enumerates the risks involved in hitting the usual places, the wife becomes incredulous and asks, "What then, day jobs?" He suggests, "Nobody ever robs restaurants—why not?" A subsequent scene shows Vincent and Jules, on the way to a hit, discussing the differences between McDonald's restaurants in Amsterdam and the United States and chuckling over the foreign name of the Quarter Pounder with Cheese, the Royale with Cheese. But their most humorous exchange occurs in the same restaurant where we have just left the married robbers. Jules is explaining that he will not eat pork because the pig is a "filthy animal." Vincent presses him and asks about dogs:

> Vincent: How about dogs? Dogs eat their own feces.
>
> Jules: I don't eat dog, either.
>
> Vincent: Yes, but do you consider a dog a filthy animal?
>
> Jules: I wouldn't go so far as to call a dog filthy, but they're definitely dirty. But a dog's got personality. And personality goes a long way.
>
> Vincent: So by that rationale, if a pig had a better personality, he'd cease to be a filthy animal?
>
> Jules: We'd have to be talking about one charmin' motherfuckin' pig. I mean he'd have to be ten times more charmin' than that Arnold on *Green Acres*.

The allusion to the television pig Arnold is perhaps the most humorous example of an inevitable feature of the dialogue: commentary on popular culture. Nowhere is this commentary more pronounced than in the scene where Vincent escorts Mia, his mob boss' wife, to dinner at a 1950s style diner, where Marilyn Monroe is a waitress and Buddy Holly a busboy. When Vincent effortlessly identifies the various Hollywood personalities working at the diner, Mia is impressed and comments, "Pretty smart." Then, in an obvious spoof of Travolta's *Saturday Night Fever* routine, Vincent and Mia enter a dance contest. What is the significance of all these references to pop culture?

In the absence of the old distinction between high and low art, sophistication now involves witty commentary on pop culture. Art has narcissistically turned in upon itself as if there were no reality independent of it. Or better, art reflects life, but life itself is now indistinguishable from pop culture. The nihilism underlying such a world suits the tone of a moderately dark comedy like *Pulp Fiction.*

Pulp Fiction normalizes the world of drugs and crime and treats it comically. Vincent's dealer promotes heroin by proclaiming, "It's making a comeback." When Vincent questions the quality of the heroin and reminds the dealer that he's been in Amsterdam, the dealer counters, "I'll take the Pepsi challenge with that Amsterdam shit anytime." After they have concluded their transaction, as if to underscore the Ozzie and Harriet normalcy of the life of drugs, the dealer calls to his wife from the bedroom, "Honey, will you get me some baggies from the kitchen?" None of the characters in *Pulp Fiction* adopts an ironic, mocking tone toward drug-free, civilized life because the life of gangsters and drug users is itself conventional.

The film follows through on the conventionality of evil more fully and more persuasively than does *Natural Born Killers.* On this score, it is interesting to note that Tarantino wrote the original script for *Killers,* but after disagreements with Stone, his name was removed from the credits. A crucial point of contention was Tarantino's penchant for leaving "things unexplained." The need to present an explanation makes Stone's *Killers* a thoroughly ambivalent, if not self-refuting, film. Stone cannot let go of the pretense of moral critique. The pointlessness of life seems to be reflected in the nonlinear structure of the film, in the impossibility of narrative unity. This, however, is but one possible interpretation of the absence of narrative unity. Leaving "things unexplained" does indeed undermine the sort of closure that characterizes most of the films we have examined thus far. Those narratives are infused with a relentless and unyielding malevolent force, a force that eliminates freedom and terrorizes our imagination by subjecting it to the aesthetics of evil. Given the sort of deterministic unity operative in contemporary treatments of evil, *Pulp Fiction's* open-endedness may be to its advantage. The film does not in fact leave us with mere chance, though stories intersect and coincidences occur. What we are to make of these intersections and coincidences might be called the central question of the film.

The issue is brought out most clearly in a sequence in which, during a hit, a gunman surprises Vincent and Jules, aims directly at them from a short distance, shoots, and misses. Jules is astounded: "We should be fucking dead . . . this is divine intervention . . . a miracle." Vincent dismissively responds, "This shit happens." In the subsequent scene, they are driving in a car when Vincent's gun goes off and kills a backseat passenger. Vincent excuses himself by stating that it was an "accident . . . the gun went off . . . I don't know why." The coupling of these two chance events, one benevolent, the other destructive, complicates Jules' claim that he "felt the hand of God." What, finally, are we to make of the appeal to the miraculous?

What we know is that the belief in divine intervention immediately puts Jules at odds with the "cool" world of evil that his partner, Vincent, still inhabits. When Jules announces that he is giving up crime to embark on a religious quest, Vincent accuses him of "deciding to be a bum." Vincent, the gangster, adopts without any hint of irony the posture of conventional society and defends its commitment to the Puritan work ethic. When this conversation occurs, we already know, because of Tarantino's reversing of temporal sequences, that Vincent will die in a chance encounter where he is shot with his own gun. Is his bad luck a divine judgment on his lack of faith, a fitting punishment for his failure to discern the work of the hand of God? Or is it all mere chance? The movie never resolves the issue; indeed, such a resolution is impossible in a world with no ultimate structure or unity, in which chance events point simultaneously in multiple and contradictory directions. But this need not be construed as evidence of failure. *Pulp Fiction*'s world of signs and wonders intelligently raises the crucial questions and prudently refuses to answer them. Shattuck's judgment that *Pulp Fiction* does not see "around or beyond the horrible actions that it portrays with the utmost cool" is only partially correct. Such a serious investigation would take us out of the world the characters presently inhabit. Jules continues to insist that he is going to do just that, retire from gangster life and wander the earth like Cain in *Kung Fu*. Here we must also recall the biblical Cain and the first fratricide. God intervened both to accuse Cain and to mark him with a sign to keep him from being killed.

Both in its vignette structure and in its explicit reference to its fictional or constructed character, *Pulp Fiction* raises fundamental questions about art and the possible unity of a narrative. On the one hand, its willingness to entertain the possibility of the miraculous points in the direction of a way out of, or at least a way through, the semiotic hell in which we find ourselves. It raises the crucial question of classical comedies: the role of chance or coincidence in opening up the possibility of a higher and more comprehensive perspective. It also implicitly raises the question of who is orchestrating events and to what end. Jules and Vincent differ over how to interpret their remarkable good fortune. Although we do not know what the ultimate result of believing in a miracle would be, the belief has already begun to transform Jules, who is seriously considering an entirely different way of life. The miracle short-circuits an otherwise unending chain of violence. Jules' interpretation of the "miracle" frees him from the deterministic gangster world. One sign that he has already begun to live that life is his change of mind about a passage from the prophet Ezekiel, a passage about the wrath of God that he quotes to his victims before killing them. He no longer interprets that passage or sees his own life in terms of divine vengeance. Moreover, he defuses potential violence in the holdup attempt in the coffee shop. Perhaps nothing more can be pursued in this story, since the quest that Jules is contemplating would take him out of the cyclical, redundant world he presently inhabits; it would set him on a new and more arduous path. So divine intervention is an undeveloped, but pregnant, suggestion. Unless we follow Jules, we are left with no code to decipher the multiple signs and symbols of contemporary life. Without that code, we might be tempted to adopt a thoroughly comic and ironic take on our nihilistic condition.

There are other clues in the film that might support Jules' claim, "God got involved." The only other character to escape the world of ordinary criminality and nihilism is a struggling boxer, Butch Coolidge (Bruce Willis), whom Marsellus Wallace has paid to throw a fight. Double-crossing Marsellus, Butch wins the fight. He returns to his apartment where he encounters Vincent Vega and kills him. Then, as he departs the scene in his car, he runs directly into Marsellus as he is crossing the street. A chase ensues, and the two men find themselves in a pawnshop, whose owners, reminiscent of the woodsmen in *Deliverance*, trap them and threaten sexual assault. Butch manages to escape, but unwilling to abandon Marsellus, he returns and rescues him. The two part on equal terms with no claim on Butch's life as long as he keeps his mouth shut and leaves town. Butch steals a chopper parked out front, picks up his girlfriend, and heads out of town relatively unscathed. Emblazoned across the side of the chopper is the word GRACE.

The character of Jules suggests the possibility of reviving the premodern, especially scriptural, conception of man as a wanderer on the earth; the New Testament reminds us that "we have here no lasting city." The Enlightenment project of creating a utopian city, where human needs are transparently detected and readily satisfied, spurns such counsel. As we noted in the last chapter, in such a context the apparently irrational quest for evil can be a sign of health or life. If *Se7en* fends off nihilism by recovering the tragic aspiration for justice in the modern world, *Pulp Fiction* suggests a way through that world by reviving the potentially comic quest. In Jules, we see the shift from God as vengeful to God as providential guide in a world where all are in need of mercy, the world we enter at the end of Milton's *Paradise Lost*. This allows for a new twist on Mickey's assertion in *Natural Born Killers* that everyone is guilty and deserving of punishment. It hints at the possibility of transcending the malevolent determinism that pervades so many contemporary films.

5

ROMANTICISM and NIHILISM

In interviews about his film version of the P. D. James novel *The Children of Men*, director Alfonso Cuarón suggested that "our culture is over-narratized" and that "we are missing one of the biggest, probably something more powerful than narrative [to] humans—that is symbols. The ability to interpret symbols."[1] The "co-reference of things," as Cuarón calls it, is precisely what makes P. D. James' novel so powerful. In fact, what James offers is a set of symbolic clues to aid us in detecting the causes of our loss of a coherent symbology. Yet the two sets of symbols are not concordant. In place of James' Christian set of signs, Cuarón substitutes the symbolic system of romanticism, the most pervasive and most powerful mythic system in our culture. So strong is the lure of romanticism that it often acts as a simulacrum for Christianity; that is to say, even in films where Christian symbols appear, they are often filtered through, interpreted in terms of, a dominant romantic vision. As we shall see more clearly in a later chapter on sacred quests, romanticism often highlights religious themes and emotions, as is evident in the hugely successful film *Avatar*. The film deploys symbols and themes from a number of world religions, but the regnant and unifying myth is that of romanticism, which embodies a set of divisions between a primitive, basically peaceful, and organic culture and an advanced, bellicose, and artificial culture.

Romanticism is a complex phenomenon, and some of that is reflected in our popular culture. For many, romanticism provides a path out of the chains of civilization back to a liberating nature, however construed. An even stronger romantic tendency is not so much toward escape as toward radical reform. This was Rousseau's great project: to reconstruct society, to reconcile instinct and reason, the individual and the community, freedom and obedience to law. Given the antithesis between nature and society with which Rousseau begins, the project seems quixotic, likely to give birth to a progressive vision of society in the form of an endless revolution and unending opposition to the alienating features of every existing civil society. One of the paradoxes of romanticism is this. Although its initial impulse is away from the rational abstractions of Enlightenment science and toward the concrete, the sensible, and the tangible, it often ends up, in the political order, advocating a set of abstract ideals: harmony, freedom, spontaneity, and authenticity. The attempted reform of society in light of these abstractions provides little in the way of prudential or moral guidance as to the appropriate means to deploy in achieving the ideals. Revolution in the form of unrestrained violence can be one consequence. Thus does romanticism have an ambiguous relationship to nihilism. On the one hand, it provides a critique, on the basis of ideal standards, of existing society. That is clearly not nihilistic. But on the other hand, the absence of guidelines for the implementation of the reform can generate destructive tendencies that court nihilism, especially when violent reform does not bring about the desired result.

HOLLYWOOD ROMANTICISM: FROM *E.T.* TO *FORREST GUMP*

In Hollywood, the tension between instinct, passion, spontaneity, and creativity, on the one hand, and repressive, bourgeois institutions, on the other, is a source of tragic drama. The conflict is rather successfully portrayed in the film *Dead Poets Society*, with Robin Williams as the inspiring poetry teacher who fosters in his students a desire for authenticity that puts them at odds with the authoritarian world of administrators and parents. When a gifted student angers his father, an emotionally distant and iron-willed man, by violating his prohibition against acting in the school play, the boy's frustration and despair lead him to commit suicide. Because the boy's plight is depicted in such noble terms, some blamed the film for glorifying suicide. From the perspective of our study, the deeper import of the film is this: it illustrates the way the conflict between civilization and the romantic authenticity of self-expression can foster the longing to transcend the societal code of good and evil. We are, admittedly, not yet at a nihilistic stage, since *Dead Poets Society* does appraise ways of life as noble or base, ranking them in terms of their authenticity. The question, as we have seen with Nietzsche, is whether the notion of authenticity or of artistic self-creation inevitably leads to nihilism.

Perhaps the greatest purveyor of the romantic vision in contemporary film is Steven Spielberg. Consider, for example, *E.T.*, the 1982 blockbuster that still ranks as the fifth highest grossing film of all time. (Adjusted for inflation, its rank is fourth behind *Gone with the Wind*, *Star Wars*, and *The Sound of Music*.) The film begins with E.T.'s spaceship landing in a dense and apparently deep forest. E.T. disembarks and, when U.S. government agents arrive to investigate, becomes separated from his fellow space travelers. The ship departs and E.T. is left to fend for himself. But the forest turns out to be a mere speck of woodland on the edge of an overdeveloped valley, a natural oasis in the midst of a technological desert.

Eventually, E.T. befriends Elliott, whose home abuts the woods. Elliott's parents are separated; when Elliott speaks the truth about his father being in Mexico with another woman, he is chastised. E.T.'s homelessness parallels that of Elliott. The symbiosis that develops between E.T. and Elliott embodies the fantasy of every forlorn, misunderstood child who hopes for the magical intervention of someone who will understand and sympathize. But Elliott's plight is not just about lonely kids. It is symbolic of an American society from which innocence has vanished (even the grade school kids in the film are already jaded), where rootlessness (captured nicely in Elliott's neighborhood, a California valley that looks like a settlement on Mars) and where technology have made nature itself an endangered species. This film depicts all of American society, except little kids fortunate enough to meet adorable aliens, as under the corrupt influence of adult civilization, science, and technology. Elliott's brother, Michael, who sports a "No Nukes" T-shirt, explains to one of the investigating scientists that E.T. and Elliott are connected. The rationalist scientist says, "You mean Elliott thinks his thoughts?" Michael replies, "No, he feels his feelings." Indeed, the film embodies a standard set of romantic oppositions: innocence versus civilization, nature versus technology, child versus adult, feeling versus reason, the organic over the artificial.

"We murder to dissect," wrote the great romantic poet Wordsworth. In *E.T.*, America is a heartless society, given to cold, scientific analysis. Elliott complains that, once E.T. is dead, the scientists will just "cut him up." The film's counter to America is E.T.'s bright, red, pulsating heart that shines through his transparent chest. At the very end, E.T. touches his heart and gestures to Elliott that he will always remain with him. The lesson is clear: home is where the heart is. The paradox is that E.T., whose civilization is far more technologically advanced than our own, is in harmony with nature. E.T. revives drooping flowers and creates no fear in animals. As if to underscore this point, the final scene of the film depicts E.T.'s spaceship vanishing into a rainbow across the evening sky. The problem with the film's underlying romantic mythology is that it never suggests how we might reach this state, how we might mediate between or reconcile reason and feeling, technology and nature, adulthood and childhood.

Romantic mythology certainly informs a great deal of left-wing politics in America, particularly in the environmental movement. Romantic themes have been prominent on the left since at least the 1960s, especially in rock music, where the romantic supposition that complex human desire and competitive zeal are corruptive of nature is prominent. It is there in John Lennon's "Imagine" and Joni Mitchell's "Woodstock," which urges us "to get ourselves back to the garden," or in Don Henley's Reagan-era lament "The End of the Innocence," with its longing for a place "still untouched by man." But none of these romantic pleas can show us the path back to unreflective innocence. We are saddled with a harsh dilemma: we must and yet we cannot return. So elusive seems this innocence, so thoroughgoing our saturation in the technological, the calculative, and the instrumental, that we may be tempted to adopt an antithetical conception of human

nature as violent, chaotic, and amoral. So too rationalism breeds fide-
ist fanaticism. As Terry Eagleton puts it, "when reason becomes too
dominant, calculative, and instrumental, it ends up as too shallow a
soil" for a healthy faith to flourish.[2]

The surprising ways romantic mythology informs our popular
culture, and not just on the left, can be seen from a comparison of
two very different films from 1994. Two of the biggest films that
year were *Forrest Gump* and *Natural Born Killers. Gump* remains one
of the highest grossing films of all time; it traces American life from
the 1950s into the 1980s and covers significant cultural and political
events: Elvis, the Beatles, civil rights, Vietnam, the birth of the Apple
computer, and every president from Kennedy to Reagan. Forrest travels through this America finding himself, Zelig-like, in the midst
of every great event. He suffers from a mental disability that ends
up being a great blessing. Unable to comprehend the world around
him, Forrest is often bemused by events and innocent of any deep
understanding of their significance. He is the exact antithesis of the
consciousness-raising protest leaders of the 1960s. Supplied by his
mother with a set of platitudes—"stupid is as stupid does" and "life is
like a box of chocolates"—Forrest faces each situation with good will
and deep-seated optimism, rooted in a faith in divine providence. Void
of critical reflection, Forrest is never confused, never hesitant about
what he ought to do. As the rest of America explodes, Forrest's faith
preserves him and anyone who associates with him. In the end, Forrest has it all: fame, wealth, and ultimately, love. Noting that Forrest's
goodwill and trust lead to success and that characters such as antiwar
protesters typify the bad guys in the film, some conservatives praised
Gump for its celebration of innocence and old-fashioned virtues like
self-reliance, loyalty, honesty, and patriotism. Writing in the *Pitts-
burgh Post-Gazette*, Pat Buchanan said the film "celebrates the values
of conservatism, of the old America, of fidelity and family, faith and
goodness. And the way of life this film holds up to be squalid and
ruinous is the way of Woodstock."[3]

Interestingly, *Gump* treats precisely that period of modern
American history that has preoccupied the revisionist films of Oliver
Stone, whose *JFK* and *Nixon* tell the tale of the downward thrust of

American public life. *Natural Born Killers* marks a sort of culmination
of that history, depicting the 1990s as an "age of absurdity." Abused
by their parents, Mickey and Mallory are the central characters in
Stone's story of love at first sight, followed immediately by a murderous rampage. Fawned over by the media, Mickey and Mallory become
cult heroes, with adoring fans holding up placards reading, "Kill Me,
Mickey." With alternating footage of contemporary murders and
1950s families gathered around TVs, Stone wants to impart the message that characters like Mickey and Mallory are the result of our
media- and television-obsessed era, even if it remains unclear what
lesson Stone ultimately wants us to derive from this.

On the surface, these two films seem to be polar opposites. But
in reality, they share core romantic assumptions: the belief that civilization, calculative reason, self-consciousness, and technology are
sources of evil, alienating human beings from nature and putting them
at odds with one another. The only escape seems to be a kind of primitive and inveterate innocence. Indeed, *Natural Born Killers* has its own
analog to Forrest's innocence: an American Indian whom Mickey and
Mallory encounter in the desert, an individual who does not own a
TV and who speaks no English, is portrayed as the only "innocent"
character in the film. If some conservatives affirmed *Gump's* celebration of the virtues of innocence, Stone's critique of media culture and
gun-obsessed violence finds a welcome reception on the left, which
sees an alienating capitalism turning human life itself into entertainment for profit.

Whereas *NBK* presents the family as the source of lecherous
instrumentalism of others and of the violent domination of bodies,
Gump suggests, in its final frames, a possible way out for the family.
Having produced a child with Jenny, who then dies of AIDS, Forrest is
left to raise the next generation. This is the kernel of truth in the conservative praise of the film for its defense of the family. But of course,
it does not free us from the dilemmas of romanticism. While *NBK*
sees the family as an institution of oppression, *Gump* retains a certain ambiguity about the family, which Aristotle describes as resulting from nature and "not from deliberate choice" and which Rousseau

describes as having an ambivalent transitional status between original innocence and the full-scale corruption of civilization.

Romantic themes are also operative in the big Oscar winner of 1997, the epic *Titanic*. The story, which can be called romantic in the sense in which that term is now ordinarily used, pits the lower-class but spontaneous and artistically gifted Jack Dawson, played by Leonardo DiCaprio, against old-world money, with its shallow formality and petty sense of superiority. On board the great ship, Dawson meets and then vies for the affection of the affluent Rose, whose disaffection from the members of her class, including her family and her fiancé, grow as she becomes romantically involved with Dawson. Their star-crossed love, fostered by their shared taste for art and free self-expression, competes with the ship *Titanic* as the central spectacle of the film. One wonders to what extent the makers of the film were conscious of the multiple significance of the ship itself. By underscoring the engineer's optimism and the crew's naive and negligent trust in his proclamations that *Titanic* is unsinkable, the film displays the tragic hubris of modern technology and Enlightenment progress. But the ship symbolizes more than the Enlightenment project of mastering nature. It is also a romantic symbol, an artifact of great beauty, deservedly inspiring awe. The sense of omnipotence the ship conveys to those on board is evident in the famous scene where Jack climbs to the tip of the bow of the ship, extends his arms, and exclaims, "I'm the king of the world!" *Titanic* allows us to see something about romanticism that the apparently heroic love between Jack and Rose conceals. In the figure of the ship itself, two forms of modern hubris (Enlightenment science and romantic rebellion) converge. Both are excessive, inordinately indulging one or another feature of human life to the exclusion of other features and other persons. The love between Jack and Rose attracts us because they are so attractive and because those they oppose are so obviously cold and callous. But it is hard to see their love as much more than adolescent and self-absorbed. Once again, romanticism fails to produce a mature and complex vision of goodness.

THE CONTRADICTIONS OF ROMANTICISM

Perhaps not surprisingly, the tensions within American popular culture reflect deeper tensions in our modern way of life, tensions going back to the very origins of modern society. Reacting against the rationalism and instrumentalism of his modern predecessors, the Swiss philosopher Rousseau took direct aim at the central thesis of early modern political theory: the idea that the state of nature is marked by acquisitiveness, competition, and perhaps even war. According to Rousseau, the competitive passions are initiated and inflamed only in advanced civilization. As Terry Eagleton puts it, "Barbarism and civilization are not only sequential but synchronic, human civilization is among other, rather finer things a 'higher' or sublimated form of violence and aggression."[4] The state of nature was the childhood of the human race, when desires were simple, when human beings sought only their "true needs," when "self-preservation" was least prejudicial to the well-being of others. Only with the development of reason could human vanity develop along with a growing sense of the indefinite number of ways our desires can be satisfied and frustrated. Rousseau adds, "the savage lives in himself; the man accustomed to the ways of society is always outside of himself and knows how to live only in the opinion of others." The result is that we have "merely a deceitful and frivolous exterior: honor without virtue, reason without wisdom, and pleasure without happiness."[5]

Romanticism leaves us in a state of permanent frustration. We become more acutely aware of our alienation, but we cannot cure it. We seem simultaneously impelled to return to Rousseau's "nature" and yet unable (and frankly, unwilling) to do so. To remedy our situation, we must deploy the very instrument (namely, human reason) which is the source of our dissatisfaction. We see technology as an enemy, yet we subject ourselves to its creations in the forlorn hope that we can re-create the visceral pleasures of pretechnological life. *Avatar*, for example, highlights the threats posed by an advanced, war-mongering, and artificial society to a primitive, pacific, and organic culture. Critics ironically tout both this ideological vision of a pristine world untouched by industrial society and the film's high-powered, cutting-edge technology evident in its mesmerizing 3-D visuals.

Since we cannot return to our original nature and cannot simply lobotomize ourselves to eliminate the adverse impact of civilization, we are caught up in contradictions from which art might seem to offer rescue. Art promises a recovery of feeling over calculation, of an orientation to the whole rather than an analysis of isolated parts; it reenchants what rationalistic science has disenchanted. In place of the petty calculation of self-interest and the treating of others as means, art puts before us an experience of the beautiful and the sublime, experiences that silence our acquisitive natures. Indeed, art not only fends off the modern sources of alienation, but it also replaces religion. As Richard Wagner put it, "It is reserved to art to salvage the kernel of religion, inasmuch as the mythical images which religion would wish to be believed as true are apprehended in art for their symbolic value, and through ideal representation of those symbols art reveals the concealed deep truth within them."[6] But of course, artifice itself is not strictly natural and always involves rational discernment of forms and means of expression (see, for example, Wordsworth's definition of poetry as the "spontaneous overflow of powerful feelings, recollected in tranquility"). In the absence of natural standards, it is difficult to see how art can guide us to what ennobles or help us to transcend the trap of having to use the very instrument of our corruption (namely, reason) as a remedy for our corruption.

In the aftermath of 9/11, the romantic impulse in popular culture has arguably grown even stronger. It is visible in our desperate hunger for the authentic and unrehearsed, for the nonstaged and nonconstructed, for an experience of intimacy that peers beneath or behind the public persona. The ever growing phenomenon of reality TV feeds precisely such longing, as does the confessional character of so much of contemporary television—from the daytime shows such as *Oprah* to prime-time specials with Barbara Walters to the narrative structure of *The Sopranos*. The best-known and most enduring of the reality TV shows, *Survivor*, offers an artificial return to a state of nature, in locales such as Borneo, the Amazon, and the outback, with groups of contestants organized into "tribes." The return to a pre- or subhuman arena is the occasion for displaying a kind of Hobbesian competition, which in turn is justified alternatively as survival of the fittest and as an expression of authenticity.

The contradictions of romanticism, the gulf it creates between, on the one hand, what we once were and in some futile way long to become again and, on the other, what we are now creates enormous tensions. One way out is not to look back but to look forward to attempt to re-create society in such a way that alienation and inequality are eliminated. But romanticism gives us no clear guidance for precisely how we can reach this state; in fact, the closer we get to eliminating undesirable features, the more we are disturbed by the lingering elements of alienation and inequality. Thus, the way is paved for the romantic restoration by means of endless revolution.

Another possibility is to live with the contradictions in such a way that one celebrates opposition to the repressive features of conventional society. Thus is born the artist as rebel. Suspecting that any positive ideal can be easily appropriated by civilized society and turned to its own ends, the artist wallows in the downward path of negation, blasphemy, and obscenity. Culture critic Camille Paglia argues that this is the revenge of Marquis de Sade upon Rousseau, the latter of whom "seeks freedom by banishing social hierarchy and worshipping uniformly benevolent nature."[7] When political and religious authorities weaken, hierarchy reasserts itself in sex, especially in the shifting hierarchies of power involved in sadomasochism. Sade, who sees cruelty as natural and construes murder as a potentially erotic activity, is not so much the antithesis of romanticism as its radicalization. Sade subjects the amorality of nature to a cold, calculating analysis in which "fantasies" are brought out "into the cold light of consciousness." He makes "visible" the results of the natural unleashing of egoistic appetite: the recognition that the body is nothing more than raw material, an instrument of subjection and subjugation for the satisfaction of one's desires, a satisfaction that gleefully obliterates the body's natural contours. Without ever reading him, many of our so-called artists are devotees of Sade. Here Enlightenment mastery conspires with the romantic impulse toward authentic experience to generate a novel form of nihilism.

Preoccupation with the unraveling of the Enlightenment permeates our popular culture, undermining not just traditional conservatism but mainstream liberalism as well. Reaction against a certain strain of the Enlightenment is a staple of the setup of a large number of science fiction films. Yet these films typically have no way of resolving the quest other than by appealing to a naive romantic affirmation of feeling over reason or by surreptitiously embracing the very technology that was accused of being the original source of our alienation. The latter sort of contradiction afflicts not only Cameron's dual boast for *Avatar* but also the plot of *The Matrix*.

As we explained at the beginning of this chapter, romanticism has an ambiguous relationship to nihilism. Because it offers an affirmative vision of a meaningful human existence, it seems antinihilistic. Because its capacity to implement the vision is tenuous indeed, it can easily breed nihilism. That was the case with Rousseau's influence on the instigators of the French Revolution. In his magisterial history of that period, *Citizens*, Simon Schama speaks of the role of romanticism in inciting citizens to reform through violence and to a repudiation of the past and all existing order: "And it was perhaps Romanticism, with its addiction to the Absolute and the Ideal; its fondness for the vertiginous and the macabre; its concept of political energy as, above all, electrical; its obsession with the heart; its preference for passion over reason, for virtue over peace, that supplied a crucial ingredient in the mentality of the revolutionary elite: its association of liberty with wildness."[8] As Dostoevsky was fond of observing, the frustrated romantic revolutionary of one generation is the nihilist of the next.

ROMANTICISM AS SIMULACRUM OF CHRISTIANITY

A suppler response to the dilemmas of humanity in a technological world can be had in P. D. James' novel *The Children of Men*. The film version departs from the book in significant and interesting ways and ends up offering its own version of contemporary nihilism and its overcoming. Assisted by the splendid cinematography of Emmanuel Lubezki, a superb performance by Clive Owen as Theodore Faron, and a lean script that throws us immediately into the midst of revolutionary activism against an oppressive political order, Alfonso Cuarón's film version of *The Children of Men* is not so much a futuristic sci-fi film as a gripping meditation on what we already are. The stunning visual quality of the film provides access to a world much darker, but not completely other, than ours—a world in which humans have been rendered rapidly and bafflingly infertile and hence face the imminent extinction of their own species, members of whose last generation are known as the Omegas. Cuarón, who has directed such solid films as *A Little Princess* and *Harry Potter and the Prisoner of Azkaban*, takes one of the many symptoms of malaise from the book—xenophobia about immigrants—and makes it the central issue of the film. For this streamlined film, the issue of immigration works as a dramatic framing device. But it also severely truncates the theological elements in the novel.

In his commentary track for the DVD release of the film, culture critic Slavoj Zizek observes that *The Children of Men* features a society without history in which everything, including human life, has become a disposable commodity. In a wonderful scene in the film, Theo visits an official to try to obtain travel permissions for Kee, a pregnant refugee seeking to escape the popular and governmental attention that her pregnancy would attract. The leader's otherwise nondescript office features Michelangelo's *David* and Picasso's *Guernica*; uprooted from all historical and cultural contexts, these works of art are merely testaments to the wealth and status of their possessor. When asked why he cares about the display of wealth, since in a short time no one will even know about such things, or anything for that matter, the leader sighs, "I try not to think about it." The disposability of all things shows up the emptiness of a consumer society. Not just works of art but also persons are commodities, as is evident in the film from the way every interest group wishes to control and manipulate the next baby. As Syd, the character who initially helps Theo and Kee to enter the prison but who soon turns on them, puts it, "Once I found that both the government and the rebels were after you, I realized you must be very desirable commodities indeed."

The future-oriented character of modern life, with its accent on equality of condition, accumulation, and physical comfort, renders the past of interest only as that which has been surpassed. As Sheldon

Wolin writes in his book on Tocqueville, modernity "fetishizes the future"; "instead of development or fulfillment of potential," we experience "the exhaustion of time in the conquest of space by beings in a hurry." Culture becomes "end-less process, the formalized method by which artifacts are produced continuously." Tocqueville's goal, according to Wolin, is to enlarge modernity's self-understanding "to include the experience of loss."[9]

Our fugitive existence renders our quest for happiness futile; yet we are not utterly bereft of self-knowledge, because we have at least the ability to recognize the disorder of our condition. Depriving us of history and tradition, modernity undermines the great countervailing forces against the exhaustion of time. It deprives us of the roots and contexts within which human life can be intelligible; the impact especially on the family, the institution through which the past is handed down to the next generation, is devastating.

As Eagleton observes, a "society of packaged fulfillment, administered desire, managerialized politics, and consumerist economics is unlikely to cut to the kinds of depth where theological questions can even be properly raised, just as it rules out political and moral questions of a certain profundity."[10] In James' novel, infertility operates as a symbol of humanity's despair, of the nihilism that lurks just beneath the surface of modern life. The questions made explicit in the infertile world are the following: For what are we living? Why do we have children? What do we want to hand on to them? But as is so often the case in science fiction, disaster and despair arise out of our greatest boasts, our technological and scientific mastery of nature. Theo Faron, the main character in the book, states, "we are humiliated at the very heart of our faith in ourselves. For all our knowledge, for all our intelligence, our power, we can no longer do what the animals do without thought."[11] Such universal failure produces despair and even a reversion to a sense of cosmic vengeance. Faron observes, "The discovery in July 1994 that even frozen sperm stored for experiment and artificial insemination had lost its potency was a peculiar horror casting over Omega the pall of superstitious awe, of witchcraft, of divine intervention. The old gods reappeared, terrible in their power."[12]

For all of its promise of protection and pleasure, the new regime seems only to exacerbate the strange mixture of fear and longing for death, even as it serves to remove pleasure from our grasp. Officially sponsored group suicide, called the Quietus, allegedly allows individuals to choose when they die; yet the book makes clear that this is subject to abuse, as the government forces death upon those who have second thoughts and offers incentives to families to ease the elderly out of this life. Cuarón's film turns this critique inside out and deprives the Quietus of any problematic status; the film's only use of the Quietus is as a private and legitimate act of euthanasia. For the increasingly tepid pleasures experienced in this world of complete sexual freedom, there is government-sponsored pornography. As P. D. James puts it in the book, one might suppose that with the "fear of pregnancy permanently removed..., sex would be freed for new and imaginative delights." But that is not the case: "Sex totally divorced from procreation has become almost meaninglessly acrobatic," characterized by "painful orgasms, spasms without pleasure."[13] The book dwells in compelling detail not just on xenophobia but also on the disorders of modern sexuality, the stultifying of human passion and feeling, the flourishing of the desire for death, and the narcissistic attitudes toward children. James describes a world in which dolls (artificial children) and pets (child substitutes) have become objects of fawning desire, christened in birth celebrations and buried in consecrated ground to satisfy "frustrated maternal desire." There is a sort of desperate romanticism operative here, an attempt to construct childhood innocence and familial affection. The adulation of the child—a cultish type of romanticism—permeates the society.

Cuarón's own comments about the film seem to contribute to, rather than correct, the penchant for cultish romanticism. Cuarón has said,

I have a grim view not of the future but of the present. I believe evolution is happening and human understanding is occurring and that the young generation is the one that is getting some new perspective of reality of what's going on in the world. The new generation will prove that the Earth is going around the sun, not the sun going around the Earth.[14]

Cuarón fails to see that this adulation of children is one of the greatest disorders in the world of the novel. James' book treats this issue with great clarity in the case of the Omegas, the last generation to be born. Both book and film begin with the fawning global media attention heaped on the death of the last person to be born, the youngest individual on Earth. James astutely observes, "It was a generation programmed for failure, the ultimate disappointment to the parents who had bred them and the race which had invested in them so much careful nurturing and so much hope."[15] Observations from the novel about the Omegas apply to the entire society of Britain: "Perhaps we have made our Omegas what they are by our own folly; a regime that combines perpetual surveillance with total indulgence is hardly conducive to healthy development. If from infancy you treat children as gods they are liable in adulthood to act as devils."[16] Surveillance and indulgence combine to sap humanity of longing and activity.

Cuarón does manage to invest the film with powerful symbols concerning children, life, and nature. One of the most telling scenes in the film occurs just after the birth of the child in a dilapidated building in the middle of ongoing war. The scene is one of two highly praised scenes in the film in which Cuarón keeps the camera rolling without a cut for a long period of time; indeed, in this one, blood from the battle spatters on the camera and remains there to distort slightly our viewing of the action. Into the middle of the battle march Theo, the mother, and the child. As the soldiers realize a newborn baby is in their midst, they cease fighting; many bow and cross themselves while the baby passes. Of course, the child departs, and vicious fighting renews.

The life of the child awakens Kee's sense of purpose. As she tells Theo, once she realized she was pregnant, she thought about the Quietus. Then the baby kicked. "It's alive. I'm alive," Kee explains. The action of the film moves in a paradoxical direction. To prepare for a new beginning, Theo, Kee, and the baby must move from freedom to imprisonment, from the status of citizen to that of refugee, and from civilized society to nature, the sea.

In the book, Theo is a reluctant seeker, someone who at the beginning of the book is a reflective but indifferent observer of the contemporary loss of meaning. He admits, "I don't want anyone to look to me, not for protection, not for happiness, not for love, not for anything." Theo identifies his own affliction in the book as *accidie,* or sloth, technically not laziness but, as Aquinas defines it, despair of the divine good. His conversion, at least in the book, is the great miracle of the story, eclipsing even that of Kee's pregnancy. As Theo observes early in the book, the "cross . . . has never been a comfortable symbol."[17] For Hollywood, it is not nearly as comfortable as the redemptive themes of romanticism, with its adulation of precivilized nature and childhood innocence. As Ralph Wood comments,

> Among the many mysteries James explores in this novel, perhaps the deepest is the mystery of conversion: How can we be transformed from self-regarding into self-surrendering people? How, more strangely still, can we find the faith to resist overwhelming evil, especially in a world without a future?[18]

The title itself, *The Children of Men,* is a quotation from Psalm 90, a prayer in the Anglican burial service for the dead: "Thou turnest men to destruction: again thou sayest, Come again, ye children of men."[19] The passage is quoted explicitly in the book during a funeral, but the film leaves viewers completely in the dark as to the origins of the title. Theo's conversion is part of a Christian, not a romantic, narrative, whose features Cuarón simply ignores. He substitutes a romantic myth about the child, akin to Wordsworth's notion that the child is the father of the man, in place of a complex Christian account of sin, conversion, and divine providence. That points up one of the chief functions of romanticism in our popular culture, as a simulacrum in the popular mind for orthodox Christian teaching.

6

DEFENSE against the DARK ARTS
From *Se7en* to *The Dark Knight* and *Harry Potter*

In the film *Se7en*, officers investigating a series of grisly murders discover odd clues and patterns in the activity of the killer and head to the library to pull out old texts of Dante and Milton. Unfolding a map of Dante's vision of hell, it is as if the map were a guide to the city inhabited by the investigators. The fleeting hope is that such texts might illumine our condition and aid us in the detection of evil and the protection of the innocent. In more recent years, Christopher Nolan's *Batman* films call to mind medieval images of gargoyles and knight's intent on pursuing justice no matter what the cost. With echoes of classic noir, Nolan refashions a comic book hero for our time, a time threatened by nihilism. Meanwhile, the most impressive publishing feat of the last fifty years, the success of J. K. Rowling's seven-volume *Harry Potter* series, revives a host of classical and medieval symbols as a means of telling a very detailed story of characters involved in a cosmic battle between good and evil. In divergent ways and with varying degrees of success, these artistic productions seek to come to terms with a problem articulated succinctly by historian and cultural critic Andrew Delbanco. He writes, "a gulf has opened up in our culture between the visibility of evil and the intellectual resources for coping with it . . . The repertoire of evil has never been richer. Yet never have our responses been so weak. We have no language for connecting our inner lives with the horrors that pass before our eyes in the outer world."[1]

As we have noted, from the late 1970s well into the 1990s, Hollywood, the dominant shaper of popular culture in America, was preoccupied with demonic antiheroes who stand beyond good and evil and inspire terror and awe in audiences or just plain entertain them. As we have also noted, a focus on evil characters in no way entails moral bankruptcy. As Hitchcock once remarked, the better the villain, the better the film, or as he refined it, the stronger the evil, the better the film. Hitchcock never takes his eye off the full human complexity of his characters, their delusions, passions, and genuine aspirations for truth and love. These aspirations and longings can be highlighted, rather than undermined, in dark narratives. In some cases, dark films give us what Telotte would call a more truthful picture of the human condition. Yet, as we have seen, too many of our contemporary explorations of evil seem to leave us speechless (or giggling) in the face of demonic evil. But this is not the whole picture of our contemporary film culture.

The greatest peril for youth in our popular culture is not so much that excessively violent films will create a nation of Columbine killers, a thesis that is reductionist in its assumptions both about culture and human choice. The real danger is the atrophying of the imagination of the young. In the place of fertile, complex, and hopeful stories about the battle in the human soul between good and evil, there are tales that make goodness simplistic and evil complex and alluring. Young persons are thus deprived of a vocabulary, a stock of images and stories in light of which to conceive their own lives and imagine their futures. In a culture where demonic evil is reduced either to a pointy-headed comic book figure (think Jon Lovitz as Satan on *Saturday Night Live*) or to a sinister but ultimately playful aesthete (think Hannibal Lecter), J. K. Rowling's series of *Harry Potter* books offers a credible figure of diabolical evil: Lord Voldemort, traitor, murderer of Harry's parents, and Harry's enduring nemesis.[2] As is true in our world, so too in Harry's world, evil often seems more attractive and complex than goodness. Quirrell, one of Voldemort's lackeys, makes clear his master's teaching: "A foolish young man I was then, full of ridiculous ideas about good and evil. Lord Voldemort showed me how wrong I was. There is no good and evil, there is only power, and those too weak to seek it."[3] The nihilistic, Nietzschean proclamation of a will to power as the truth about existence presupposes the bankruptcy of all existing moral codes, which are deemed merely conventional human constructs. This is the proclamation of The Joker in *The Dark Knight*, who insists that "codes" are merely rules of convenience and that, if pressed, ordinary citizens will "eat one another."

Dark quests for redemption, whether religious or secular, abound in contemporary culture. As Nolan's films indicate, these quest films owe a great debt to classic film noir, which takes aim at some of the treasured assumptions and promises of modernity. In noir, the modern world, embodied in an urban setting, is hardly the world of light, happiness, and peace that utopian thinkers of the Enlightenment foretold. Modernity is about human beings exercising control over nature and thus taking control of their destinies; in our modern technological project, knowledge and power are one. The postmodern turn in the quest accentuates the experience of the loss of control, the absence of intelligibility, and the threat of powerlessness. But the quest also has something premodern about it—a sense of human limitations, of the dependence of human beings on one another and on events not in their control. In this world, the outcome of the quest is tenuous and uncertain. In contrast to Nolan's films, *Harry Potter* offers much more in the way of resolution, which is made possible by the presence of a rich conception of justice and love. In defiance of nihilistic teaching, Harry and his friends learn to make distinctions between good and evil, between virtue and vice, and between the tools of magical power and the deeper magic of sacrificial love, a magic that, in voluntarily accepting death for the sake of a higher good, defeats death itself.

In this chapter, we will look at the way these films, and books in the case of *Harry Potter*, engage without succumbing to nihilism; these works attempt to provide characters and viewers with defenses against the darkest of the dark arts, the arts counseling nihilistic despair over the good and the amoral pursuit of power. Before turning to the contemporary scene, we examine briefly some classical accounts of evil, accounts that seek to render evil in grandly mythic terms and to depict evil as a kind of death wish, inevitably bringing about its own nothingness. Yet this entire tradition of thinking about evil has been called into question. The objection is that the penchant for myth necessarily falsifies the phenomenon of evil, bestowing upon it a grandeur and depth that it lacks. By way of introducing the grand tradition, we consider briefly Hannah Arendt's famous banality thesis about evil.

ARENDT'S BANALITY THESIS

German-born Jewish philosopher Hannah Arendt crafted the phrase "banality of evil" to describe the phenomenon of Adolf Eichmann, architect of the Nazis' final solution. On her way to Jerusalem to report on his trial, Arendt expected to encounter a modern-day Iago or Macbeth but found neither.[4] What Arendt discovered in Eichmann was a shallowness of motive, a failure to take thought, and more specifically, an inability to adopt the point of view of another. Instead of a complex and mysterious demon, he was simply a law-abiding citizen doing his job, concerned to advance his career. His "normalcy was more terrifying than the atrocities" he committed. In his testimony, he alternated between, on the one hand, claiming that no one can be criticized for doing what he did (that is, for doing his duty) and, on the other, flippantly dismissing the entire affair. He boasted that he would jump in his grave laughing about his orchestration of the final solution. His insouciant manner of relating his crimes was both "horrible and funny."

From her encounter with Eichmann, Arendt developed the apparently novel thesis that evil has "neither depth nor any demonic dimension." Conversely, "only the good has depth and can be radical."[5] Along with her mentor, Karl Jaspers, she focuses on evil's "total banality" and "prosaic triviality" and regards "any hint of myth . . . with horror." Jaspers goes so far as to say that Shakespeare's "aesthetic sense would lead to a falsification" of evil.[6] Certainly, there are dangers, some of which we have discussed, in any aesthetic or dramatic approach to evil. But one wonders whether these risks can be completely avoided. Even Arendt's rather staid retelling of the Eichmann trial involves an artistic reconstruction of some sort. The key question is this: does myth necessarily lead to a glorification of evil, to an exaltation of it, and thus to a covering over of its "prosaic triviality"? As we shall see, this is not the case in Shakespeare's *Macbeth* or in Milton's *Paradise Lost*, nor is it the case in *Se7en*, *The Dark Knight*, or *Harry Potter*. These works begin with the apparent grandeur of evil only to reveal its fundamental emptiness.

Arendt's association of evil with banality has been seen as trivializing Eichmann's actions and to some extent exculpating him, since it seems to deprive him of freedom and responsibility. Even if Arendt were right about Eichmann, there are good reasons to resist the universal application of her position. The description of evil as a "mere technique of management," resulting from a failure to think and a willingness to treat humanity itself as if it were superfluous, is best suited to the sort of evil endemic to modern bureaucratic regimes. As she notes, banality marks the final stage in the totalitarian annihilation of the world, others, and the self. In spite of these limitations, Arendt's account of evil is highly suggestive. We have already seen that it coincides at least in certain respects with our view of the trajectory of the aesthetics of evil, with its tendency toward a mixture of comedy and horror that renders heroic evil dubious and farcical. These films reveal that the banality of evil need not be limited to totalitarian regimes; some version of it may surface in liberal democracies, where the last residues of human greatness have been lost, where life becomes an end in itself.

Both Shakespeare's Macbeth and Milton's Satan provide instructive comparisons with Eichmann. The characters are not trivial or simple; initially at least, they possess complexity, depth, and grandeur. Nevertheless, both illustrate the way crime is its own punishment. Macbeth fails in his attempt to place himself beyond the human condition, and his embrace of nihilism at the end of the play is the logical term of an unyielding pursuit of evil. In that sense, Shakespeare's Macbeth ends up partially confirming Arendt's view that evil lacks depth, that only the good is radical. The same can be said of Milton's Satan, who in spite of his apparent grandeur actually deprives himself of nobility, beauty, and power by pursuing evil, by making evil his good.

When we first meet Macbeth, he has just proven his bravery in battle. On his return, he encounters the weird sisters, the three witches, who inform him of his immanent promotion and predict his future ascent to the throne. Although his prudent comrade, Banquo, warns him that the "instruments of darkness tell us truths, / Win us with honest trifles, to betray's / In deepest consequence" (I iii:124–26), he is so taken with their promise that he begins to contemplate helping fate along. His ambition soon cools, however, and were it not for his wife's prodding, he likely would have remained content with his subordinate status. When he expresses reservations about their plan, she questions his manhood and accuses him of cowardice. The warrior seems a wimp by comparison with her clarity of purpose and courageous resolve: "I have given suck, and know / How tender 'tis to love the babe that milks me: / I would while it was smiling in my face, / Have plucked my nipple from his boneless gums, / And dashed the brains out, had I so sworn as you / Have done to this" (I vii:54–58). Lady Macbeth invokes supernatural aid to "unsex" her, to free her from feminine compassion. But she badly overestimates the power of masculine resolve; indeed, she is mistaken about the true nature of courage. In terms of self-knowledge, she is her husband's inferior. After the murders, she rapidly deteriorates, entering a trance-like state, haunted by images of blood she cannot wash off her hands. She cannot bear consciousness of her deed.

While Lady Macbeth loses herself rapidly, Macbeth experiences in excruciating and vivid detail his own progress in evil and descent into nothingness. Initially overwhelmed by his murderous deeds and by the impending threat of vengeance, late in the play he is unmoved by shrieks in the night. By the end, he has "supped full with horrors" and "almost forgot the taste of fears." No longer assaulted by visions of the dead, he gains a kind of self-control. But this proves another deception. The more he pursues absolute power, the more he finds himself in the clutches of the evil sisters. When he is told of his wife's death, he utters the oft-quoted words,

She should have died hereafter;
There would have been a time for such a word.

Tomorrow, and tomorrow, and tomorrow
Creeps in his petty pace from day to day,
To the last syllable of recorded time;
And all our yesterdays have lighted fools
The way to dusty death. Out, out, brief candle!
Life's but a walking shadow, a poor player
That struts and frets his hour upon the stage
And then is heard no more. It is a tale
Told by an idiot, full of sound and fury,
Signifying nothing. (V v:18–28)

This is one of the most eloquent nihilistic speeches of all time. Macbeth no longer has anything to live for; time itself is empty, void of hope or regret, merely an objective succession of moments. Macbeth experiences the narrative of human life as a cruel and unintelligible antiprovidence, a "tale told by an idiot." Nihilism is not, however, the final word of the play; given Macbeth's multiple defeats, we have reason to associate his nihilism not with the nature of things but with the consequences of his traitorous and murderous acts. Even though he chooses to fight on and "will not yield," he is hardly possessed of his former grandeur of spirit. The banality of Macbeth at the end is not the almost comic absurdity of Eichmann, who excuses himself by appeal to the fulfillment of a function in society. Instead, it is the despair of a noble soul who suffers the consequences of having embraced evil. *Macbeth* asserts the viability of natural standards of right and wrong, of the subtle, but nonetheless dramatic, links between human society, human nature, and the larger cosmos.

What makes this a peculiar tragedy is that Macbeth is aware from the start that his actions will prove his undoing; wicked deeds "return to plague the inventor." In the standard Greek tragedy, the hero commits a deed at least partially in ignorance and only later recognizes what he has done and its consequences. Macbeth's recognition comes immediately after the murder, perhaps even in his reflections prior to the deed. He apprehends that nature will counter his revolt with a revolt of its own: "Blood," he notes, "will have blood. Stones have been known to move and trees to / speak." Macbeth's flaw, if we have to pinpoint an outstanding defect in his character, is his lack of true courage. He succumbs to the entreaties of the witches and his wife not just out of ambition but out of weakness. And yet he is in many respects a noble character. His eloquence is more than mere rhetorical flourish. He has a fertile imagination and a capacity to perceive his own situation even as he thrusts himself further into misery. Macbeth's grandeur, then, does not result from evil itself but from the residual nobility and excellence of his soul. As he pursues his illusions of omnipotence further, he becomes more impotent and less complex. He thus approaches the simplicity of evil, its inherent nothingness.

The remainder of the play portrays his descent into a living hell and the way equivocation and lies destroy not only one's relationships to others but the very meaning of one's life. Having revolted against the codes of nature and civil society, his own nature revolts against him. Soon after the murder, he comments that he has given his "eternal jewel" to the "common enemy of man," the devil, and that death would be preferable to the "restless ecstasy" he now endures. The further he proceeds in his tyrannical task of murdering all potential threats to his power, the more indifferent he becomes to the fate of his own soul, "to return were as tedious as to go over."

The play illustrates something very much like the traditional doctrine of natural law. Nature is so constituted by God that violations of its laws lead inevitably to punishment. The link between the natural and the supernatural, wherein rebellion against order in the state is simultaneously a violation of nature and God, precludes the possibility of envisioning the divine as an arbitrary, omnipotent, and inscrutable being, the dark God of late medieval voluntarism and Descartes' *Second Meditation*. Macbeth's punishment is at once willed by God and self-inflicted. His nature avenges itself on him. In a reversal of Nietzsche's view of nihilism as arising from the attempt to live in accord with an objective and transcendent order of truth and goodness, Macbeth's nihilism is a direct result of his repudiation of such order.

Lest we suppose that the play provides too clean a resolution to the problem of evil, we should recall that the supernatural forces of evil have not been eliminated. They await another soul on which to prey. In such a world, vices leave us vulnerable to assault by preter-natural evil powers. Furthermore, although nature rebels against Macbeth, the punishment of nature is insufficient to defeat him and vindicate the good or the innocent. Instead, human beings, especially those with responsibility for the community, must defend themselves against the likes of Macbeth. Finally, there is the possibility that someone more resolute, less complex than Macbeth might actually succeed in attaining and holding power. He fails in part because he remains human, incapable of fully cutting himself off from the nature he shares with other members of his species. Only at the end, when he loses all sense of feeling and conscience, does Macbeth approach satanic evil. For most of the play, he suffers from a debilitating division between his calculated ambition and his human feelings of sympathy and fear. The worst evil is not to be found in those who harbor a conflict within them but rather in those whose passions are under the complete control of their reason and who have a clear apprehension of their goal and the means to its attainment.

While Iago in *Othello* supplies the chief example of such pure malevolence in Shakespeare's plays, perhaps the most famous and most influential demonic character in the history of Western literature is the Satan of Milton's *Paradise Lost*. The epic is one of the chief sources of the romantic fascination with the devil, for it sets a dubious precedent of attempting to depict the devil directly. Some readers find Milton's Satan so much more captivating than God, the angels, or Adam and Eve that they have accused Milton of being of the devil's party. Whatever the flaws in the presentation of the good characters may be, Milton's depiction of satanic evil is indeed hard to rival, but not perhaps for the reasons usually given.

Milton's Satan has the grandeur and apparent glory of a Homeric hero. Immediately after turning against God and being thrust out of heaven, he notes his lost glory but counters, "All is not lost; the unconquerable will, / And study of revenge, immortal hate, / And courage never to submit or yield" (I.106–8). He adds, "Though all our glory extinct, and happy state / Here swallowed up in endless misery" yet "mind and spirit remains / Invincible, and vigor soon returns" (I.139–42). In Satan's celebration of his invincible will and courageous rebellion, there is a striking anticipation of the model of demonic heroism that we detected in *The Exorcist, Cape Fear, The Silence of the Lambs,* and *Se7en.* In presenting Satan in this way, Milton explains why we find evil so alluring and awesome. Moreover, by allowing Satan to voice his own complaint against God, the source of all good, he allows us to recognize that we are often sympathetic to evil. But Milton does not leave it at this. He proceeds to undermine the project of the aesthetization of evil.

Interspersed with the images of Satan's glory and within his words of self-justification are images and words that reveal a much darker and cowardly intent: to prey upon weaker creatures. The satanic goal is to reverse the strategy of providence, which is to bring good out of evil. Attempting to confound the divine plan, the demons devise an antiprovidence and plot to bring evil out of good. Their plot itself makes an important concession: goodness is a primordial given; it precedes and makes evil possible. The fundamental division is between the grateful and the ungrateful.

The attentive reader begins to discover in Satan a malicious intent masked by a remarkable capacity for deception, not only deception of others but also deception of self. Milton describes in some detail Satan's self-destruction, the way giving oneself to evil involves a negation of one's being, life, and intellect. On this view, evil is non-being, the absence of an appropriate perfection or goodness. A successful depiction of evil presupposes a rich and supple narration of goodness. Like Shakespeare, Milton captures both the apparent grandeur of evil, its alluring and glittering surface, and its fundamental poverty and emptiness. Evil is nothing.

Just as in *Macbeth,* so too here supernatural evil remains, awaiting another opportunity to try to bring evil out of good. *Paradise Lost* provides a more explicit anticipation of the final defeat of evil by the supreme power of goodness, but it leaves humanity in a world where its future is uncertain, where each individual risks being defeated by, or conspiring with, evil. The book ends thus:

> The World was all before them, where to choose
> Their place of rest, and Providence their guide:

They hand in hand with wandering steps and slow,
Through Eden took their solitarie way. (XII.646–49)

There is no facile transcendence in these works; the only way to overcome the tragedy is go through it, to defeat evil not by avoiding it but by comprehending it. The strategy in such dramas is to make the "complete" and presently unrealized "pattern" of life so appealing "that it . . . leaves the audience wishing to live their incomplete and as yet potentially tragic lives in the light of the enacted ideal."[7] We live with a tempered hope, not with the self-possessed certainty of success. We aspire to be "lowly wise."

Most artists have not been as daring as Milton in their attempts to depict demonic evil. Instead, they portray merely human evil, the struggle in a noble but imperfect soul between good and evil. The advantage is that human evil can be complex, whereas satanic evil is as close to simple evil as is possible. Even Milton gives us a strikingly human devil who deliberates, expresses doubt, and embodies human vices. But Satan's grandeur is residual; it is precisely the depth and complexity of his being, of his original God-given goodness and excellence that makes his turning to evil so apparently powerful and magnificent. Both Shakespeare and Milton confirm rather than disprove Arendt's thesis that only the good has depth. Revealing its banality, the perverse pursuit of evil as good undermines and negates itself.

DEADLY SIN AND THE QUEST FOR JUSTICE

Se7en, with its contemporary urban setting, as a film noir is much less secure. And yet it succeeds in bringing the virtues of noir to bear upon what might otherwise be a standard serial killer story. *Se7en* pits Somerset, a seasoned, intelligent, somewhat jaded member of the New York homicide department, and Mills, a young, brash, and mildly idealistic detective, against a serial killer whose motif is the seven deadly sins. While it continues the narrative of the serial killer as antihero, whose explosive crimes are judgments on a corrupt society, it suggests other and richer possibilities for the construal of the nature and meaning of evil. If anything, this film is more chilling than the ones we have discussed thus far. Its response to the problem of the artistic presentation of evil in a nihilistic world is to reassert with a vengeance the primacy of the tragic construal of evil. By the use of clever and veiled artifice, the film makes it impossible for the audience to adopt a detached, ironic point of view. More than the previous movies, this film attends to the development of character and especially to the question of why someone would fight against evil in a world where its power seems invincible.

Adopting a standard strategy in detective stories, the film introduces the two main characters as polar opposites. It pairs a young, enthusiastic detective with an old and jaded mentor: Somerset is old, reflective, and nearly cynical, whereas Mills is young, idealistic, and emotional. Somerset drinks wine, Mills has beer. Somerset wants out and is in fact seven days from retirement when the first murder occurs. He is tired and describes his job as ineffectual, as just "picking up the pieces." He describes poetically the seeming pointlessness of detective work, the elusiveness of justice, thus: "So many corpses roll away unavenged." Yet his intellect is piqued by odd clues; once he glimpses the design of the latest serial killer, whom he describes as "methodical, exacting, and patient," he goes to the library to read texts like Dante's *Inferno* and Milton's *Paradise Lost*. Nicholas Christopher notes that *Se7en* mythically conflates New York and hell. It is as if Dante's *Inferno* is a map of the city.[8] Somerset never indulges in psychological speculation about the killer. Mills, by contrast, is naive and brash. Thinking he might make a difference, he fought to get reassigned from upstate to the city. He thinks the killer is a lunatic and opts for CliffsNotes over the poetry of Dante, whom he dismisses as a "poet faggot." The negative view of Mills as combative, ignorant, and cocky is tempered when his wife reveals to Somerset that she knew he was the one for her the day they met because he was the "funniest" guy she'd ever known. He is also not without insight; he sees through Somerset's repeated claims of indifference and despair, countering, "You don't believe this."

While Mills is most obviously engaged in a kind of contest with the killer (he unknowingly berates the killer, who shows up at a murder scene disguised as a cameraman and is later nearly killed by him in a chase scene), the deeper parallels are between the killer and Somerset. He is the first to pick up on the clues and to trace them to the didactic medieval literature on sin, in which the punishment mirrors the crime. Somerset realizes early on that the tortures and murders have both a proximate and an ultimate goal. The former is "forced attrition," wherein one regrets one's sins but not because one loves God. The latter goal is the same as the didactic end of medieval sermons: to convert the world. Somerset's complaint that we "embrace and nurture apathy as if it were virtue" anticipates the killer's indictment of modern society. Somerset counters Mills' view (and the dominant American view, at least in the media) that freaks and nuts are responsible for evil with the observation that evil is an everyday occurrence, the stuff of ordinary life.

As they zero in on the killer, they realize why he has been so difficult to trace. He shaves the skin off his fingers to avoid leaving fingerprints even in his own home, which he has turned into a cheesy, baroque Catholic, religious shrine, full of crosses, bibles, and rosaries. In an act symbolic of his martyrdom, he has taken the name John Doe. Like Cady in the later version of *Cape Fear*, John Doe appears to suffer from religious pathology. Were it not that other characters in the film share something of his appraisal of his victims, indeed of modern urban life, we might be inclined to think that his project is the result of his religious fanaticism, a fanaticism that generates excessively elevated and unrealistic standards for human behavior. The frustration at the failure of others and perhaps of oneself to meet these standards sometimes leads individuals to lash out at others. But this is not the appraisal the film leads us to make. Although the police hunt for the killer, they share his disgust at the lives of his victims. For example, when the victim accused of sloth, a drug-dealing pederast, whom the killer has kept barely alive in his bed and tortured for a year, is brought to the hospital in a coma, the doctor first comments that the victim has "experienced as much pain and suffering" as a human being is capable of. He adds, "He still has hell to look forward to." The detectives are repulsed by the vanity of another victim, a gorgeous model, whom the killer cleverly tortures by cutting off her nose, tying her to her bed, and then gluing a phone to one hand and a bottle of pills to the other. Unwilling to call for help, since that would mean living with her disfigurement, she commits suicide.

Another way the film leads us to adopt the perspective of the killer is in its presentation of the victims. We see them as the killer would have us see them. We see neither their torture and death nor the grieving of disconsolate relatives and friends. We see them only after they are dead and only through the lens of the killer's commentary on their lives, a commentary that argues for the fittingness of their punishment. The vile body becomes a means of instruction, as it is the site of punishment and a physical manifestation of the vices of the soul. The movie thus gives us maximum sympathy with the killer's perspective, with the theatrics of his morality play, lifted largely from Dante. He is almost a highbrow version of the vigilante made familiar in numerous Charles Bronson films. In contrast to those films, which are preoccupied with the question of the justification of vigilante methods, there is no real debate about John Doe's style of working outside the law. The American justice system is not so much corrupt as utterly powerless; reform is no longer a credible project. Besides, such debates would be a distraction from the film's unrelenting focus on the terrifying mystery of evil.

The mood of the entire film, which is bleak and oppressive, reflects the genre of film noir; nearly all the action occurs in rain and darkness. It's as if the entrance into the city is an entrance into a nihilistic hell. Urban life is so terrifying and enervating that there seems to be nothing worth handing on to the next generation. Devoid of hope for the future, the present seems pointless. Near the middle of the film, Somerset receives a call from Mills' wife asking him to meet her for a talk. She reveals to him that she is pregnant and contemplating an abortion because she "hates the city." Somerset confides that he once got a woman pregnant. While she was committed to having the child, he feared bringing the child into the world and gradually "wore her down." Somerset's ambivalence about life reaches its pinnacle in his comment that he knows he "made the right decision" but that every day he "wishes he'd made a different one." Reason and prudence militate against properly human aspirations. The city is inimical to life itself. The quotation from Milton, which the killer leaves at one of the crime scenes, is apt: "Long is the way and hard that out of hell leads up to light."

The ending of the film will tragically vindicate Mills' wife's cynical view of modern urban life. When John Doe unpredictably turns himself in at the police station, the detectives are suspicious but utterly unprepared for what he has in store for them. The careful viewer is given a hint of what is about to unfold, when just before the killer enters the police station, a clerk yells to Mills that his wife called. John Doe soon reveals that there are more bodies and offers to take Mills and Somerset to them. As they drive to a remote field, he articulates his vision and denies that his victims are innocent. Only in a society as corrupt as ours would practitioners of vice be called innocent. He complains that we "tolerate" deadly sin. Insisting that he will soon be forgotten, Mills taunts and mocks the killer, who calmly informs Mills that he will indeed be impressed once he sees the complete performance. In the final act, our worst fears are realized as John Doe has the severed head of Mills' wife delivered to the field. He then provokes Mills into killing him. What are we to make of this depiction of evil?

One possible interpretation of *Se7en* is as a modern-day Greek tragedy. Mills' own destruction is at least in part a result of his own everyday evil. It is significant, for example, that Mills' wife couldn't talk to him about her predicament. In his naiveté and inexperience, he simply wouldn't have understood her hesitance about bringing life into the living hell that is the modern city. In his imprudent and rash desire to confront evil, he seems to bring the final catastrophe upon himself. His unwillingness to submit his mind to the knowledge of Somerset, his proud taunting of the killer, and his naive assumption of his own security from vice—all these ordinary evils contribute to his demise. Of course, there is no proportion between Mills' vices, which are admittedly mixed with certain virtues, and the punishment that he undergoes. But that disparity is precisely what makes the cultivation of virtue so crucial; in a world awash in depravity, vices, especially those that foster presumption in us, render us vulnerable. It would undoubtedly have been difficult for anyone in Mills' position at the end of the movie to restrain himself; for Mills, it was impossible. Character is destiny. The character to which Mills aspires is that of supercop; his wife jokingly calls him Serpico at one point. But the contemporary American city is not hospitable to heroes. Because Mills doesn't yet possess the wisdom that comes from suffering, from years of dreary confrontations with evil, there is a kind of suitability to his downfall. His pride leaves him open to tragedy. He is a classic tragic hero, whose desire for knowledge blinds him to himself. He is so captivated by the killer, by his desire for a fight, that he fails to see his own vices and flaws. He suffers from a debilitating lack of distance and critical reflection. Somerset, who understands the killer better than Mills does, has the proper distance, which allows for understanding but avoids the perils of excessive sympathy and self-forgetfulness.

The echoes of classical tragedy and the complex artifice of *Se7en* have led some to identify it as neo-noir, a genre that sends its main character(s) on a quest, whose goal is unclear and whose completion is unlikely, through the labyrinth of the modern city. But *Se7en* is even more restrained and emotionally stultifying than were the productions of film noir. In that genre, an alluring and mysterious female usually plays an important role in the plot, joining the man at a crucial point in his search. Of course, the alluring female often proves to be an instrument of the demise of the protagonist. The presence of a captivating but deceptive female reinforces his tragic situation because she arouses desires, and not just of the sexual sort, whose satisfaction is thwarted. By contrast, *Se7en* does not even admit the possibility of any significant erotic element; there is none of this in the marital relationship between Mills and his wife or in the friendship between Somerset and Mills' wife.

To say that the film is restrained is not to say that it suggests no clues as to how we ought to understand its narrative. The deadly sins provide us with a criterion for understanding the evil of John Doe. The seven capital sins are called deadly not only because they lead to damnation after this life but also because they kill the soul here and now. Vice inflicts its own punishment and issues an invitation to nonbeing. Of course, human beings are forgetful animals, and the further we sink in vice and indifference, the more we are in need of dramatic reminders. The artistic match between the punishment and the sin of the damned is but a way of making more explicit what is already implicit in the way of life they adopted while on Earth. This is John Doe's task.

Yet his vocation does not go unquestioned. During their drive outside the city, amid the taunting of Mills, Somerset interjects the question of whether the killer's enjoyment of his act is compatible with martyrdom. Instead of being a martyr for the eradication of evil, he is actually an embodiment of the vices traditionally associated with the devil: envy and pride. His own envy is dramatically realized in his act of killing Mills' wife. By putting Mills in a situation where Mills will kill him, he admits his own vice and arranges for his own punishment. But he is also proud, even though that sin has been disposed of already. Not only does he take judgment and execution into his own hands but he also lures and tempts Mills into sin, even as he ensures that he will have control over his own punishment. He is afforded the gift of nonbeing that evil inevitably seeks. His punishment is the slightest of all those meted out in the film. But it should have been the severest, following the principle—articulated in Dante and Milton—that the corruption of the best is the worst.

During one of their discussions, Somerset comments to Mills that the only thing that would meet their expectations of this killer is if he were the devil himself. Somerset quickly adds that he's just human. But it is not clear that Somerset is entirely right. The combination of reflection and creativity with a complete lack of sympathy or clemency makes John Doe something more than merely human. The way he skillfully corners Mills so that he has no way out but to become evil is reminiscent of diabolical evil. The ending of the film seems to reverse the initial pattern of establishing an identity between our perspective and that of the killer. This is mostly because the film develops the characters of Somerset, Mills, and Mills' wife so that we sympathize with them; their misfortune is in some measure our own. They are the only victims we know independently of the killer's appraisal. In spite of the apparent victory of the demonic criminal in *Se7en*, the film does not finally engender in its audience feelings of sympathy for him. In this way, *Se7en* comes closer than *The Silence of the Lambs* or Scorsese's

Cape Fear to making us feel the horror of evil, to inducing in us feelings of anger toward the demonic criminal. But we cannot take refuge in venting our feelings of rage, lest our anger turn to self-destructive vice, as in the case of Mills. Insatiable curiosity, an appraisal of criminals as crazies, and an inordinate desire for knowledge in the form of direct experience of evil—all this is characteristic not just of Mills but of average viewers of movies like *Se7en*. But average viewers are likely to be so transfixed and numbed by *Se7en* that they will fail to reflect upon themselves. Thus, they will duplicate Mills' vices.

As always, there is a flip side to the horror induced by demonic wickedness of the amoral superhero: a subtle admiration for his power and artistry. In his superior artistic control over the entire drama, if not in his purported intentions, John Doe resembles Lecter. The ending underscores the triumph of the artisan serial killer, whose final act overshadows all else. There is little satisfaction of our desire for justice. Only endless torture would be condign punishment for this sort of villain, who is incapable of remorse. In spite of his protestations, his artistry is exhibited not in the renewal of life but in vivid destruction. John Doe's theology is a heretical version of the medieval view of the role of sermons on the sins. Those sermons presuppose that God's love grants us the freedom to opt for vice instead of virtue and in so doing to reject him. By reminding us of God's justice, the sermons call us back through his mercy. But John Doe's sermons have no place for freedom or forgiveness; the primary power in *Se7en*'s world is not Dante's "love that moves the stars" but a mechanical and malevolent necessity. For all its reliance upon medieval motifs, *Se7en* suffers modernity's chief affliction, the silence of God. Since there can be no call to conversion, the hell of *Se7en* is one without prospect of purgatory or paradise. The advantage of *Se7en* over its predecessors is that we feel the loss of that larger vision, the absence of what Edmundson calls an affirming myth of eros or love.

We are thus left with the signs and symbols of medieval theology but with no available way of life in which the signs might make sense. No merciful and provident God speaks through the signs and symbols. In the modern world of *Se7en*, God is effectively dead. The loss of that authoritative voice is not liberation but enslavement to new forms

of tyranny. Without providence to bring good out of evil, evil endlessly begets evil. Dante's *Inferno* is a more accurate guide to the modern city than are the architectural blueprints of the utopian designers
of the American city. The rain, darkness, and filth that saturate the
modern city reflect the bog outside the city of Dis in Dante's hell,
where the wrathful, sunk in the mire, struggle to thrash one another.

There is no good life to which one can aspire in this world; the
American dream has become an unrelenting nightmare. *Se7en* allows
for no ironic distance or detached levity. Malevolence is unrelenting,
and the best we can do is cultivate certain virtues to fend off disaster. Neither behaviorist psychology nor autonomous creativity offers
a way out. The only substantive hope available to us consists not in
succumbing to the meaninglessness of it all but in keeping alive our
sense of the injustice and disorder of contemporary life. Somerset
exercises a kind of ancient Greek moderation, a practice of reining
in one's ambitions and expectations that is prudent in a world that is
tragic at best. As we noted above, there is something transcendent and
ennobling about classical tragedy because it educates us about virtue
and vice and because it presupposes and fosters natural human feelings of pity, fear, and sympathy. By contrast, *Se7en* provides no purga-
tion or catharsis; its ending is oppressive and emotionally stultifying.
Unlike the exalted nobility of Greek heroes, Somerset is admirable
only because he is unable to give in to apathy, the vice that modern
America equates with virtue.

The final note of *Se7en* is, however, sober and not entirely negative. After Somerset tells the police chief that he wants to provide
whatever Mills needs, he acknowledges that he will "be around," that
he is no longer planning to get out. The movie ends with his quoting Hemingway's statement: "The world is a fine place and worth
fighting for." He comments, "I agree with the second part." We might
restate Somerset's view in this way. Hemingway is wrong about the
world. It's not a fine place; the world is wicked, nonetheless it is worth
fighting for. The great temptation? Apathy. The great task? To exercise a moderation that is not to be confused with apathy, to act out
of a chastened passion for justice, a passion that we know in advance
will never be satisfied. This puts Somerset dangerously close to being

engulfed by nihilism. The key question is why he has not succumbed. He is noble not because of what he achieves but because of what he cannot quite bring himself to do: abandon Mills and the world that has destroyed him. Given all that has transpired, the great mystery is not the existence of evil but the residue of goodness in Somerset, his unquenched thirst for justice.

There is, we can be grateful, no necessity in following the horror genre into its degradation through self-parody or the rise of the surface aesthetics of bodily vivisection. The most promising alternatives in the quest for evil in recent years have involved filmmakers working at the margins of the horror genre, such as M. Night Shyamalan, and those reinventing the superhero genre, such as Christopher Nolan. Indeed, in the first decade of the twenty-first century, the biggest box office successes included the *Lord of the Rings* trilogy, films from Rowling's *Harry Potter* books, *Spider-Man* films, and the *Star Wars* prequels, all fantasy films that feature a grand battle between good and evil and that have identifiable heroes and villains. These box office successes indicate that there is an appetite among American audiences for films that have something to say about the necessity and nobility of fighting evil for the sake of justice.

In *The Myth of the American Superhero*, John Lawrence and Robert Jewett argue that superhero stories embody a monomyth, a simplistic dualism of good and evil, a naive faith in human heroes endowed with miraculous powers, and an affirmation of violence as the only effective means of purging society of evil.[9] They also foster spectator democracy. The worry is that the success of these films, far from being evidence of a healthy appetite among Americans, signals an American retreat from the complexities of world politics into the comforts of fantasy, the great temptation of which is to see all opposition to America's virtuous aims as constituting a demonic other. Similarly, Delbanco bemoans the fact that, into the cultural vacuum we have created on the topic of good and evil, evil often returns as a "demonized other." The chief alternative to such dualism is to construe evil in what Delbanco rightly calls Augustinian terms, as "a pocket of nothingness in a good world."[10]

How do our fantasy stories stand up to the objections articulated by Lawrence and Jewett? Are they all equally susceptible to the criticisms? At the end of the book, we will look at the film versions of *Lord of the Rings*, which is generally regarded as the greatest work of fantasy in the last century. In the remainder of this chapter, we will examine Nolan's *Batman* films and Rowling's *Harry Potter* books, neither of which is vulnerable to the just-mentioned objections.

GARGOYLE IN GODLESS GOTHAM: NOLAN'S *BATMAN*

With the record-setting release of *The Dark Knight*, his sequel to *Batman Begins*, Christopher Nolan is making a claim to be our most inventive and most philosophical filmmaker. He has certainly surpassed M. Night Shyamalan, who seems bent on destroying his career. Both Nolan and Shyamalan focus on dark tales of human quest in which characters set out to solve a crime or set things right in the face of seemingly insuperable evil, are beset with doubts, and are tempted by despair or—what is worse—by the temptation to become the evil they are fighting against. Whereas Shyamalan has descended into unintentional self-parody in his last few films, Nolan's filmmaking and storytelling skills are on the rise.

Nolan first gained his notoriety with *Memento*, his remarkable indie neo-noir film starring Guy Pearce as a man trying to solve his wife's murder while suffering from short-term memory lapses. Shot in brief segments, to mirror the amount of time Pearce's memory could remain intact, and in reverse chronological order, the film raised all sorts of interesting questions about personal identity, knowledge of the past, and the significance of human choices. The examination of moral issues was even more at the forefront of Nolan's next film, *Insomnia*, starring Al Pacino as a compromised cop, whose insomnia reflects his uneasiness with the state of his own soul. Pursuing a wily suspect (Robin Williams), Pacino's character is forced to reckon with questions about what differentiates him from the criminal. Consciously making use of classic noir thematic and stylistic elements, Nolan specializes in the dramatic portrayal of quests for which there is no possibility of a traditional happy ending or a complete recovery of what has been lost. The best that can be hoped is, as Pacino's character puts it, that we "not lose our way."

A similar premise undergirds Nolan's retelling of the Batman myth, starring Christian Bale as Bruce Wayne. Among the many visually entrancing scenes in *Batman Begins,* Christopher Nolan's grand and mesmerizing tale of how Bruce Wayne became Batman, perhaps the most striking are those of Batman standing motionlessly on the perches of tall buildings. Shrouded in darkness, looking downward, a sentinel who blends perfectly into the environment, the Dark Knight resembles the gargoyles from the great medieval cathedrals. Nolan's version of the Batman legend results in a superb film that repeatedly takes great risks and, except when it falls prey to the temptation to turn Bruce Wayne into a philosopher of the death and rebirth of great American cities, almost always reaches the heights to which it aspires.

In Nolan's version, the figure of the Batman—selected by Bruce Wayne as a "dramatic example . . . an elemental symbol" to turn violence and ugliness against those who trade in violence and ugliness—functions as a gargoyle in a godless city, a creature of darkness protecting the innocent from other creatures of darkness in a city bereft of any natural or religious framework for justice or hope. The buildings from which Batman overlooks the city are like cathedrals stripped of all their symbolism except that provided by the menacing bat. That Batman-style justice is the best we can do in such a context is made clear in a terrific scene in which Batman seizes and interrogates a criminal. To convince Batman that he is telling him the truth, the criminal screams, "I swear to God." Batman gets right in his face and angrily demands, "Swear to me."

An early scene in the film introduces the central theme of fear; since every viewer knows what Bruce Wayne will become, it also hints at the answer to the question of how to overcome fear—become what one fears. A young Bruce Wayne tumbles down a well and into a bat cave, where alarmed bats swarm over him, leaving him haunted by nightmares.

Not long after this event, the affluent and dignified Wayne family travels to Gotham to attend an evening performance at the opera, whose story sparks in Bruce bad memories of the bat attack. Leaving early from the theater, the Wayne family enters the filthy, desolate, crime-ridden streets to encounter a mugger who shoots both parents. In a marvelously edited scene, a petrified Bruce stands amid the crumpled bodies of his parents as his father breathes his last words, "Don't be afraid."

From the opening, rather distant shots of Gotham through Batman's infiltration of the city to the final, sizzling chase scene, Gotham is magnificently rendered, fully realizing Nolan's wishes for Gotham as "New York cubed," a city where you find yourself "completely immersed to the point that you do not feel its boundaries." In early scenes, the city has the look and feel of the American metropolis in Charles Bronson's *Death Wish* films, with trash strewn everywhere, dilapidated buildings, and desperate figures stealthily moving about.

The generation gap between the Wayne parents and son marks a transition from detached liberal philanthropy to engaged conservative crime fighting. Bruce's generous parents live at a safe distance from the city in a protected mansion. Bruce converts to conservatism the old-fashioned way—a liberal mugged not so much by reality as by, well, a mugger who kills his parents. Delicate, liberal philanthropy collapses in the face of violent evil; Bruce is left with fear and nihilism, the pointlessness of his life. His response is to create a purpose for his life by exploring and striving to overcome his fears.

Some years later, after a parole hearing for his parents' murderer, who is himself shot down by mobsters against whom he had promised to testify, Bruce reenters the city and visits Falcone, the local mob king. When Bruce proclaims his fearlessness, Falcone (Tom Wilkinson) schools him on his ignorance of city life: "You think you have nothing to lose. This is a world you can never understand, and you always fear what you don't understand." He has Bruce beaten and tossed into the streets.

Bruce then vanishes, immerses himself in an international criminal underworld, and eventually resurfaces in a Bhutanese jail, from which he is freed by Ducard (Liam Neeson), head of the League of Shadows, a vigilante group that mercilessly executes justice and conspires to push modern cities into acts of self-destruction, after which there might be a possibility to start anew. According to Ducard, civilization at its very pinnacle breeds corruption. Ducard trains Wayne in ninja-style combat and educates him to overcome fear. He taunts Bruce that his parents' death was not his fault but rather that of his father, who was not prepared to act in the face of evil.

The opening third of the film, which alternates between flashbacks to Bruce's youth and scenes in the jail and Ducard's training camp, is the segment of Batman's life that Nolan sought to tell. In a sense, the film's justification rests on the success of this initial segment and how well it paves the path for Batman's appearance in Gotham. Nolan takes enormous risks here in the use of an Asian setting and in the attention given to the philosophical probing of fear, power, and justice. The setting—much of it was filmed on a glacier in Iceland—is a jarring contrast to Gotham, yet its very remoteness and physical austerity set an appropriate mood. Neeson aptly describes the glacier as a "gorgeous Beckett wasteland."

References to a "Beckett wasteland" are quite apt. Nietzschean themes run through the film. Bruce Wayne aspires to make himself extraordinary by becoming more than a man and by shattering the conventional distinction between the legal and the illegal, hence his time among the criminals performing illegal acts without ever becoming a criminal. He also strives to transform himself into pure performance. He gives a radical twist to what might otherwise seem a mere platitude in the film, "It's not what you are underneath but what you do that defines you." But Batman is not finally an amoralist; he resists rather than welcomes nihilism. He aims to defend and inspire those ordinary citizens whom the League of Shadows, in fine Nietzschean fashion, deems useless and expendable.

Nolan's Batman may be a bit too reflective for traditional devotees, although they will find that they have not waited in vain for the Gotham combat scenes or the Batmobile car chases. Others may object that Bruce Wayne's musings are not entirely coherent, but the discussions of justice, never separated from the topic of the exercise of physical force, have a point. They underscore the sheer difficulty of gaining any clarity about justice in such a forlorn world. Bruce Wayne's refusal to join the League of Shadows indicates that he sees some limitations to, or restraints upon, his own enforcement of justice. He has not given up hope for the inhabitants of modern cities such as Gotham. In this respect, the hopeful idealism of his parents maintains a crucial, if residual, influence on him.

Another way Batman distinguishes himself from the members of the League of Shadows is that he is never completely cut off from those operating within the civilized world; he does not desire to be isolated in this way. Batman teams up with one of the only decent cops left, Jim Gordon (Gary Oldman), a cop, near despair, whose initial suspicions of Batman give way to hope and collaboration. There is also Rachel (Katie Holmes in a performance that only makes you think of *Dawson's Creek* a couple times), Batman's childhood friend, who now works as a prosecutor and persistently reminds Bruce of his parents' legacy. Finally, there is Alfred (played flawlessly by Michael Caine), the family butler who continues to act as a father figure for Bruce and who, at a crucial point in the film, counsels him not to get "lost inside the monster." That is precisely the risk for someone who has consciously chosen to become a monster, a gargoyle in godless Gotham, whose goal is to fend off monsters, to intimidate through fear those who would terrorize the innocent.

Ambitious to make a sequel that would rival in quality the second films in *The Godfather* and *Star Wars* trilogies, Nolan focuses in *The Dark Knight* on the "idea of escalation," the way Batman's dramatic persona, with its violent heroism, calls forth a greater, more creative response from the criminal element. It would be hard to imagine a more compelling embodiment of the escalation of evil in Gotham than what Nolan and actor Heath Ledger have created in the character of The Joker, whose insouciant embrace of chaos eclipses the malevolence of Hannibal Lecter from *The Silence of the Lambs* and John Doe from *Se7en*. What makes Nolan's latest film such a success is not, however, Ledger's compelling presentation of evil, on which critics have focused their attention, but the way he uses that character to bring out the depth and complex goodness of the other characters in the film, including Batman. The title of the film is not *The Joker* but *The Dark Knight*.

Still, Ledger's performance as The Joker is a chilling and memorable one, superseding all other villains in the superhero genre. To account for The Joker, Nolan adverts to no childhood trauma or scientific experiment gone awry. All such explanation is beside the point. In the film, The Joker asks one of his victims whether he wants to hear the story of how he got his scars. He proceeds to explain that his father was a "drunken fiend," who fought with his mother, one night to the point of cutting her with a knife. Having done so, he turned on his stupefied son and, putting the knife to his mouth, asked, "Why so serious?" Then, in a subsequent scene, The Joker tells quite a different story about the source of his scars. The point is clear—there is no "reason" for The Joker's love of chaos. As Nolan commented, The Joker has "no arc, no development"; he is an "absolute." As he sets fire to a huge pile of money, The Joker chastises the astounded criminals in his midst for their petty love of money. When Bruce Wayne tells Alfred that criminals are "not complicated" and that they just need to find out "what this one wants," Alfred responds, "Some men just want to watch the world burn." There is no ultimate purpose to The Joker's mayhem; he delights in it for its own sake, as is evident in one particularly chilling scene when Batman tries to beat him into revealing his plans. As The Joker cackles with glee at the pain, he taunts Batman, "You have nothing to frighten me with."

Beyond good and evil, The Joker is off the human scale. In preparation for the role, Ledger studied the voices of ventriloquist dummies, aiming for a chilling effect in which the voice itself sounds "disembodied." Ledger and Nolan looked at Francis Bacon paintings to try to capture the look of "human decay and corruption." If there were a purpose, it would be akin to that pursued by Mr. Glass (Samuel Jackson) in Shyamalan's *Unbreakable*, whose amoral destruction has as its goal the discovery of someone at the other end of the spectrum, his complement. As The Joker says to Batman, "Why would I want to kill you? What would I do without you? You complete me." So he taunts Batman, "You're just like me—a freak."

The Joker espouses a nihilist philosophy concerning the arbitrariness of the code of morality in civilized society; it is but a thin veneer, a construct intended for our consolation. If you tear away at the surface,

"Civilized people will eat each other." As The Joker puts it, "Madness is like gravity; all it takes is a little push." In a wonderfully comic take on a Nietzschean sentiment, he sums up his beliefs, "Whatever does not kill you makes you stranger." His character also illustrates the parasitic status of evil and nihilism. A thoroughgoing nihilist could not muster the energy to destroy or create. As The Joker puts it at one point, he's like the dog chasing a car; he has no idea what he would do if he caught it. The Joker's attempt to bring down the entire system of civilization has the scope and feel of terrorism.

Nolan shares Shyamalan's sense that true suspense and fear require restraint in the direct depiction of gore and the development of characters with whom the audience is sympathetic. In addition to Batman, there are a number of other admirable characters in *The Dark Knight*. In a film brimming with terrific performances, three stand out: Lieutenant and then Commissioner Gordon (Gary Oldman), the assistant D.A. Rachel (Maggie Gyllenhaal, replacing Katie Holmes from *Batman Begins*), and especially the fearless crime-fighting D.A. Harvey Dent (Aaron Eckhart), whose tragic undoing at the hands of The Joker is the "arc" upon which the plot pivots. These three illustrate the costs of defending the innocent and fighting against evil, the costs borne by those who would be decent in an indecent world. If in certain prominent instances in this film the hopes of the audience for these characters are dashed, the film does not succumb to The Joker's vision. The film is not nihilistic; instead, it affirms the ineradicable human longing for justice. As Batman put it in the original film, "Gotham is not beyond redemption."

The title of Nolan's latest Batman film calls to mind medieval chivalry in a postmodern key. The dark knight embraces extraordinary tasks and fights against enormous odds; his quest is to restore what has been corrupted and to recover what has been lost. In so doing, he takes upon himself a suffering and loneliness that isolate him from his fellow citizens and inevitably court their misunderstanding and scorn. He is a *dark* knight, in part because the world he inhabits is nearly void of hope and virtue and in part because some of the darkness resides within him, in his internal conflicts between the good he aspires to restore and the means he deploys to fend off evil. Of the many filmmakers designing dark tales of quests for redemption, Christopher Nolan is currently making a serious claim to being the master craftsman.

MUTILATED SOULS, HEROIC VIRTUE, AND SACRIFICIAL LOVE
IN *HARRY POTTER*

Rowling's books merit consideration because of their widespread influence on popular culture. Perhaps only the books of Dan Brown have come close in recent years to receiving the popular recognition of Rowling's books. Her work is not without detractors. Some object to the style or her imperfect control over the slew of symbols and themes she weaves into the plot; others, notably some Christians, have voiced reservations about the role of magic in the books. Now, the books will never rival Shakespeare or Tolkien, but they are well-crafted stories that draw in rich and suggestive ways on themes from classical litera-ture. The series constitutes one of the few examples in recent years of literature that mediates between low and high culture. The religious objections are even wider off the mark. In fact, Rowling's series is not only not part of the problem, but it is part of the solution to what ails our popular culture, especially our youth culture.

The impressive account of evil in Harry Potter is inserted within a complicated series of plots involving the main character's quest to solve riddles and to escape from a series of labyrinths. It is not a stretch to suggest that classic noir themes figure prominently in the books and films, not just the themes of the labyrinth and the quest but also the theme of the wrong man, the wrongly accused character who often comes to share the suspicions others have of him. Harry must pro-ceed through secret passageways, chambers of secrets and mazes, as he endures many a test of character. Moreover, Harry shares so much in common with his evil nemesis that he suffers from the doubts of others and from occasionally lacerating self-doubt. Harry is haunted by events from his past, events in which he was not an active par-ticipant; he worries that the past has predetermined his present and thwarted the possibilities for his future. The difference here is that the bad memories do not leave him desolate. He has other memories con-cerning his parents' love, their acts of courageous virtue, and in most cases, the assistance of friends and virtuous adults. The call to battle has an intrinsically social dimension to it. Harry and his friends must learn to exercise certain kinds of virtues in defense of the innocent and in opposition to those bent on destruction of the good.

One of the virtues operative in the stories has to do with the recognition of the limits to, and appropriate use of, power, especially the sort of power provided by techniques, in most cases techniques of magic. Rowling here draws out similarities between magic and technology. The quixotic project of overcoming mortality through technological power is also a violation of limits, for example, the limits imposed upon us by the bodily conditions of human life. The modern world is given to extremes on the topic of death and the body, from the resolute refusal to acknowledge or embrace aging and mortality to a nihilistic celebration of the death wish. What is striking in the final book is the prominence of the theme of reverence for the dead body. In *Goblet of Fire*, Harry risks his own life to return the murdered body of his friend Cedric to his parents; then, in *Half-Blood Prince*, after Dumbledore's death, Harry wonders, "Had they taken Dumbledore's body yet? Where would it rest?" and announces his plan to visit his parents' grave. In *Deathly Hallows*, much is made of the fact that, instead of using magic, Harry physically digs the grave of one of his fallen fellow warriors. Reverence for and remembrance of the dead are hallmarks of virtue and of a well-ordered community.

Our attitude toward death defines in many ways how we live. The medieval theme of *memento mori*, the virtuous cultivation of the memory of death, acts as a counter to modernity's vacillation between unhealthy obsession and tragic forgetfulness. *Harry Potter* does more than simply avoid falling into nihilism; it exhibits a vision of what a purposeful life in common with others might look like. That vision also avoids the romantic temptation to dismiss advanced technological society—in some cases, the entire adult world—as alienated and corrupt. Despite its focus on children, *Harry Potter* does not fall prey to a naive adulation of youthful innocence. The principal setting for the chief events in the story is a school, Hogwarts School of Witchcraft and Wizardry; the task of the virtuous adults at Hogwarts is to aid children in making the transition to the adult world.

THE SYMBOLISM OF EVIL

As Nietzsche himself puts it, the fundamental drive in human life is "to have and to want to have more." A "living thing seeks above all to discharge its strength—life itself is will to power; self-preservation is only one of the indirect and most frequent results." In place of the traditional moralities devised by Jews and Christians, Nietzsche proposes the establishment of a new rank ordering of values; indeed, he proposes an endless creation or revaluation of values. We want to restore an "order of rank according to strength." It is a "measure of strength to what extent we can admit to ourselves, without perishing, the merely apparent character of the world," the "necessity of lies."[11] This is precisely the insight and strength of will that Voldemort arrogates to himself.

On the issue of nihilism and its overcoming, Nietzsche's thought becomes embroiled in a series of contradictions. He wants to encourage the spread of nihilism, the "unwelcome guest," precisely because it will undermine faith in any transcendent standard of good and evil. While the advent of nihilism will further erode the confidence of the many—the petty masses of humanity, who follow what Nietzsche calls a slave morality—it will embolden the few—the active, rather than the passive, nihilists. In society's confrontation of nihilism, the war of the many against the few, of the resentful leveling instincts of democracy against the aristocratic tastes of the few, can be reversed. Nietzsche's position involves a kind of aesthetic self-fashioning wherein both good and evil, as these are regarded from the perspective of slave morality, become instruments of artistic creation. With his repudiation of any shared, objective standard of good and evil, Nietzsche would seem to have deprived himself of any basis whatsoever for judgment or discrimination. Yet he insists upon introducing a new standard, a new rank of higher and lower. The problem is that, after nihilism, any way of life seems equally valuable (and of course, equally bankrupt). As we have already urged, Nietzsche's remedy for nihilism would seem to exacerbate the situation, to immerse us more fully in meaninglessness.

In its own way, Rowling's *Harry Potter* series illustrates the self-defeating character of nihilism, of the attempt to live beyond good and evil. For all their ability to wreak havoc, to spread a culture of death (Voldemort's very name means "death wish"), evildoers in the Potter universe are either pathetic, weak sycophants or malevolent beings who rule through fear, hatred, and preying upon the innocent. Indeed, the very act of attempting to kill the infant Harry (an attack that left Harry with his trademark lightning bolt scar) backfires on Voldemort, rendering him impotent, barely alive, forced to lead a vicarious, parasitic life, feeding off and inhabiting the very bodies of others, hoping desperately to regain his power. The attraction and power of evil are present, but evil is never glorified as an end itself; instead, it is shown to be empty. The world of *Harry Potter* does not leave us with the banality of goodness and evil; instead, it confirms Hannah Arendt's thesis that "only the good has depth," that goodness is fundamentally more captivating and more complex than evil.

The plot of the first book hinges upon a search for the philosopher's stone, a magical source of money, power, and endless life. The stone is hidden somewhere at Hogwarts, the school for magicians that Harry attends. Harry and his friends, Hermione and Ron, have strong suspicions that Voldemort is trying to secure the stone to reinvigorate his life and power, which had been depleted in his attempt to murder an infant Harry after having already killed his parents. In the climactic scene, Harry confronts Professor Quirrell, a stuttering, apparently innocuous professor and secret servant of Voldemort. As Quirrell unwraps his turban and turns around, the back of his skull emerges as a face, Voldemort's face. "You see what I've become? See what I must do to survive? Live off another. Be a parasite."[12] Voldemort's self-induced demotion from aristocratic nobility and regal military command is shocking and instructive; it mirrors the path followed by Milton's Satan from Homeric hero to impotent parasite.

In an echo of the culminating scene of *Star Wars*, Voldemort invites Harry to join him. "Together we'll do extraordinary things," he promises. The last words recall one of the opening scenes of the film, in which the wand seller in Diagon Alley helped Harry select a wand suitable to him. They eventually settle on a wand, or rather the wand settles on Harry, since the custom is for the wand to choose its owner, not the reverse. Harry's "destiny" is a wand made from the same material out of which Voldemort's was constructed. The wand seller then tells Harry that he expects great things from Harry, since "he-who-must-not-be-named did great things, terrible yes, but great."[13] Harry repudiates Voldemort's offer. "Never," he shouts. Voldemort responds with cynical detachment: "Bravery. Your parents had it too." The dialogue touches here upon the complex connection between virtue and power. The books offer a supple reflection on greatness, which can accompany both goodness and evil. The books do not succumb to a least-common-denominator celebration of mediocrity, nor do they suppose that the magnificence that resides beyond good and evil is the only type of grandeur available to us.

Harry Potter's complex account of good and evil rests upon its subtle and elaborate system of symbols of virtue and vice, redemption and damnation, symbols derived from the medieval Christian world and the pagan world that preceded it. There is Lucius Malfoy, that is, Lucifer, whose last name means "bad faith," as well as his son Draco, whose name is Latin for "snake." We have Slytherin House, again the snake. By contrast, we have Gryffindor House, based on the griffon, the medieval symbol of Christ.

The most striking symbol is the unicorn, the medieval symbol of purity and innocence. When Hagrid and the children tell Ronan the centaur that a unicorn has been injured in the forest, Ronan responds by saying, "Always the innocent are the first victims. . . . So it has been for ages past, so it is now."[14] In *The Sorcerer's Stone*, Rowling modifies the traditional meaning of the symbol by adding to it the notion that the blood of the unicorn gives life. To slaughter a unicorn and drink its blood is thus a "monstrous" crime. Another centaur explains to Harry, "Only one who has nothing to lose, and everything to gain, would commit such a crime. The blood of a unicorn will keep you alive, even if you are an inch from death, but at a terrible price. You have slain something pure and defenseless to save yourself, and you will have but a half-life, a cursed life, from the moment the blood touches your lips."[15] Although Rowling never explicitly adverts to Christian doctrines, the image of drinking the blood of the slaughtered unicorn calls to mind the slaughter of Christ. On a trip to the forbidden forest, Harry confronts a dark, hooded creature feeding on the blood of a unicorn. A centaur, Firenze, arrives and explains to Harry that the blood of the unicorn can keep someone alive but at a grave cost. Here we see evil not as a demonic other but, in the Augustinian terms deployed by Delbanco, as "a pocket of nothingness in a good world."[16]

The use of the snake as a symbol for the tempter, the deceiver, and for Satan himself is well known. The basilisk that Harry encounters at the end of *Chamber of Secrets* is identified in medieval tradition as Satan, looking into the eyes of whom would turn one to stone. Fawkes' blinding of the basilisk, which Harry describes as the King of Serpents, changes that equation. "Harry looked straight into its face and saw that its eyes, both its great, bulbous yellow eyes, had been punctured by the phoenix."[17] The phoenix, rumored to rise from its own ashes and thus a symbol of the resurrected Christ, blinds the beast, and Harry slays it with the sword of Godric Gryffindor. The phoenix weeps on the basilisk's poisonous bite and keeps Harry from dying. "He felt the bird lay its beautiful head on the spot where the serpent's fang had pierced him. 'You're dead, Harry Potter,' said [Voldemort's] voice above him. 'Dead. Even Dumbledore's bird knows it. Do you see what he's doing, Potter? He's crying.' Harry blinked. Fawkes' head slid in and out of focus. Thick, pearly tears were trickling down the glossy feathers. . . . 'So ends the famous Harry Potter,' said [Voldemort's] distant voice. . . . Alone in the Chamber of Secrets, forsaken by his friends, defeated at last by the Dark Lord he so unwisely challenged. You'll be back with your dear . . . mother soon, Harry. . . . If this is dying, thought Harry, it's not so bad. Even the pain was leaving him . . . But was this dying? Instead of going black, the Chamber seemed to be coming back into focus. Harry gave his head a little shake and there was Fawkes, still resting his head on Harry's arm. A pearly patch of tears was shining all around the wound—except that there *was* no wound—."[18] Here, too, Rowling adopts and adapts a traditional symbol by adding the theme of the healing power of the tears of the phoenix.

This is the dominant contrast between good and evil in the book, a contrast that includes but transcends the exemplification in various characters of a set of virtues and vices. Indeed, Rowling draws freely upon classical symbols contrasting goodness understood in terms of sacrificial love with evil as the deceitful, parasitic, and self-indulgent activity of demonic evil. In the second book, Tom Riddle, another manifestation of Voldemort, manages to resurrect his past life by preying upon the naiveté and loneliness of Ginny Weasley, Ron's younger sister, who has just arrived at Hogwarts and who innocently begins writing a diary in a magical book that secretly contains Riddle's memories and the potential to renew his life.

In the climactic scene of the fourth book, *The Goblet of Fire*, which marks the transition from the first half of the series to the second, Voldemort discovers and implements a plan designed to bring back his life. He needs the flesh of a servant, which the pathetic Wormtail supplies, the bone of his father, which is easily retrieved from his father's grave, and "the blood of the enemy forcibly taken," which Wormtail extracts from Potter. As Voldemort rises, Harry stares into "the face that had haunted his nightmares for three years. Whiter than a skull, with wide, livid scarlet eyes and a nose that was flat as a snake's with slits for nostrils."[19] Just as he has kept himself from death, on the fringes of life, by feeding on unicorn blood and inhabiting the body of Quirrell, so too he is brought back to life by preying upon the body and blood of others. Evil has no life of its own and can sustain itself only by being parasitic on the good and the innocent.

The books combat simplistic accounts of evil in a number of ways. The temptation to construct a clearly defined "other" and label that group evil is most evident among the members of Slytherin, the house that produced Voldemort and that now houses the petty and nasty Malfoy family. Slytherin's crowd likes to conceive of all those who are not of pure wizard blood as contaminated or impure. They mock Hermione, who is the offspring of a mixed marriage of Muggle and wizard, as a "mudblood."

It is interesting that the negative judgment about Voldemort and his followers does not engender the proposal that the House of Slytherin, the source of most of the diabolical characters, should be eliminated from Hogwarts School of Witchcraft and Wizardry. The reason for this is not just tradition. Slytherin House embodies the aspiration for human greatness, something in itself noble and necessary. In Hogwarts' annual initiation for new students, a magical Sorting Hat hovers above the head of each student to discern the house in which they belong. With Harry, the Hat first suggests Slytherin, proclaiming to him, "You could be great . . . Slytherin will help you on your way to greatness."[20] Harry resists, requests Gryffindor, and the Hat complies. The words of the Hat continue to haunt Harry, especially when other similarities between himself and Voldemort emerge. In *The Chamber of Secrets*, as a classmate is being attacked by a snake, Harry manages to fend off the reptile. But he does so by using snake language, Parseltongue. Harry, who is at first not even aware of having spoken a different language, becomes an immediate object of suspicion at Hogwarts. Since no one could understand his language, it looked initially as if he was commanding the snake to kill; moreover, Parseltongue is a language spoken by very few and most notoriously by Voldemort.

The way others are suspicious of Harry and the way he becomes suspicious of himself suggest an overlap between *Harry Potter* and themes from film noir; the consequence here is that readers and viewers cannot become too comfortable in their assumptions about any particular character. The motif of the "wrong man," of the innocent man who is falsely accused or, conversely, of the guilty thought to be innocent—this theme is operative on a number of occasions in *Harry Potter*. In the fourth book, *The Goblet of Fire*, Dumbledore hires a new Defense against the Dark Arts teacher, his trusted friend, Alastor Moody—known as Mad-Eye Moody for the way his eye rotates at odd angles. Harry and friends are inclined to think they can trust Moody, but at the end of the book, it is revealed that Moody is the one who has been attempting to orchestrate Harry's destruction at the hands of Voldemort. What is more, Moody is not Moody but an impostor who has taken his place. The most dramatically effective use of the 'wrong man' is at the very heart of the plot of *Prisoner of Azkaban*, which turns on the question of what role Sirius Black, a notorious criminal, recently escaped from the maximum security prison of Azkaban, played in the plot to kill Harry's parents. The story is that Black, Harry's godfather, betrayed his parents to Voldemort and killed their good friend, Peter Pettigrew. His escape from prison now presents him with an opportunity to finish the job for Voldemort by killing Harry. As Harry peruses a family photo album in his dorm at night, he comes across a picture of Black and wonders, "Had he already been working for Black when this picture was taken? Was he already planning the deaths of the two people next to him?" Harry lies in bed fuming:

> A hatred such as he had never known before was coursing through Harry like a poison. He could see Black laughing at him through the darkness . . . He watched as though somebody was playing a piece of film, Sirius Black blasting Peter Pettigrew into a thousand pieces. He could hear . . . a low, excited mutter. "It has happened, My Lord" . . . And then came another voice, laughing shrilly.[21]

It turns out, however, that Sirius was framed for the crime, that he had tried desperately to save the Potters, and that the real criminal is Pettigrew. More than a simplistic division of characters into good and evil is required in the Potter universe.

VIRTUE AS DEFENSE AGAINST THE DARK ARTS

Although the *Harry Potter* stories, in both book and film forms, are always clear about the difference between good and evil, the contrast is never simplistic. There is a spectrum of character types, embodying a host of virtues and vices. Even those who are on the side of good can find themselves tempted by vice, momentarily uncertain as to whether their path is the right one. So struck is Harry by certain unsettling similarities between himself and Voldemort that he begins to doubt his destiny. As he often does in times of trouble, Harry turns to Dumbledore, the wise headmaster at Hogwarts, whose courage and force (he's repeatedly said to be the only wizard Voldemort fears) remain concealed behind his gentle, avuncular visage. Harry continues to be troubled by the fact that the Sorting Hat at first wanted to put Harry into Slytherin, the school that produced Voldemort and many of his followers. Harry wonders out loud about the "similarities" between himself and Voldemort. Dumbledore suggests that in the initial attack, Voldemort must have "transferred some of his powers" to Harry. Aghast, Harry concludes that "the Sorting Hat was right. I should be in Slytherin." In the film version of this exchange, the musical soundtrack moves back and forth between eerie, nervous notes as Harry speaks and calm, harmonious tones as Dumbledore offers reassuring clarifications. Dumbledore responds calmly, "It's true, Harry. You possess many of the qualities that Voldemort prized . . . determination, resourcefulness, and, if I may say so, a certain disregard for rules." To Dumbledore's question, "Why then did the Sorting Hat place you in Gryffindor?" Harry responds, "Because I asked it to." A relieved Dumbledore concludes enthusiastically, "Exactly, Harry. Exactly. Which makes you very different from Voldemort. It is not our abilities that show what we truly are. It is our choices."[22]

The film affirms in multiple ways the complex connections among choice, habit, character, and destiny. Indeed, those who criticize the presence of magic in the books fail to see the way the stories underscore the inherent limitations to magic. Those who stand with the truth will at times find themselves at a disadvantage in their battle against those who believe that the use of any means is justified as long as it serves the end of their own aggrandizement and power. But this means that those who fight against dark forces must be ever vigilant in their exercise of the virtues of courage, loyalty, prudence, and justice. Those in the front lines of the battle need more than just knowledge of virtue, however; they also need to be aware of the methods the enemy is likely to use against them. As Moody explains,

> Curses. They come in many strengths and forms. Now, according to the Ministry of Magic, I'm supposed to teach you countercurses and leave it at that. I'm not supposed to show you what illegal Dark curses look like until you're in the sixth year. You're not supposed to be able to deal with them. But Dumbledore's got a higher opinion of your nerves, he reckons you can cope, and I say, the sooner you know what you're up against, the better. How

are you supposed to defend yourself against something you've never seen?[23]

With that introduction, Moody proceeds to initiate the students into the use of various curses. Although Moody has them discard their textbook, its name is significant, *Dark Forces: A Guide to Self-Protection.* Harry learns to defend himself against these darkest of arts and to deploy them when necessary against the most hateful of foes.

But the virtuous do not have the same license in the use of the dark arts. At the end of the third book, after the truth has been revealed about Sirius Black's innocence, Harry assumes that, having spelled everything out to Dumbledore, the headmaster will fix everything. When Dumbledore expresses skepticism, Harry assumes that he doubts the story. Dumbledore assures Harry that he does believe him but that he has "no power to make other men see the truth, or to overrule the Ministry of Magic." Of course, Dumbledore does have a plan that will minimize the harm done to the good, but Harry is nonetheless stunned at Dumbledore's confession of limitations to his power: "Harry stared up into the grave face and felt as though the ground beneath him were falling sharply away. He had grown used to the idea that Dumbledore could solve anything."[24] "The truth," as Dumbledore says at the end of the first book, "is a beautiful and terrible thing, and should therefore be treated with great caution. However, I shall answer your questions unless I have a very good reason not to, in which case I beg you'll forgive me. I shall not, of course, lie."[25]

Intellectual training is insufficient and not just because it could, in the wrong hands, be put to evil use. The role of moral, in addition to intellectual, virtue is on display in the various challenges the threesome of Harry, Ron, and Hermione must confront and overcome in their path to finding the Philosopher's Stone. In the most striking scene, Ron takes the lead ("I'll be a knight") in helping them win the chess match. At a crucial juncture in the competition, Ron realizes that the only way for them to win the game is for him to sacrifice the character he's riding. "Once I make my move, the Queen will take me." When Harry explains to Hermione that Ron is "going to sacrifice himself," she screeches, "No! There must be another way." But there is no other way, and as his chess figure is destroyed, Ron collapses in a heap on the ground. Hermione starts to move toward him, but Harry urges her, "Don't move. Don't forget. Stop. We're still playing." Harry then announces the final move of the match and "checkmate."[26] He now must proceed on his own, without Ron's or Hermione's assistance. When he commends Hermione, she responds, "Me. I'm all books and cleverness. There are more important things," such as "friendship and bravery."[27] Her response indicates that she possesses these virtues and others, such as prudence and even a dose of humility.

Flawed in other ways, Chris Columbus' film version of the first book does a decent job, especially in its culminating scenes, of exhibiting the scale and sophistication of the obstacles facing Ron, Hermione, and Harry as they attempt to solve mysteries and protect the innocent. Before they can gain access to the stone, they must traverse a sort of labyrinth; they must pass a ferocious, huge, three-headed dog that Hagrid has fondly named Fluffy, then avoid the Devil's Snare— an intricate web of roots that attempt to strangle any who enter into its trap—and finally, pass a life-size chessboard on which loss may mean death. The film captures nicely the way the sheer size of the chessboard characters dwarfs the children; effective use is also made of sound, as in the thunderous crashing of the giant chess pieces, and high and low camera angles, as in the scene where the children plummet into the room beneath Fluffy's chamber and directly into the grasp of the Devil's Snare. In the case of Fluffy and the Snare, Hermione's learning enables the children to outsmart the threatening creatures. The practical relevance of Hermione's book learning indicates that libraries contain a forgotten wisdom about good and evil and offer a vicarious training for battle against the threats that pervade the adult world.

As if to underscore the importance of the public and communal recognition of virtue, the first film ends with the entire school of Hogwarts gathering for its annual closing academic banquet and the awarding of the House Cup to the house within Hogwarts that has accumulated the most points in a variety of competitions during the year. Dumbledore begins by noting the current score, which has Slytherin comfortably in the lead and Gryffindor near the bottom of the rankings. But then he states that more points are to be awarded in light of the recent events at Hogwarts. Hermione receives points for the "cool use of intellect when others were in grave peril," Ron for the best-played game of chess in the history of the institution, and Harry for "pure nerve and outstanding courage."[28] The points given to Gryffindor now place them in a tie with Slytherin for the House Cup. In a sort of democratic affirmation of the multiple contributions to the common good, not all of which can be construed in straightforwardly heroic terms, Dumbledore awards points to Neville Longbottom, the brunt of many jokes and the schoolmate Hermione had momentarily to petrify to keep from coming on the final quest with them: "It takes a great deal of bravery to stand up to your enemies, but just as much to stand up to your friends."[29]

It is an instructive fact that Hollywood's translation of books to the screen can go astray not only in the usual way, by departing radically from the intentions of the author, but also by attempting too literal a rendering. The latter flaw was on display in the first two Hollywood versions of the *Harry Potter* books, in films directed by Chris Columbus of *Home Alone* fame. Columbus' versions of *Harry Potter and the Sorcerer's Stone* and *Harry Potter and the Chamber of Secrets* were all too bookish. For the third installment in the series, *Harry Potter and the Prisoner of Azkaban*—whose opening weekend box office take exceeded that of the first two films—Alfonso Cuarón assumed directorial duties. Cuarón's production is visually magnificent and dramatically stirring.[30] The film is especially good at probing the following questions: How do the young develop confidence? How does one do something difficult for the first time? Confidence is a matter of envisioning a future in which one's fears have already been overcome. But this is a film in which subtle lessons about courage, confidence, friendship, and the value of truth abound. Is not this among the things young readers find so attractive in the *Harry Potter* books, an invitation to participate in a series of quests, to find their proper place, their dramatic role, not alone but in friendship with others, in the battle between good and evil?

Even apart from his great battles with Voldemort that reach a zenith in the final book, Harry must exercise virtue in response to external and internal threats. Harry's vulnerability and trepidation, grounded in the clear knowledge of what sorts of forces are allied against him, render his courage all the more palpable. In the film version of *Prisoner of Azkaban*, Harry fears not only Black but also the presence of the Azkaban guards, now at Hogwarts on the lookout for Black. These guards, the dementors, bear a striking physical resemblance, at least on film, to the Ringwraiths from *Lord of the Rings*. A deathly chill in the air announces the arrival of dementors, whose mode of attack involves sucking the soul from the mouth of a victim. The scene in which Harry first encounters a dementor, on the train to Hogwarts, is expertly handled to deliver subtle scares. Sitting in a railcar, Harry, Ron, and Hermione notice the windows begin to cover with ice; they feel a cold chill in the air and then perceive the approach of a dark hooded creature. The dementor takes a particular interest in Harry, who barely escapes having his soul sucked from his body. Harry remains petrified, and with good reason. As Ron puts it with a terrified expression, the dementors make you feel as if you'd "never be cheerful again."

What the film provides in visual images the book supplies in concrete language. Of Harry's first encounter with a dementor, on the train to Hogwarts, Rowling writes, "Standing in the doorway . . . was a cloaked figure that towered to the ceiling. Its face was completely hidden beneath its hood. Harry's eyes darted downward, and what he saw made his stomach contract. There was a hand protruding from the cloak and it was glistening, grayish, slimy-looking, and scabbed, like something dead that had decayed in water."[31] Harry comes very close to this fate at the end of the story. As the encroaching dementor raises its hood, Harry sees "where there should have been eyes, there was only thin, gray, scabbed skin, stretched blankly over empty sockets. But there was a mouth . . . a gaping, shapeless hole, sucking the air with the sound of a death rattle."[32] On page or screen, the dementors, cloaked, hollow figures, are reminiscent of the Dark Riders in *Lord of the Rings*. Both Tolkien and Rowling underscore the notion that evil is vacancy, loss, absence, precisely in its most threatening manifestations.

Rumors quickly circulate that Harry Potter swooned and fainted on the train, a rumor of which Malfoy makes maximal, mocking good use. So Harry must learn to overcome his fears even as he is subjected to doubts, external and internal, as to his ability to succeed.

THE DEEPER MAGIC OF HARRY POTTER

Among the most prominent philosophical themes in Rowling's series is the project of controlling nature and overcoming death. As Alan Jacobs notes, magic is not so much an attempt to seduce readers to the occult as it is an invitation to reflect on technology and the modern project of rendering humanity masters and possessors of nature—the goal, Descartes famously boasted, of his scientific method. As Jacobs puts it,

> The counterfactual "secondary world" that Rowling creates is one in which magic simply works, and works as reliably, in the hands of a trained wizard, as the technology that makes airplanes fly and refrigerators chill the air—those products of applied science being, by the way, sufficiently inscrutable to the people who use them that they might as well be the products of wizardry. As Arthur C. Clarke once wrote, "Any smoothly functioning technology gives the appearance of magic."

The fundamental moral framework of the Harry Potter books, then, is a familiar one to all of us: it is the problem of technology. (As Jacques Ellul wrote, "Magic may even be the origin of techniques.") Hogwarts School of Witchcraft and Wizardry is in the business of teaching people how to harness and employ certain powers—that they are powers unrecognized by science is really beside the point—but cannot ensure that people will use those powers wisely, responsibly, and for the common good. It is a choice, as the thinkers of the Renaissance would have put it, between *magia* and *goetia*: "high magic" (like the wisdom possessed by the Magi in Christian legend) and "dark magic."[33]

Another way to express Jacobs' point is in terms of C. S. Lewis' contrast between the deep magic of vengeance and power and the deeper magic of sacrificial love. *Harry Potter* contains a critique of the vices that can attend self-indulgent fantasy, the dark magic promised in so much of our popular forms of media today and in our scientific quest, through plastic surgery and self-help medications, to achieve an elusive state of perfection. The most powerful guard over the philosopher's stone is the Mirror of Erised ("desire" backward). Peering into the mirror reveals to the viewer the "deepest and most desperate desires of our heart," as Dumbledore explains. Discovering the mirror, Harry sees in it an image of his parents smiling happily back at him. Appearing at just the moment when Harry most needs instruction, Dumbledore tells Harry that the "happiest" person would look into the mirror and see only himself. But he proceeds with a grave warning to Harry. The mirror "gives neither knowledge nor truth." "Men have wasted away" staring into the mirror and "gone mad." It "does not do to dwell on dreams and forget to live."[34] The substitution of fantasy for life has always been a temptation for human beings; our own age differs only in the variety and immediacy of the means by which we can escape into the world of instant gratification of fantastic desires. The fulfillment fantasy of sexual desire is but one form of wish fulfillment made instantaneous by technology. By comparison to these various forms of quick and easy gratification, the truth we need to lead a good life is hard and elusive. Achieving a good life means paradoxically sacrificing one's present conception of happiness for a more adequate understanding of the human condition, an understanding in which sacrifice and the acknowledgment of insuperable limitations are pivotal.

Of course, the capacity for imagination plays a crucial role in the Potter universe; indeed, it is constitutive of it. The first film begins in a setting designed to introduce us to a world of great mysteries. Late at night, as the music of chimes plays, a tall, bearded man in a long cloak appears on a dark suburban street. The juxtaposition of magical and Muggle, or nonmagical, worlds suggests that there are mysteries and adventures in our midst. Some Muggles, such as Harry's relatives the Dursleys, lack the imaginative sympathy to perceive this magical world. So afflicted are they with a kind of bourgeois pettiness that they are habitually blind to the magical world; when they are forced to confront it, they label it abnormal, dangerous, and evil. The Dursleys are a sort of community of Nietzsche's "last men," the pusillanimous individuals whose lives are consumed in the enjoyment of petty plea- sures and whose opinions are determined by the common herd. If the film invites us to transcend the narrow conventions of good and evil, as folks such as the Dursleys understand it, it does not promote a Nietzschean transcendence of the categories of virtue and vice, of all notions of good and evil. As we have seen, the film repudiates the identification of virtue with sheer power, understood exclusively in terms of the magnitude of one's control over external events and individuals.

This is precisely the sort of control promised by the philosopher's stone, an alchemical stone that can turn base metals into "pure gold." It also contains the Elixir of Life, providing immortality to those who consume it. Here alchemy, as Alan Jacobs suggests, is a stand-in for modern science and its most ambitious goal, the conquering of death. Dumbledore had been saving it for his friend Nicolas Flamel, who is near death. After Harry's altercation with Voldemort, in which Volde- mort came very close to seizing the stone and thus restoring himself to full power, Dumbledore explains to Harry the reason the stone came to Harry and not to Quirrell or Voldemort. Dumbledore had set things up so that "only a person who wanted to find it but not use it would be able to get it." He then pauses, smiles wryly, and adds, "One of my more brilliant ideas, if I do say so myself."[35] He tells Harry that the stone is no longer a threat because Dumbledore, after consulting with Flamel, decided to destroy it.

In the book, there ensues an explanation from Dumbledore that death is nothing to fear, at least for the "well-organized mind"; instead, it is the "next great adventure." In fact, it is not death itself but the dis- organization of our lives, through the inordinate desire for money and utter deathlessness—the two promises of the stone—that we should fear. Dumbledore says, "You know, the Stone was really not such a wonderful thing. As much money and life as you could want! The two things most human beings would choose above all—the trouble is, humans do have a knack of choosing precisely those things that are worst for them."[36] The film preserves none of this philosophical teaching of Dumbledore, although he does frankly and without the least hint of panic admit that the destruction of the stone means that his friend Nicolas must soon die. By contrast, in the film, the conversation immediately moves to a consideration of a mystery greater than that concerning the power of the stone or the human desires for money, endless life, and power. It is a mystery why Quirrell's attack on Harry—at Voldemort's instigation—failed; indeed, each time Quirrell tried to touch Harry, his hands began to burn. Then, as Harry began to fight back against Quirrell, the fused team of Quirrell and Voldemort burns and disintegrates. Dumbledore explains that what protected Harry was his mother's love, which is precisely what had repelled Voldemort's attack on him as an infant, leaving him with his trademark scar. Harry is and continues to be "the boy who lived," as the title of the opening chapter of the book proclaims, because of his mother's love, exemplified in her willingness to "sacrifice herself" for Harry's sake. "That kind of act leaves a mark," Dumbledore concludes.[37]

The love that leaves a mark runs through the entire series of books. Unlike the physical mark resulting from Voldemort's attack, the mark of Harry's mother's love is invisible. As Dumbledore explains, "your mother died to save you. If there is one thing Voldemort cannot understand, it is love. He didn't realize that love as powerful as your mother's for you leaves its own mark. Not a scar, no visible sign . . . to have been loved so deeply, even though the person who loved us is gone, will give us some protection forever. It is in your very skin. . . . It was agony to touch a person marked by something so good."[38] The sense of a spiritual connection that transcends the limitations of mere matter is often suggested in the books. So the spell *expecto patronum* means "I await a defender," "I hope for an advocate." It turns out that the answer to his prayer is his father. Harry is saved by this prayer and then sees himself standing next to the stag on the bank across the lake. Later, Dumbledore explains, "Your father is alive in you, Harry, and shows himself most plainly when you have need of him. How else could you produce that *particular* Patronus? Prongs rode again last night." In *The Chamber of Secrets*, for example, the bureaucratic nitwits at the Ministry of Magic remove Dumbledore from power and force him to leave the school grounds. Despite his physical absence, he tells Harry, "I'll only have left Hogwarts when none remain loyal to me." These words console Harry and foreshadow Harry's being saved at the end by Dumbledore's phoenix, Fawkes. In *The Prisoner of Azkaban*, just as Harry is beginning to piece together the truth about what actually happened to his parents, who was loyal to them and who was not, he defends Peter Pettigrew from an attack. When he later comes to realize the extent of Pettigrew's treachery, Harry regrets having saved his life. But Dumbledore describes the act as a "very noble thing." He observes that "when one wizard saves another wizard's life, it creates a certain bond between them. . . . This is magic at its deepest, its most impenetrable."[39] He cautions Harry that he may come to be grateful for having saved Pettigrew's life. The magic of love or mercy is deeper, more mysterious, and ultimately more powerful than the magic of evil.

THE LAST ENEMY

"The last enemy that shall be destroyed is death." This passage, without a reference to its scriptural source (1 Cor 15:26), appears nearly halfway through J. K. Rowling's *Harry Potter and the Deathly Hallows*, the final book in her hugely popular series.[40] *Deathly Hallows* marks a satisfying completion of the series, more dramatically captivating and more effectively orchestrated than any book in the series since *Harry Potter and the Goblet of Fire*. As both the title and the scriptural reference indicate, the book is preoccupied with death. While addressing our peculiarly modern obsessions, the reflection on death and its possible overcoming is hardly morbid. Ultimately, it is not even tragic; instead, it is a comic affirmation of the triumph of life over death, love over hate, and community over isolation.

The early pacing of *Deathly Hallows* is superb; because the central characters (Ron, Hermione, and Harry) are no longer attending Hogwarts School of Witchcraft and Wizardry, in the wake of Dumbledore's death and Voldemort's takeover of the institution, the plot is freed from having to follow the rhythm of the academic year. In saving the big battle for the finale, previous plots also delay the deaths of major figures. In *Deathly Hallows*, there are significant casualties early, middle, and late and important revelations early, middle, and late. Through it all, Harry, much more clearly and forcefully than in the previous books, comes into his own as he grows in confidence and judgment. What was becoming a bit tiresome in the last few books—the bottomless teen angst and Harry's internal horrors—here achieves equilibrium between external challenge and internal preparedness. In short, he becomes an adult and a leader.

Despite great loss, suffering, and sacrifice, *Deathly Hallows* has a comic, not a tragic, ending. A clue that this might happen was inserted into *Half-Blood Prince*, which ends with general mourning for Dumbledore and with fear over Voldemort's increased control of the wizard world. But it also ends with plans for a wedding, precisely the communal celebration with which many classic comedies conclude. Harry finds the prospect of a wedding in the midst of so much anger, fear, and sorrow "incredible and yet wonderful."[41] That's the note of joy in the midst of sorrow that the final book, quite fittingly, hits more regularly and more accurately than have any of the previous books.

This theme is powerfully coupled with repeated dramatic illustration of the unnaturalness of the project of overcoming death by any means whatsoever and of the way the practice of evil arts, murderous arts, destroy the practitioner. In the *Half-Blood Prince*, Dumbledore informs Harry that Voldemort's pursuit of immortality has "mutilated" his "soul beyond the realm of what we might call usual evil."[42] The passage beyond customary evil illustrates one of the classical claims about virtue and vice, namely that vice is its own punishment, that it harms the perpetrator as well as, if not more than, the victim. As in *Macbeth*, so too here the nihilism espoused by one of the main characters is a result of an overweening desire for power; mutilation of soul is the inevitable result of such a pursuit. There is an affirmation of the Augustinian thesis that evil is nonbeing, that its very existence is dependent on the prior existence of goodness. In a telling scene toward the end of *Half-Blood Prince*, when Draco Malfoy threatens to kill a disarmed Dumbledore, Dumbledore instructs a stunned Malfoy, "It's my mercy, and not yours, that matters now."[43]

Readers of the final book are left to puzzle over not just the mysterious powers of mercy and self-sacrifice but also explicit references to the New Testament. Visiting Dumbledore's familial gravesite in Godric's Hollow on Christmas Eve, Harry discovers the epitaph from Corinthians cited above and a passage from Matthew, "Where your treasure is, there will your heart be also."[44] Nearby, he discovers his own parents' grave and reads their epitaph: "The last enemy to be destroyed is death." When he wonders whether the saying has something to do with the Death Eaters, Hermione responds, "It doesn't mean defeating death in the way the Death Eaters mean it, Harry. . . . It means . . . you know . . . living beyond death. Living after death." Harry is skeptical: "But they were not living. . . . They were gone. The empty words could not disguise the fact that his parents' moldering remains lay beneath snow and stone, indifferent, unknowing. And tears came before he could stop them, boiling hot then instantly freezing on his face, and what was the point of wiping them off or pretending?" He looks down and ponders his parents' ignorance of his presence, "his heart still beating because of their sacrifice and close to wishing, at this moment, that he was sleeping under the snow with them." This is a marvelous expression of a child facing the death of his parents, facing the apparent nothingness of death, its sheer, chilling absence.

This is also one of the most touching passages in the friendship between Harry and Hermione. She takes his hand and grips it "tightly." As he wishes he had brought something to adorn the gravesite, she suddenly raises her wand and makes "Christmas roses" blossom before them. Arms around one another, they depart in silence past the graves of those dear to them. Because there are so many battles and quests in the series, we are apt to think of friendship in terms of reliable courage in battle, of loyalty to one's friends in the face of mortal peril. The pilgrimage to the gravesite makes clear that friendship is also at work not only in moments of fighting against death but also in moments of its acceptance, in shared mourning and commiseration, and in the attempt to interpret the meaning of death.

Harry encounters scriptural statements on tombstones and knows neither their source nor their precise import. In that respect, Harry is a stand-in for most modern readers, who have a sense that the words of Scripture are significant but not much in the way of a context by which to interpret them. Although he never explicitly formulates it this way, Harry's great quest in *Deathly Hallows* leads him toward an understanding of the meaning of these scriptural passages, an understanding not just theoretical but eminently practical.

Beyond her creation of memorable characters and plots that will likely remain part of the cultural vocabulary for years to come, Rowling has crafted a mythical universe at whose center stands the cultivation of the virtues of remembering, and preparing for, death—perhaps the strongest antidote to nihilism in our contemporary culture.

7

GOD GOT INVOLVED
Sacred Quests and Overcoming Nihilism

As noted earlier, at least one contemporary philosopher, James Edwards, argues that nihilism is now our normal condition: "we are all now nihilists," leading "lives constituted by self-devaluing values."[1] As a solace against despair, Edwards proposes the cultivation of a secular sacramental mentality. The contrast with Nietzsche is instructive. Where Nietzsche emphasizes alternately the ennobling, tragic confrontation with nothingness and the affirming laughter of the value-creating soul, Edwards is somber and restrained, modest and joyless. The idea of a sacrament without its vivifying source—the religious sacrifice—is an empty husk. Secular sacraments foster the bad faith of those who want the aesthetics of religion without its dogmatic, moral, and transcendental burdens. Edwards would give us a new civil religion to clothe the naked public square; the problem is that the square is already populated with demonic heroes. Nietzsche sees more clearly the great confrontation between his anti-Christ and the Judeo-Christian tradition. How much of popular culture is but a dramatic and violent inversion of the gospel of peace, an immersion in sadomasochistic sex and impersonal egoism? As Walker Percy observes, we are living in the "dread latter days of the old violent beloved U.S.A. and of the Christ-forgetting Christ-haunted death-dealing Western world."[2]

In his perceptive study of contemporary popular culture, *Nightmare on Main Street: Angels, Sadomasochism, and the Culture of the Gothic*, Mark Edmundson persuasively argues that ours is not the age of chaos that many decry and others celebrate. Instead, it is "shot through with a significant dialectical pattern," a conflict between the Gothic and the genre of "facile transcendence." Among the salient features of the Gothic are a thorough critique of conventional authority, a preoccupation with revenge plots, with the unrelenting and disproportionate punishment of even the most minor of sins or flaws, and an obsession with the supernatural, especially in the form of haunting and possession. Facile transcendence, by contrast, dismisses the Gothic as juvenile and embodies the hope of an easy way out of contemporary confusion.

Edmundson thinks that the primary reason for our contemporary preoccupation with the Gothic has to do with the cultural decline of religion. There is, I think, more to this remark than he realizes. An argument can be made that the artistic power of the Gothic and the romantic is in some measure derivative of a Judeo-Christian worldview. This is, of course, a Nietzschean claim. In fact, Edmundson concedes and laments that ours is a "debased Gothic." We have its emphasis on haunting, on crime and punishment, without its counterbalancing accent on regeneration.[3] Our Gothic resembles nothing so much as a dismembered *Divine Comedy*. It is equivalent to Dante's inferno without any prospect of purgatory or paradise, a world of unrelenting punishment, the work not of a just and merciful God but of a malevolent and arbitrary force.

Edmundson thinks that the Gothic is composed of a set of dichotomies: between surface and depth, appearance and reality, and ego and id. Although Freud is now passé, Edmundson makes a persuasive case for the lingering influence of Freudian language on our discourse. Certainly, there is a residual presence of Freudian language, but one wonders how much resonance it has. Few, if any, contemporary productions are more preoccupied with tracing out the roots and significance of sexual desire than is *Seinfeld*, but the quest leads to no great insight or self-knowledge, not even to terror. This is also the case with our contemporary heroes who stand beyond good and evil and whose attempts at terror seek to unmask the illusions of conventional morality. But the amoral hero substitutes surface for surface because the notion that evil has depth is itself an illusion. Evil is revealed as banal. If there is a secret truth, it is that there is no truth. What these narratives retain is a shape, a pattern, a structure, and so the question about the unifying power or author of the story inevitably arises. Thus does the dark God come continually to the fore in contemporary popular culture. We moderns sometimes fancy ourselves beyond the crude and superstitious visions of an inscrutable, avenging divinity. An analysis such as Edmundson's belies that confidence.

Like Edwards, Edmundson is unwilling to investigate further the theological dimensions of our current culture. Indeed, his account seems a bit dated now. He makes sense neither of the enduring power of the romantic religious vision nor of the recovery of Jewish and Christian narratives. He may be right that the religious element is too often "intolerant and literal-minded,"⁴ but his dismissal of the possibility of a religious response is sweeping and dogmatic and deprives him of an important conceptual resource. The loss here is not just religious but human as well. Accompanying the decline in grand, providential narratives is the shrinking and flattening of the human world: the exaltation of the human ends in its debasement.

To discern the theological themes in our popular culture, we need to attend to a Nietzschean point: that wherever there are unifying cultural forces at work, there is a divinity present. The most patently deconstructive elements in Nietzsche aim at undercutting the possibility of a return to Judeo-Christian monotheism. This is a daunting task, as Nietzsche himself acknowledged: "we haven't rid ourselves of God because we haven't rid ourselves of grammar." What sort of deity do we now have? Given the complex and contradictory culture in which we live, there is no simple answer. However, I think there are three currents on the God question in our popular culture. The first, already discussed in some detail, is the romantic religious sensibility; here the divinity is immanent rather than transcendent and sometimes construed in pantheistic terms. The second is the proclamation of lesser gods or at least a diminution in stature of the one God so that we end up with a diminished divinity that is often subject to derision.

In the place of a truly transcendent God, there is a divinelike being, higher than us but far from perfect. This is the image of the creator present in *The X-Files*, with its myth of alien intervention in human evolution, and in Ricky Gervais' comic send-up of the divine lawgiver, the Man in the Sky, in *The Invention of Lying*; tellingly, it is also the version of God criticized in the books of the new atheists.

Perhaps the most instructive lesson to take away from the religious themes in recent films is the way our popular culture seems to vacillate between essentially empty conceptions of a transcendent God and increasingly fertile notions of divine immanence. Given that choice, the attraction of the immanent deity of romanticism is clear. In nature, palpably in a film such as *Avatar*, we encounter a mysterious other whose regal power is palpable. But these are not the exclusive options. There is yet a third conception of God and divine providence operative in our popular culture; it hearkens back to Jewish or Christian narratives of redemption and can be found in different forms in films as diverse as *The Pursuit of Happyness*, *The Book of Eli*, and *Lord of the Rings*.

REVERENT ROMANTICISM

In "My Heart Leaps Up," nineteenth-century romantic poet William Wordsworth writes of being inspired from the time of his youth by the mere sight of a rainbow. He proceeds, "The Child is father of the man; / And I could wish my days to be / Bound each to each by natural piety." Religiously reverent romanticism continues to exercise a strong influence on our popular culture. We have already discussed romanticism in some detail and seen intimations of its religious sensibility, its natural piety, in the film version of *The Children of Men*. Hence, we need attend only briefly to religious romanticism in this chapter. If the box office is any indication, the most compelling portrait of divinity in the films of 2009 is not the Man in the Sky but the Lady in the Tree—the goddess Eywa who is worshipped by the Na'vi on the planet Pandora in James Cameron's *Avatar*. The much-touted look of the film is, indeed, mesmerizing, but the visuals work largely because Cameron is so effective in constructing an entire world, that of the Na'vi tribe. The very blue inhabitants of Pandora are deeply bound, one to another, and to a particular place, especially to the sacred tree and the goddess who dwells there. The tree happens to grow on mineral deposits that are valuable to the militaristic capitalists who want to relocate the tribe, by diplomacy or war (preferably the latter), so as to exploit Pandora's natural resources. The film delivers its share of politically pointed clichés, as when the merciless military commander announces a policy of "fighting terror with terror." What is more telling is the way *Avatar*, like many recent sci-fi films (*The Matrix* and *The Children of Men*, for example), deploys symbols and themes from a number of world religions. The dominant and unifying myth, however, is that of romanticism. *Avatar* embodies a set of standard romantic divisions between a primitive, basically peaceful, and organic culture, on the one hand, and an advanced, bellicose, and artificial culture, on the other.

In some ways, the film is not so much a departure as a continuation of a trend in recent filmmaking. In the last decade, in the annual ranking of box office success, large-scale, mythic quest stories have most often dominated: *Star Wars, Harry Potter, Lord of the Rings*, and now—one mythic blockbuster to rule them all—*Avatar.*

The hero of the story, and the vehicle through which the audience comes to experience the world of Pandora, is a partially paralyzed marine named Jake Sully—who takes on an avatar, an artificial body of the Na'vi, in the Avatar Project. His goal is to infiltrate a tightly knit community, uncover information about it, and perhaps even persuade its people to relocate so that the military can secure a desirable natural resource called "unobtainium." When Sully's efforts are not as successful as hoped, the military commander threatens "shock and awe" and promises to fight "terror with terror."

The connection of the inhabitants of Pandora to one another is woven into their biological constitution; they possess ponytail tendrils that enable them to bond with each other. They are also intimately bound, in this life and beyond, to the Tree of Souls, wherein dwells the goddess Eywa. The malevolent pursuers of unobtainium are nothing more than caricatures of evil, but the plight of the Na'vi is a sympathetic one, and the Na'vi characters are engaging and even admirable. Not only is their deity immanent but she is also the locus of the souls that have passed into the afterlife. The sacredness of the place is thus the holiness of nature, people, and eternity. *Avatar* provides an attractive pantheistic vision. There is some question in the film as to how impersonal the deity Eywa is. In the course of the big battle between the indigenous creatures and the military industrial complex, the Na'vi at first believe Eywa is indifferent to the course of events. But the way the battle turns in their favor leads to a reinterpretation of Eywa's intentions, or rather to the view that Eywa has intentions. This points up another of the inherent tensions in romantic pantheism: the natural human longing for a caring deity versus the demands of honest pantheism, which eschews the consolations of a personal deity.

The visual quality of the film is indeed stunning, but mere artistry would have proven tiresome were the world of the Na'vi not such a fascinating one. In the journal *Image*, Jeffrey Overstreet aptly comments, "Pandora is a whole new world of breathtaking beauty, exploding with wild new life forms that soar, spark, prowl, pounce, gallop, and graze. Borrowing heavily, and brilliantly, from what he's seen in deep-sea exploration, Cameron has built the most enchanting magic kingdom since Dorothy first stepped into Technicolor Oz."[5]

The threat of irrevocable loss is quite credible. Here the film taps into a sentiment that has often been at the heart of conservatism, at least the strain of conservatism inspired by the likes of Tocqueville: the worry that gambling on cosmopolitan forces of progress not only carries with it unintended consequences but also exacts a cost in the erosion of traditional customs and the destruction of intermediate institutions. The problem here is that there seems to be no possibility of the Na'vi incorporating elements of modernity without destroying their community. Thus, we, if not the Na'vi, are faced with an impossible dichotomy: either modernity and its technology or primitive fidelity to place and people.

The word *avatar* has religious origins (it's a Hindu term referring to the descent of a deity), but its more common contemporary use has to do with artificial or second lives and role-playing in social media. From its title and from the fact that its main character takes on an artificial body and identity through the use of highly developed technology, then, one might have expected the film to probe this issue. For a film that was many years in the making, it is remarkably void of self-awareness. It never faces squarely the way in which technology is necessary to allow viewers to experience and come to know this primitive world. The contradictions of romanticism may well undermine the hopes of the makers of *Avatar*, but that does not mean that religious romanticism will fade from the scene of our popular culture anytime soon. It offers a diagnosis of what ails our culture and a rich symbolic alternative.

CHILDREN OF LESSER GODS

If romantic narratives supply fertile depictions of an immanent deity, many other productions offer incredible and nearly vacuous conceptions of divine transcendence. In a famous eighteenth-century dialogue on religion, the skeptical philosopher David Hume mounts a sustained attack on the traditional conception of God as an infinitely perfect being. He sardonically suggests the following substitute: "[the universe is the] first rude essay of some infant deity, who afterwards abandoned it, ashamed of his performance; it is the work of some dependent, inferior deity, and is the object of derision to his superiors."[6] In our situation, the derision aimed at this inferior deity often comes from Hollywood and from the so-called new atheists.[7]

Ricky Gervais' *The Invention of Lying* might be said to articulate the common thesis of the new atheists: God is the big lie. Gervais plays Mark Bellison, a struggling scriptwriter in a world where lying does not exist and is, indeed, for everyone except Bellison, inconceivable. In a world without fiction, scriptwriters are reduced to constructing bland recitations of historical fact. Bellison is not a success either in his writing career or in his pursuit of attractive women like Anna (Jennifer Garner). For overweight, unattractive guys like Bellison, universal honesty is painful. This is made clear in the phone conversation Anna has with her mother during a date with Bellison. Seated across the table from him, she recounts his physical defects and announces that she won't be sleeping with him.

Experiencing inner conflict and some sort of genetic transformation, Bellison eventually seizes on an opportunity to lie. The pivotal scene in the film occurs as Bellison visits his dying mother in the hospital and strives to console her. After hospital workers overhear him describing the pleasures of the afterlife, they spread the good news. Soon crowds are camped outside his house, demanding further information about the Man in the Sky and his criteria for deciding who gets to live in a mansion in the next life. Gervais/Bellison appears on his porch with a pizza box on which he has written a set of commandments. If this were a Monty Python film, such a scene would be rife with comic possibility. Not here. One friend, realizing that all he has to do to gain eternity in a mansion is to avoid serious wrongdoing, decides simply to stay home, drink beer, and watch TV. Although the film introduces tensions between fact and fiction, truthfulness and lying, it is so devoid of imagination that it simply does nothing with these tensions. Gervais seems to want to poke fun at the banality of religion, but the dullness of this and other scenes points to the banality of his own humor.

One wonders whether Ricky Gervais was an adviser for the Coen brothers' film *A Serious Man*, which stars Michael Stuhlbarg as Larry Gopnik, a physics professor awaiting a tenure decision. A sort of postmodern Job, Gopnik is in a bad way; up for tenure, he is receiving secret letters attacking his prospects. His wife is having an affair with a friend of the family, and his kids are deadbeats. On a quest to read the signs of the times, particularly as they apply to his own cursed life, he consults various rabbis, who wander from reflections on the difficulty of seeing *Hashem*—that is, God—in the world to oracular recitations of Jefferson Airplane lyrics: "When the truth is found to be lies." But the Coens have not updated Job; they have served up a dramatically diminutive version and paired him with a vastly diminished divinity. Gopnik somberly muses about God and the uncertainty principle, which, according to his version, means "you can never know what's going on." One searches the screen for Gervais' pizza box when Gopnik concludes, "The boss isn't always right, but he's always the boss."

A more somber and more creative take on the arbitrariness of the big boss—divine, human, or alien—can be had in *The X-Files*. The show features Dana Scully and Fox Mulder as FBI agents in charge of investigating unsolved cases involving unexplained phenomena. By pairing these two, the FBI hopes that Scully's bent for scientific proof, cultivated during her training as a forensic pathologist, will temper Mulder's passion, inspired by his youthful witness of his sister's abduction by aliens, for unraveling the government cover-up of alien infiltration of the planet. Despite their different backgrounds and inclinations, Mulder and Scully forge an alliance, a friendship that transcends a prurient, even romantic, interest in one another. Whatever eros there is in their relationship is sublimated into the search for truth. The quest—encapsulated in the show's motto, "the truth is out there"—imposes an ascetical restraint, a willingness to sacrifice personal well-being and success. It also demands truthfulness, at least toward those who assist us in the search.

Truth proves not only elusive but contradictory. What at one moment seems innocent or trustworthy can, and usually does, turn corrupt and insidious the next. One critic sees the show as a metaphor for humanity in the technological age of television. Scully and Mulder are "literally and figuratively alienated, penetrated, and probed to the molecular level by omniscient and omnipotent forces who have infiltrated like television and, now, computers, virtually everything in our lives. . . . Scully and Mulder trust each other. . . . Yet virtually everything they think they know is wrong. Television has taught them the arts of insight but not how to formulate a point of view. It has sent them on a quest for identity, but taught them also never to trust what they find. . . . The media-driven milieu of *The X-Files* suggests that the whole world is now the same place, all of it accessible, all of it at once safe, dangerous, restricting, liberating. The North Pole is not more or less threatening than the New Jersey woods or a cheap motel room."[8] The persistent plot reversals and illusory characters render the quest for truth problematic. "The truth is out there" competes for lead billing with other slogans like "trust no one" and "believe the lie."

The series tends to reverse and thereby unsettle traditional stereotypes; for example, the woman plays the hard-headed realist, while the man is credulous. But Scully and Mulder are less antithetical than complementary. Even before Scully shows signs of sharing Mulder's faith, the show illustrates the subtle link between skepticism and credulity in the absence of any clear basis for preferring one to the other. As Tocqueville notes, the confrontation with implacable, cosmic forces deprives the individual of a sense of control over his own life. The result is psychic inertia. Amid incessant investigative activity and in the face of the most horrifying revelations, both Scully and Mulder retain an almost icy detachment. *Entertainment Weekly* notes Scully's "open, blank stare" and Mulder's "pin-eyed zombie cool." There is something oddly mesmerizing and consoling about the conspiratorial artistry of the show. The experience of one's personal history, perhaps of the history of humankind, as the effect of the malevolent stratagems of some grand experiment conducted by aliens, the government, or some amalgam of the two (the syndicate) induces a universal paranoia that has an inoculating quality.

The fragility of identity in the world of *The X-Files* often revolves around the family. Yet, as one observer notes, families "scarcely matter except as plot devices." Perhaps what is more important, the question of family identity is always backward (toward uncovering the truth about the death of Scully's sister, about who abducted Scully and rendered her infertile, about the disappearance of Mulder's sister and the relationships of his father and mother to less than savory individuals associated with the government conspiracy) and never forward (toward the possibility of marriage and child-rearing). As is often the case in film and on television, in *The X-Files*, the family is a microcosm. In both the global and the local narratives, there is a desperate longing to recover what has vanished, a sense of belonging, of trust, and stability. Both the cosmos, wherein human life issues from genetic manipulation by alien life forms, and the family, which is now at cross-purposes with itself, have suffered a cataclysmic blow which we seem unable to rectify or even to name clearly. How can we go on in a universe where the only thing that is trustworthy in the end is the insubstantiality or nothingness of what is most important and most personal, most universal and most immediate?

If there is a grand narrative to the series—and the revelations in the film and subsequent television episodes point rather strongly in that direction—it has to do with an alien plot to reclaim Earth. The planet's original inhabitants had a crucial hand in the evolution of the human species and in the crafting of our civilization's most important religious documents. In place of the no longer credible big myth about creation ex nihilo, in order to account for the present state of things, we construct a new myth featuring a creator higher than us but hardly a rival to the God of the two testaments of Scripture. Myths seem necessary to account for the present state of things. But the active making of myths, the construction of images, symbols, and stories, diminishes the power of myth, which is no longer seen as a revelation or insight into the nature of things and history but as a mere human construct. This is yet another source of our suspicion of images, our worry that what seems real is but a deceptive construct. Despite its noir-ish elements, *The X-Files* often serves up a comical and satirical take on its fanciful theories, even on the quest for truth, thus providing further confirmation of the comic trajectory of contemporary treatments of evil.

There is an odd coincidence here of skepticism and credulity. In *Truth and Truthfulness*, British philosopher Bernard Williams describes the current unrest about truth in our culture in this way. He detects "an intense commitment to truthfulness—or, at any rate, a pervasive suspiciousness, a readiness against being fooled, an eagerness to see through appearances to the real structures and motives that lie behind them." This request for transparency, for hearing the whole story, pervades our political and media culture. Yet it is not exactly the same as a commitment to truthfulness, because it entails only a demand that others tell the truth. Paired with this demand, Williams observes, "there is an equally pervasive suspicion about truth itself: whether there is such a thing; if there is, whether it can be more than relative or subjective" and "whether we should bother about it."[9] In a similar vein, another secular British philosopher, Simon Blackburn, in *Truth: A Guide*, contends that a soft, democratic form of relativism has given our contemporaries a "green light to believe what they like with as much conviction and force as they like." An influential British philosopher with distaste for religion, Blackburn laments the current forms of dogmatism: "Astrology, prophecy, homeopathy, Feng shui, conspiracy theories, flying saucers, voodoo, crystal balls, miracle-working, angel visits, alien abductions, management nostrums and a thousand other cults dominate people's minds."[10] Can we add, and perhaps move to the front of the queue, the cult of Dan Brown's *The Da Vinci Code*?

Of course, many readers and viewers of the story are simply interested in it as a mildly entertaining yarn; many are drawn in by the controversy itself. If media reports are even marginally accurate (and Amy Wellborn has collected quite a bit of anecdotal evidence from responses to her own book about the *Code*), then many, many individuals are inclined to take large portions of the book as offering a true picture of the history of Christianity and of our greatest works of art and architecture. Although Brown has recently urged that his book is just fiction, the book contains a page entitled "FACT" which lists alleged facts about the antiquity of the Priory of Sion and about Opus Dei and then makes the bold claim that "all descriptions of artwork, architecture, documents, and secret rituals in this novel are accurate."[11]

The cult of *The Da Vinci Code* is a marvelous illustration of both these contemporary impulses concerning truth. It purports to offer transparency, an unveiling of things kept hidden by powerful institutions. It simultaneously feeds our skepticism about truth, since it deflates the greatest claims to truth in the history of human civilization. This is why conspiracy theories are at once superficially so satisfying and essentially so vacuous. And Brown's conspiracy theory has a clever hook; it invites us, as readers, to participate in the solution of the great mysteries through the deciphering of a series of codes.

There are now travel guides organized around the plot of *The Da Vinci Code*. But the impact on travelers is less elevating than it is unintentionally comic. Inhabitants of the modern world are increasingly ignorant of the wider world—geography, politics, world religions, and great works of art. But we have the nagging sense that something significant must be at work in history, in religion, and in art. Brown's story fulfills our desire to have things fit together, to have the great events of history, the great religious teachings, and the greatest works of art and architecture woven into an intelligible story. Brown's story also feeds our (utterly unearned) modern sense of superiority; we can see further than our predecessors not because we stand on the shoulders of giants, whom we have spent our lives trying to master, but because we suppose that we can see through them. In place of the old Christian myth, Brown gives us a New Age myth, a quasi-feminist myth of the royal bloodline of Mary Magdalene, wife of Jesus.

How little any of the myths of deficient divinities have to do with orthodox Christianity is evident from Terry Eagleton's *Reason, Faith, and Revolution: Reflections on the God Debate*, an engaging, witty, and largely successful critique of the new atheists, especially Christopher Hitchens (author of *God Is Not Great*) and Richard Dawkins (author of *The God Delusion*), whose delusional grandiosity earns them the hybrid nickname Ditchkens.[12] From Ditchkens, one would never know that there are forms of Christianity reducible neither to fundamentalism nor to effete Unitarianism. There has been a sustained Christian tradition of scriptural commentary that acknowledges the autonomy of science and is quite self-conscious about its own hermeneutics. Ditchkens reduces God to a sort of Loch Ness monster for whose existence there is no convincing evidence. As Eagleton clarifies, with help from Thomas Aquinas and contemporary interpreters such as Herbert McCabe, God is not the big, bad daddy in the sky, "the largest and most powerful creature." Nor is theology intended to explain the operations of nature. But it does respond to questions concerning "why there is anything in the first place, or why what we do have is actually intelligible to us."[13]

Of course, some contemporary Christians are easy targets for Ditchkens. They are not spared Eagleton's wrath: the comic irrationality of the "young earth" movement, the theological despair of those who care more about securing a religious America than about their own religion, and the advocates of a Gospel of Success that skips Good Friday and turns Easter Sunday into a shopping spree at an upscale mall. By contrast, what Eagleton sees in the Gospels is a persistent reminder that the "truth of history" is a "mutilated body" of a "tortured innocent." There is "no self-fulfillment that is not a self-divestment."[14]

Eagleton's devastating critique focuses on Hitchens' and Dawkins' theological illiteracy, ignorance of how science works, and naive faith in rational progress. The crisis of Enlightenment reason, which was apparent to secular philosophers long before it became part of the popular Christian response to modernity, is little noted in Ditchkens. Having exalted himself above nature and placed himself at the high point of history, Enlightenment man falls prey to the chief "bourgeois fantasy," that of the "self-authorship." He can "extract from the world only the values he has placed in it."[15] The deracination of traditional sources of meaning in our increasingly rational civilization sends citizens scurrying to the realm of culture. The privatization of sex, art, and religion has freed these up as sources of cultural meaning independent of politics and as weapons of political critique, but at a great cost. "Isolation from the public world causes them to become increasingly pathologized."[16]

Civilization, Eagleton insists, never fully leaves barbarism behind; purely instrumental, technical reason, having no roots in anything other than itself, can easily generate barbarism. Even science has roots; following a host of contemporary philosophers of science, Eagleton argues that science is built on assumptions, on a certain kind of faith. Even as it bestows enormous benefits—political, scientific, medicinal—modernity occludes from view certain incorrigible features of the human condition. Ditchkens is forced to treat the nonreligious political horrors of the twentieth century as mere blips in the unfolding of evolutionary progress.

In response to naive beliefs in progress, Eagleton notes that Christian theology affirms the "possibility of transforming history without the hubris of the idea of Progress." The grand narrative of redemption will be seen only "retrospectively." He quotes the philosopher Walter Benjamin, "Only a redeemed mankind receives the fullness of its past."[17] But here we come to the problem that plagues Eagleton's entire project: the failure to face squarely the truth claims at the heart of the Gospel. Indeed, on this question, Ditchkens is at least more forthright than Eagleton.

THEOLOGICAL QUESTS

Romantic pantheism and diminutive deities do not, of course, constitute the whole picture of religion in film in recent years. Amid a revival of classic quest films in the last decade, *Lord of the Rings* stands out as the most ambitious, the most artistically compelling, and the most philosophically and theologically astute. Eclipsing even the *Harry Potter* books in execution and in addressing the nihilistic dangers of the modern age, Peter Jackson's trilogy manages to overcome the divide between immanent and transcendent conceptions of divinity, even as it encompasses romanticism within its grand design. But *Rings* is not alone; other less ambitious films feature quests in a theological key: a quest for the American dream as an expression of a civil religion in *The Pursuit of Happyness* and a prophetic quest amid the ruins of modern civilization in *The Book of Eli*. These films testify to the enduring attraction of classic theological themes even in advanced Western culture.

The pursuit of the American dream and the overcoming of threats to its realization have recently resurfaced in Hollywood. One of the most popular recent films, an Oscar nominee, is John Lee Hancock's *The Blind Side*, an upbeat true story of the life of Baltimore Ravens offensive lineman Michael Oher and the white, upper-class family that adopts Oher and gives him a chance at living well. Criticized in the mainstream media for its "selective charity," the emotionally predictable but nonetheless enjoyable film depicts the southern and Christian Tuohy family as thoughtful, industrious, generous, and good humored.

The threat overcome in this story is not so much nihilism, certainly not philosophical nihilism, as it is the all too common temptation to despair in the face of bad luck and overwhelming odds. Such an experience can lead to nihilism, to indifference toward the lives of others and one's own life, even to a life of violent opposition to the world. This is precisely the sort of violence-saturated, drug-infested male inner-city world from which the Tuohy family rescues Big Mike. In its exercise of personal charity, the Tuohy family itself is saved from the sort of hollow, snidely racist, upper-class life that is seen as a source of nihilism in so many Hollywood films.

The success, indeed the very existence, of a Hollywood film such as *The Blind Side* is a sign of a change in Hollywood, which seems to be slowly overcoming its aversion to making uplifting stories about contemporary ordinary Americans. Perhaps an even more important film of this sort is the 2006 film *The Pursuit of Happyness*, a quintessentially American success story, and a true story, about San Francisco salesman Chris Gardner (Will Smith). In the early 1980s, just as the national economy goes into rapid decline, Gardner makes a risky investment; he purchases new bone-density scanners. When he fails to sell them, the ensuing familial financial crisis prompts his wife, Linda (Thandie Newton), to leave him and their son, Christopher (Jaden Smith). A chance encounter with an executive from Dean Witter, whom Chris impresses by rapidly solving a Rubik's Cube, leads to an internship opportunity with the firm. Unfortunately for Chris and his son, the internship is unpaid; when the IRS seizes nearly all of his remaining savings for back taxes, the two are left homeless. At one point, they sleep in a bathroom at a BART station. They do find regular shelter at the Glide Memorial United Methodist Church, at least on those nights when Chris can make it there from work before all the beds are taken. Meanwhile, Chris continues his internship and, defying various protocols, manages to land a number of high-profile customers. Never letting on to coworkers about his homelessness, Chris is eventually rewarded with a full-time position at Dean Witter, on the basis of which—the epilogue informs viewers—he went on to set up his own multimillion-dollar brokerage firm.

Gardner's story is a quintessentially American tale about upward mobility through industriousness and fidelity. A story about a self-made man, Gardner's life is the antithesis of the life of Don Draper. The pursuit of happiness is a kind of quest. As Gardner wonders aloud at one point in the film, "I started thinking about Thomas Jefferson, the Declaration of Independence, and our right to life, liberty, and the pursuit of happiness, and I remember thinking, 'How did he know to put the pursuit part in there?' That maybe happiness is something we can only pursue, and maybe actually we can never have it, no matter what. How did he know that?" Here happiness is a quest and a puzzle. The film embodies a kind of civil religion. Chris' son likes to tell a joke: "There was a man who was drowning, and a boat came, and the man on the boat said, 'Do you need help?' and the man said, 'God will save me.' Then another boat came and he tried to help him, but he said, 'God will save me,' then he drowned and went to Heaven. Then the man told God, 'God, why didn't you save me?' and God said, 'I sent you two boats, you dummy!'" Not so much an affirmation of the principle that God helps those who help themselves, the joke illustrates the need to be attuned to, and eager to seize, the opportunities divine providence puts before us. Indeed, the civil religion here is hardly of the deist variety; perhaps the most powerful scene in the film is a worship service at a gospel church. As the choir sings an emotionally stirring version of Mahalia Jackson's hymn, "Lord, Don't Move That Mountain," Gardner weeps and affectionately embraces his son. The opening stanza is

> Now Lord don't move my mountain
> But give me the strength to climb
> And Lord, don't take away my stumbling blocks
> But lead me all around

This is not facile transcendence but redemption in and through suffering endured for the sake of the good; here as elsewhere in religious quest films, fulfilling ordinary duties often demands the exercise of extraordinary virtue.

Themes of religious quest also surface in dour apocalyptic quest films such as *The Road* and *The Book of Eli*. Cormac McCarthy's *The Road* is one of the great novels of recent years, yet the film version fails to capture the poetry of the novel and ends up as a brutal story of cannibals. Another postapocalyptic film released not long after *The Road*, *The Book of Eli*, an early 2010 release, features Denzel Washington on a postapocalyptic path to deliver a mysterious book to a place where it can become the basis of a new civilization.

There are hints in this film of the power of reading and of authoritative words—especially when those words emerge from the Word—to undergird political deceit or, by contrast, to provide the seeds for a renewal of civilization. Washington's performance as a man gifted with supernatural powers of self-defense and an undivided will to fulfill the command of God is surprisingly credible. He makes the viewer believe that he has heard the Word and been called. Like McCarthy's novel *The Road* (but not the film), *The Book of Eli* manages to portray God as mysterious and more worthy of our obedience than the jejune Man in the Sky of *The Invention of Lying* and other films.

In search of water, Eli enters a town run by Carnegie (Gary Oldman), who rules by fear and violence and has his lackeys scouring the area for a book whose authority, Carnegie believes, will give him greater political control over people. After gang members threaten Eli in a bar, he takes them on and kills them one by one. He then meets Carnegie, who, intrigued by Eli's rare literacy, demands that he stay with them. Carnegie commands Solara (Mila Kunis), the daughter of the blind concubine Claudia (Jennifer Beals), to spend the night with Eli and seduce him. Fearing retribution against herself and her mother, Solara tries to seduce him but he refuses. Instead, he invites her to eat with him, and before they begin, he reaches out, grasps her hands, and begins to pray. She is befuddled by the hospitality and especially by the prayer. The next day, as she eats with Carnegie and her mother, she mimics Eli and begins to pray. That makes Carnegie suspicious, and as he sends his men to set a trap, Eli escapes and heads west. The remainder of the film is a chase scene through the desert. Despite his insistence that he must travel alone, Solara follows Eli, who saves her from an assault and then hides out with her in a cave. She becomes inquisitive about the book, asking whether he reads the same book every day and whether he will let her see the book. When he resists, she persuades him to tell her some of what is in the book. Eli begins reciting from memory Psalm 23:

> The Lord is my shepherd; I shall not want.
> He maketh me to lie down in green pastures:
> he leadeth me beside the still waters.
> He restoreth my soul: he leadeth me in the paths of righteous-
> ness for his name's sake.
> Yea, though I walk through the valley of the shadow of death,
> I will fear no evil.

When he finishes, she asks, "Did you write that?" Eli relates his experience of God's calling and explains that, before the destruction, people had "more than what they needed and didn't know what was precious."

As he begins to trust Solara, Eli tells her that he saw a hole in the sky and heard a voice that urged him to go to a place where he would find a book. He did and there he found a book. He was then commanded to head west to a place where he would find a safe location for it. Although there is an image of a cross on the Bible that Eli carries, the film has a more Old Testament feel to it. Eli is a blind prophet obeying a mysterious command of God in a postapocalyptic world that has forgotten God and has failed to learn even from its own self-destructive tendencies. He uses violence against those who threaten to take the book.

An uneven film with a minimal plot and not much in the way of special effects, *The Book of Eli* nonetheless succeeds as a meditation on the psalm. Denzel Washington plays a credible prophet who reveals himself in words and signs even as he continues to hide from mere mortals. Indeed, only the blind fully see. As numerous clues indicate that Eli is a blind prophet, his astonishing powers of perception and ability to fend off attackers give evidence of supernatural gifts. More than his physical capacities, his faith in the authoritative call of the invisible God is compelling. Eli's God is not part of creation, nor is he to be identified, as in pantheism, as the whole; instead, he transcends the whole as its author and reveals himself in words and deeds heard and seen by those open to his message. One might say of Eli's life what Jules says of the miracle in *Pulp Fiction*: "God got involved." Apparently random, seemingly chance events reveal an order otherwise hidden to the eyes of mortal men.

In the orthodox Christian vision, to which Eagleton directs us at various points in his analysis of our current cultural malaise, there is no contradiction between transcendence and immanence, between the God who transcends the whole as its author and the God who is manifest in and through the created order. The closest any recent cultural phenomenon comes to capturing the possibility of divine transcendence and immanence is Peter Jackson's *Lord of the Rings*, a remarkable achievement. Despite occasional flaws in the translation from Tolkien's book to the screen, Jackson has produced a marvelous film trilogy, a fitting testimony to the book that British citizens have voted, in a BBC survey, the "nation's best-loved book." In an early review of Tolkien's trilogy, poet W. H. Auden had these words of praise, words that give some indication of how the book could be seen as engaging, without succumbing to, nihilism: "If, as I believe, Mr. Tolkien has succeeded more completely than any previous writer in this genre in using the traditional properties of the Quest, the heroic journey, the Numinous Object, the conflict between Good and Evil while at the same time satisfying our sense of historical and social reality, it should be possible to show how he has succeeded. To begin with, no previous writer has, to my knowledge, created an imaginary world and a feigned history in such detail."[18]

It is no small matter to say that Jackson's films come nearly as close in the world of film to achieving these same aims as does Tolkien's text in the world of popular literature.[19] Forced to condense a long and sprawling narrative, the filmmakers, especially in the opening, have chosen wisely. The film begins with a voice-over that provides the history of Middle Earth and the rings of power, crafted to aid rulers in their respective realms. Meanwhile, another ring has been secretly forged in Mordor; the ring with the power to rule all other rings is under the control of Sauron. As Sauron wages war and free lands fall, some, particularly the lands of men and elves, resist. In battle against the ring bearer, Sauron, Isildur slices off the finger bearing the ring and has, at that moment, the opportunity to destroy the ring. Being of the race of men, who "above all else desire power," Isildur is "easily corrupted" and elects not to destroy the ring. The ring is eventually lost and passes out of all memory. As history becomes legend, which, in turn, becomes myth, the present is described as a time of deprivation of the knowledge of the past: "things that should not have been forgotten were lost." But chance, which plays a crucial role in the action of the story, occasions the finding of the ring by Smeagol, whose possession affords him "unnatural long life" and "poisons his mind." The narrator describes the ring as having conscious intentions, as ensnaring its new possessor. Yet we are promptly told that "something happened next that the ring did not intend," namely, the discovery of the ring by the hobbit Bilbo.

From that brief history lesson, we move to the present and to the lush, simple lives of the hobbits in their Shire, a setting wonderfully realized in the film. The diminutive creatures live peaceably and in harmony with nature; their dwellings are in fact built into the natural landscape. With the exception of Bilbo, whose desire for adventure led him out of the Shire and enabled him to find the ring, hobbits generally show little interest in the world beyond the Shire. But as the narrator informs us, a "time will soon come when the hobbits will shape the fortunes of all." As the action begins, Frodo, a relative of Bilbo, awaits the arrival of a great wizard, Gandalf.

In the presence of the ring, Gandalf nearly cowers. When Frodo suggests that he use the ring, Gandalf responds that, although he would seize the ring with a "desire to do good," it would, through him, "wield a power too great and terrible to imagine." That Gandalf should be more afraid of the ring than Frodo indicates both his greater awareness of danger and his appreciation of the principle that the corruption of the best is the worst. Cognizant that Sauron has heard rumors about the ring's presence in the Shire, Gandalf requests that Frodo, accompanied by fellow hobbit Sam, flee the Shire with the ring.

Gandalf reports that Sauron is not dead, that, with the assistance of the corrupt wizard Saruman and the Dark Riders, he now seeks to recover the ring and restore himself to power. As is true in the book, so too in the film Sauron is depicted as a great eye surveying surrounding lands. It is striking that Tolkien chooses as his image of evil an almost all-seeing eye, an image that has sometimes been associated with God. But the eye, as the story makes clear, is not an especially apt image for the true God. The fiery, hollow, nearly disembodied eye captures nicely the impersonal desire to monitor, control, and destroy or manage all that falls under its purview.

Before they have even left the Shire, the hobbits encounter the Ringwraiths, dark, hooded creatures riding horses, emitting a chilling shriek. The Nazgul, as they are known, are a corrupt race of men, the "most terrible servants" of Sauron. There is much talk early in the film and the book about the easy corruptibility of the human race; yet, along their path to Rivendell, they meet up with Strider, Aragorn, who is the true heir of Isildur and of the throne of Gondor. He is the remaining link to the ancient line of kings. Deeply aware of his own human weakness, he proves himself a wise leader, a worthy colleague, and a supremely courageous warrior. After a decision is made at Rivendell, one of the last remaining free realms, to send the hobbits, with Aragorn and others, to Mordor to return the ring to the fires from which it was forged, the members of the fellowship of the ring set off on their journey. They are soon beset by Orcs and split up. Frodo and Sam must now set off toward Mordor on their own.

Although he does not explore it as deeply as Tolkien does in the book, Jackson does not neglect the role of chance and providence in the plot. We have already mentioned the opening reference to chance in the determination of the possessors of the ring. Later, as Frodo sits with Gandalf in a cave on the way to Mordor, they discuss Smeagol/Gollum, whose emaciated, hairless body with bulging eyes has appeared trailing them on their way. Frodo curses Smeagol/Gollum and wishes that he were dead. Gandalf gently chastises him for being too eager to make judgments of life and death. Besides, Gandalf adds, the unfortunate creature may have some role to play before the end. The notion that not everything is predetermined—by God, the fates, or the necessary causal order of nature—underlies every great work of fiction; dramatic literature hinges upon the gravity of the free choices, however limited, of characters. But agents do not act in a vacuum; instead, their acts are embedded within an external order of nature and other agents. In that larger context, many things happen apart from, and even against, the intentions of particular agents. Yet chance events can contribute to the narrative shape of events not just in the sense that they alter the course of events in unanticipated ways but also in the sense that they seem over the course of time to constitute a new sort of order. The repetition of chance events that seem to align in an intelligible way raises the question of whether something other and higher than mere chance is at work. It raises the question of providence, the very possibility proposed by Gandalf in his conversation with Frodo.

Of course, the ending of the entire story confirms Gandalf's suggestion about Smeagol/Gollum's role, but not in the way we might have anticipated; the shape of the story suggests that events are under the control of a benign providence that brings good out of evil. Followed by Smeagol/Gollum in their journey to Mordor, Frodo and Sam eventually enlist his help in guiding them along paths unknown to them but known to Smeagol/Gollum because of his previous journey to Mordor. Jackson does a marvelous job in the physical portrayal of Gollum and even more in portrayal of his divided will. Perhaps because of his own growing sense of the burden of the ring, Frodo has increasing sympathy for Gollum and takes up the habit of calling him by his original name, Smeagol. The attempt to remind him of what he was and might be again seems to inspire hope in Smeagol/Gollum. In contrast to Frodo's disposition, Sam expresses increasing distrust and hatred of Gollum. In an especially compelling scene, Jackson captures the Smeagol/Gollum divide by showing Smeagol/Gollum in an argument with himself, as one side of his personality vies with the other. The camera angles make it look as if there were two distinct individuals facing one another in a hostile way. Gollum tries to tear down not only Smeagol's trust in Frodo but also Smeagol's incipient confidence in his own ability to convert from evil. He shouts accusingly at him, "Murderer!"

The arduous demands of the journey, the lack of food, the increasing threat of Sauron's minions, and mounting suspicions within their own group exacerbate the tensions among Sam, Frodo, and Smeagol/Gollum. The strain shows on the faces of Frodo and Sam. They manage in the end to fulfill the goal of destroying the ring and thus to defeat Sauron, but not in the way that was planned. At the last moment, as he stands above the fires of Mordor, Frodo cannot bring himself to part with the ring; he puts it on even as Sam urges him to destroy it. Just at that moment, Gollum reappears, attacks the invisible Frodo, finds his ring finger, and bites it off. Now holding the ring and with an expression of demented glee on his face, Gollum jumps jubilantly on a ledge above the flames of Mordor, trips, and falls into the consuming flames. As the ring melts in the fire, Sauron's eye dissolves into nothingness. The good end comes about in direct opposition to the intention of the agents involved; that, in a narrative as deliberately planned as Tolkien's, is sure confirmation that a transcendent providence is at work.

Among the many achievements of Jackson's trilogy, his display of the humor of the book has to rank very highly. The dialogue between characters captures Tolkien's witty repartee. For example, toward the end of the film, Aragorn counters Gandalf's despairing prediction of defeat by urging his comrades to run directly toward enemy forces. He hopes thereby to turn Sauron's eye to the field of battle and away from Mordor and the hobbits. In response, the high-spirited dwarf Gimli deadpans with a smirk, "Certainty of death, small chance of success, what are we waiting for?" The plot works. Sauron turns his attention to the battle, and the hobbits make their way with the ring to the fires of Mordor. Auden's review of the book contains an apt comment about this scene and what it tells us about the nature of evil. He writes, "Evil . . . has every advantage but one—it is inferior in imagination. Good can imagine the possibility of becoming evil—hence the refusal of Gandalf and Aragorn to use the Ring—but Evil, defiantly chosen, can no longer imagine anything but itself. Sauron cannot imagine any motives except lust for domination and fear so that, when he has learned that his enemies have the Ring, the thought that they might try to destroy it never enters his head, and his eye is kept toward Gondor and away from Mordor and the Mount of Doom."[20]

Also impressive is the film's rendering of Tolkien's many fabulous creatures. One of the most entrancing is Jackson's creation of Treebeard, the member of the Ents from Fangorn Forest. It is exceedingly difficult to personify a tree without having it come off as camp; here Jackson manages to capture the gravity of Treebeard who eventually decides, along with his fellow Ents, to enter the battle against Saruman, Sauron's ally. After initially deciding to continue the policy of avoiding entanglements in the wars of other creatures, Treebeard comes upon a forest once populated by his friends but now devastated by the fires of Saruman. As they march on Isengard, the trees tear down the dam of a river and thus unleash a flood on Saruman's kingdom. Tolkien once quipped that he had constructed the scene of the marching trees out of disappointment with one of the final scenes in Shakespeare's *Macbeth*. He spoke of "the bitter disappointment and disgust from schooldays with the shabby use made in Shakespeare of the coming of 'Great Birnam Wood to high Dunsinane hill': I longed to devise a setting by which the trees might really march to war." However much he may have harbored reservations about that scene, his work shares with Shakespeare's *Macbeth* the insistence that acts contrary to nature bring about their own punishment. With trees and water overwhelming Isengard, the film makes clear that malefactors will end up undone by the very nature they had sought to violate.

The accent on nature in Tolkien has generated numerous ecological and environmental interpretations of *Lord of the Rings*. From the evidence of various interviews, this seems to be the interpretation favored by Peter Jackson and his actors. It holds that the difference between good and evil in *Lord of the Rings* hinges upon different relationships to nature, with the good existing in harmony with nature while the evil are indifferent or hostile to nature, using it as raw material to satisfy inordinate longings for greed and power. The interpretation finds support in the film and perhaps even more in the book. Greed is undeniably a deadly vice in *Lord of the Rings*; the Dwarves lust for riches in the mines of Moria awakens an ancient evil. Recall the scene in the film where the traitorous wizard Saruman, once friend and now nemesis of Gandalf, commands his underlings to destroy the trees to feed the fires he needs to forge a new creature, a mixture of human and Orc. What ensues is a panoramic shot of massive deforestation.

But the ecological interpretation, especially if it is understood in a standard liberal way, misses the mark. The greatest danger is not the depletion of natural resources but the moral destruction of the human species and other rational species. Tolkien's heroes are not autonomous creators but those who humbly embrace their role within a natural and even a supernatural order not of their own devising. Saruman's cloning project, his attempt to remake life, even human life, in his own image and likeness, or at least to serve his own needs, mirrors the project of Sauron himself, who is animated by a "will to dominate all life." Is there a contemporary analogue to this? Certainly. It is already underway in the proclamation of a disembodied sexual liberty, in the practice of selective abortion, and in the push for greater freedom in genetic experimentation, which even includes cloning. Of course, these practices are pursued not in the manner of Sauron, out of a malevolent intention to dominate the world; instead, their supporters appeal to progress, freedom, and compassion. But the presence of the best of intentions, if we are to take seriously the teaching of *Lord of the Rings*, in no way ensures that we will not wreak a great and terrible evil.

The philosophical and theological understanding of nature and the human person implicit in Tolkien's *Lord of the Rings* is articulated in quite fresh ways in recent Catholic encyclicals. Both John Paul II and Benedict XVI advocate a close link between natural ecology and moral ecology, between environmental conservation and the preservation of a culture befitting the dignity of human persons. Both popes trace the roots of our current environmental quandary to problems of anthropology. So confusion about our use of natural goods reflects confusion about the human good. But is the converse true? Can we trace the erosion of moral culture to a failure in our attitudes toward the external world? Benedict affirms the reciprocal influence explicitly in *Caritas in Veritate*: "The way humanity treats the environment influences the way it treats itself, and vice versa."[21]

The recovery of that understanding of human nature provides an alternative to the Enlightenment exaltation of human beings above nature and romantic submersion of human persons within nature.

Having lost the sense of natural order, we veer from one extreme to its opposite in our attitude toward nature. As Benedict observes, "we end up either considering nature as an untouchable taboo or, on the contrary, abusing it. Neither attitude is consonant with the Christian vision of nature as the fruit of God's creation."[22] We vacillate between, on the one hand, an Enlightenment view—what Benedict calls the Promethean view—that exalts human beings above nature as raw material at our disposal and, on the other, a view that engulfs humans within nature—what Benedict calls a new pantheism and John Paul decries as an "egalitarian" claim about the dignity of all living beings. Twentieth-century American poet Robinson Jeffers, who was both an environmentalist and a sort of modern pantheist, labeled this view "inhumanism."

Jeffers and others may well object to the language of the dignity of man because they see in that very terminology an invitation to human tyranny over nature. Dignity indicates a certain distinctive stature. As Kant put it, only the rational creature has dignity and merits being treated as an end in itself; everything else has a price. While Kant did not draw this conclusion, one might infer from this conception of human dignity that the human person has the freedom to do whatever he or she wishes with everything that is not human.

But this is not the church's understanding of human dignity. As John Paul II made splendidly clear in *Veritatis Splendor*, the Catholic understanding of human dignity is not rooted in an absolute autonomy but in a participated theonomy. As Thomas Aquinas puts it, human persons are "ruled rulers." Between the extremes of Promethean manipulation and romantic inhumanism is the integral humanism of Benedict XVI, a humanism rooted in "biblical anthropology," which depicts human creatures as custodian of the environment, as having "dominion" over the earth (Gen 1:28, Wis 9:1, and Ps 8:6-8).

Increasingly in the modern world, we are inclined to treat both external nature and our very selves as property that we have the right to dispose of however we wish. The popes see the roots of this attitude in the transformation of the attitudes toward nature in the early modern period. In a wonderful address to a conference on environment and health, delivered in March 1997, John Paul II spoke of the tension between environment as "resource" and environment as "home," the former of which increasingly threatens the latter. Strains of modern science, aiming at "power over nature," and economics, the conception of nature as raw material for "unlimited profit seeking," preclude the possibility of encountering nature in a contemplative mode, as a source of wonder and admiration. Early modern philosopher and scientist René Descartes famously proclaimed that his method would "render us masters and possessors of nature." In the fields of politics and economics, John Locke, in his hugely influential discussion of property, goes so far as to claim that "each man has property in his own person." The chief danger with modern laissez-faire capitalism is not profit or the market but the way it conspires with the decline in cultural mores to insinuate itself into all aspects of life.

Attentiveness to what John Paul II and Benedict XVI say about the environment reveals both a philosophically astute analysis of modernity and a perceptive account of the intimate link between how we understand and treat the environment and the human person, the natural and the human. Tolkien has much in common with this vision. That is not to say that he simply dismisses the impulses that motivate, or the insights that inform, romanticism. He embraces the rich return to nature, the critique of the Enlightenment, and the central role of the moral imagination in human life, but he does so without lapsing into the various dichotomies so often celebrated in romanticism.

Tolkien's work is postromantic and postmodern. As we have seen repeatedly in this book, nihilism arises from the demise of the Enlightenment project, the decline in the credibility of its boasts to rational necessity and linear progress. Irrational, unpredictable chance seems to rule in the wake of pristine order. But chance, as is perhaps most powerfully evident in *Lord of the Rings*, opens the possibility of a higher order, an order apprehended through myth and religious faith rather than reductionist science. Thus does the theological quest make a surprising reappearance at modernity's end.

As Auden's comments indicate, *Lord of the Rings* addresses the central concerns of the modern age about good and evil and about the threat of the vanishing of purposeful living. Its impact on our current culture is less in its written than in its visual form. What, in recent years, Harry Potter has been in the medium of writing, *Lord of the Rings* is in the medium of visual art: a compelling antidote to nihilism.

8

FEELS LIKE the MOVIES

In *Amusing Ourselves to Death*, Neil Postman argues that the influence of TV on our contemporary mode of life is so thoroughgoing that it shapes us unconsciously, without our taking note of it. The role of TV in our daily lives seems wholly "natural." We rarely advert to the phenomenon of TV itself, its mode of communication; instead, we talk about what is on TV. Postman's insights are many, particularly about the unreflective way that visual media, especially TV and film, often operate on us. Yet he offers us little in the way of discrimination among the types of stories available to us on TV and in film. At times, Postman comes close to the totalizing and deterministic view of the culture industry that was once a centerpiece of Marxist cultural criticism.[1] The warnings about unconscious passivity are well taken; yet we need something more and different in the way of engagement with popular culture.

One of our finest living film critics, David Thomson shares some of Postman's worries about TV, a medium that proclaims there are all sorts of things happening to which you do not have "to pay attention" and in which you have no responsibility to "take part." As a counter, Thomson proposes an education in the moving image. He wonders, how many of us have had any "education in the nature of moving imagery, its grammar, its laws or lawlessness" or how can we be "expected to distinguish news from fantasy, art from deception?"[2]

Thomson is among a group of contemporary media critics, secular and religious, who stress the religious features of film. Assertions about the connection between film and religion range from claims (a) that films are largely about characters seeking one type of redemption or another, (b) that the phenomenon of watching film is a quasi-religious experience, with films providing a kind of ritual appropriate to religion, and (c) that the historical rise of film occurs at the moment in our cultural history when religion's public role is in rapid decline. These three strands can be seen in the writings of the contemporary culture commentators Godawa, Lyden, and Thomson.

In *Hollywood Worldviews*, Brian Godawa, a Christian and an award-winning screenwriter, aims to offer a path between the extreme groups in their attitude toward popular culture: "cultural gluttons," who mindlessly imbibe whatever form of entertainment comes their way, and "cultural anorexics," who fear a corrosive, secular culture and thus shun it entirely. Godawa counters that Christians need to engage in critical analysis and begin to watch films with "wisdom and discernment."[3] Godawa also argues that film as narrative is almost always about redemption.

A more ambitious thesis about the tie between film and religion can be found in John Lyden's *Film as Religion*.[4] Lyden argues that different films, like different religions, offer a pluralism of worldviews. There is no doubt something to this, but how much is unclear. If films offer religious experiences and yet are irreducibly pluralistic in their vision, then it is hard to see how the ritual formation of believers could take place. With no central myth, one that is available repeatedly to a wide audience, films could at best suggest contradictory images and stories, so intermittent and so distant from the world of human action that they could not decisively shape our ways of being in the world. Lyden's argument for the overlap between film and religion works to the extent that religious experience itself becomes a spectator sport for consumers seeking consoling or intermittently inspiring entertainment.

In *The Whole Equation*, David Thomson focuses squarely on the problematic ethics of the moving visual image. Thomson is at once immersed in, fascinated with, and horrified by Hollywood. Unlike most contemporary critics of Hollywood, Thomson locates Hollywood's questionable influence on culture not in the late twentieth century with the rise in explicit violence and sexuality but in its glory days. He focuses on the "enormous . . . tidal pull toward new dreams" and the consequent and far-reaching "romantic transformation" wrought by the influence of film and TV in the twentieth century.

As viewers, he asks, are we "watching heightened things—great danger, great desirability, intense loveliness—without being tied by the responsibilities that attach to real onlookers?" "We are," he suggests, "like voyeurs, spies, or peeping toms."[5] In contrast to literature, which actively engages the imagination to probe the "meaning behind events," film involves the "fetishization of appearance." Film is less about glimpsing hidden meaning than about "what happens or appears next." It thus suffers from "the crushing restriction of visibility."[6]

Here Thomson puts his finger on the crucial ethical question regarding Hollywood, indeed regarding film itself as a cultural artifact. Hollywood film, "the professional craft of pretending," comes to the fore just as our sense of identity becomes "destabilized by the slippage of religious belief."[7] Hollywood offers its own "images to worship," as it reveals "rather ghastly fake gods." The new model for humanity becomes the actor, with his infinite variety. Still, Thomson sees much to engage in Hollywood's products, even if he is skeptical as to whether today's youth feel the "stealthy rapture" of film or are "inclined to take it seriously."[8]

What is or might be the "stealthy rapture" of film? It is the sense that a new world is opening up before our eyes. However much we might not directly articulate it, we are being moved by a story, by characters in which we ourselves are in some measure invested, and we might discover or rediscover some truth about ourselves. In this sense, for something to "feel like the movies" is to experience an enhancement of the possibilities for human life, an enlivening of the imagination, and an elevated expansion of human desire. In Walker Percy's *The Moviegoer*, the main character, Binx Bolling, a stockbroker and film fan who enjoys coastal drives in his MG and seducing his secretaries, has the intermittent sense that there is or could be something more to life. When this happens, he embarks, however briefly, on a quest.

What is the nature of the search? You ask. Really it is very simple, at least for a fellow like me so simple that it is easily overlooked. The search is what anyone would undertake if he were not sunk in the everydayness of his own life. This morning, for example, I felt as if I had come to myself on a strange land. And what does such a castaway do? Why, he pokes around the neighborhood and he doesn't miss a trick. To become aware of the possibility of the search is to be onto something. Not to be onto something is to be in despair.

Movies are onto the search, but they screw it up. Their search always ends in despair. They like to show a fellow coming to himself in a strange place—but what does he do? He takes up with the local librarian, sets about proving to the local children what a nice fellow he is, and settles down with a vengeance.[9]

Partly inspired by his habit of moviegoing, Binx has a glimmer of the quest. He is not in complete despair because, as Kierkegaard defines it in the epigraph to *The Moviegoer*, "the precise character of despair is this: it is unaware of being despair." Thomson thinks that contemporary film is even less likely than classic American film to produce or inspire characters like Binx. The mysteries present in great filmmaking have migrated further to the margins of the industry, which itself has moved steadily in the direction of attracting a young audience for whom camp, irony, endless motion, novelty, and spectacle are the real draws. Audiences now seem enraptured by special effects, by the "capacity of the visible to exceed reality" rather than illumine it.

But here we must face the problem of culture itself. As Eagleton observes, "Culture becomes the new absolute, bottom-line, conceptual end-stop, or transcendental signifier. Culture is not able to fill the role of an ersatz religion, which is one reason the idea of culture has come under so much strain in the last couple of centuries."[10] The cultivation of memory, of our link to the past, is no longer something that comes naturally to us. It takes conscious effort, and given the options, it is an onerous task that can too easily be seen as constricting our freedom. And what we encounter is too often transformed beyond recognition. In "The Crisis in Culture," Hannah Arendt notes that because the "entertainment industry must offer new commodities," it "ransacks the entire range of past and present culture," for material which in turn "must be altered" from its original form "in order to become entertaining."[11]

The deeper problem with our culture is this: the hippest, the cleverest, and the most humorous films and television series are laced with references to pop culture itself, as if there were no world beyond that culture. The title of this chapter comes from the popular song "Iris" by the Goo Goo Dolls: "when everything feels like the movies, you bleed just to know you're alive." The self-lacerating violence described in the lines from "Iris" can result from a despairing sense of unreality brought on by the insight that the real is unreal. Many of the most popular Hollywood products are self-consuming artifacts, where the only model of human excellence is the skimming ironic mode of detached, clever humor about pop culture itself. Thus, culture no longer points beyond itself but becomes involuted, specializing in the self-canceling insights of those who are in on the endless litany of allusions to its own constructs.

If works of art do not allow for the sort of self-awareness that suggests ways of transcending the world we have made, the givenness of convention, then all we are left with is an impotent self-consciousness. If everything is artifice, with no intelligible guiding purpose behind it, the very notion of nature becomes inconceivable and there is nothing independent of conventions and preferences to which we might appeal. Art becomes narcissistically turned in upon itself, unable to provide any insight into an order not of its own devising. Such a conception of culture easily reduces to an understanding of human life in terms of aesthetic self-creation, the Nietzschean problematic with which we began and whose nihilistic tendencies we have detailed.

The spectacle of the self-canceling insights of self-made humanity is by turns amusing, captivating, enervating, and horrifying. Dare we add instructive? Do we not witness all around us the astonishing consequences of our attempt to become masters and possessors not just of external nature but also of our very selves?

Of course, our best artists see the predicament, and some of them see beyond the self-imposed limitations of a self-enclosed culture. In most cases, what they offer is not a grand, comprehensive vision of human life but rather what Flannery O'Connor calls "limited revelation." She writes,

> Unless we are willing to accept our artists as they are, the answer to who speaks for America today will have to be the advertising agencies. They show us our unparalleled prosperity and our almost classless society. They could never be accused of not being affirmative. Where the artist is still to be trusted, he will not be looked to for assurance. Those who believe art proceeds from a healthy and not a diseased faculty of mind will take what he shows them as a revelation, not of what we ought to be but of what we are at a given time and under given circumstances, that is, as a limited revelation but a revelation nonetheless.[12]

O'Connor is not urging artists to abdicate their traditional role as revealers of truth about the human condition. The question concerns the scope and types of truth the artist is currently capable of displaying. O'Connor wants artists to resist the temptation to grasp for comprehensive, affirmative visions where only negations and partial insights are possible.

Novelist, scriptwriter, and sometimes film critic Graham Greene thought it was a mistake to denigrate film because of the democratic tastes it sought to meet. "Cinema," he wrote, "has to appeal to millions." Its "popularity is a virtue not to be rejected as vile."[13] In all his work, Greene moved with ease between written words and moving images, between high and low culture, between philosophical and theological questions and popular film. Sustaining the link between high and low, between the popular and the elite, is crucial to the vitality of any artistic culture. The nation's leading philosophical commentator on film, Harvard's Stanley Cavell, notes that while we lack "a common inheritance of high culture," the study of film and philosophy allows us "to move between high and low, caring about each also from the vantage of the other."[14]

Cavell's philosophical approach to film is through ordinary language philosophy; the accent is on film as probing the same sort of questions that arise for ordinary human persons about the shape, meaning, and significance of their lives. Such an approach presupposes that art and cultural artifacts are not coextensive with human life; they do not exhaust the purpose and meaning of human life. The approach allows us to see film as offering a limited revelation, significant, in some cases indispensable, but limited. Such an inquiry into philosophy and film might lead us back to a proper understanding of culture. Its origins, as Hannah Arendt points out, are Roman. The Latin verb *colere* means "to cultivate, to dwell, to take care, to tend and preserve." Culture as cultivation involves a "loving care" that contrasts with "all efforts to subject nature to the domination of man."[15]

The notion of culture as cultivation, of both the earth and the human soul, calls to mind Tolkien's *Lord of the Rings*. In that vision, environmental and moral ecology complement one another. With the possibility of a few other select examples, *Lord of the Rings* may be the exception that proves O'Connor's rule concerning the impossibility of anything other than limited revelation. Only in the rare cases where mythic discourse rises to the level of premodern literature is something more than a limited revelation feasible.

Limited revelations, tragic and comic, will provide the ordinary artistic sustenance in our time. For a comic example, we might return to Woody Allen, whose thoughts on nihilism and its relationship to film initiated our investigation. The film *Play It Again, Sam* (1972) opens with Woody's character, Allan Felix, sitting alone in a movie theater, enraptured at the final scene at the airport in *Casablanca*. In this film as in others, Allen plays the overly self-conscious failed wooer of women. Longing to be Bogart, he conjures up an imaginary Bogey to advise him in his relations with women. Much of the humor in the film derives from the contrast between Bogey's tough guy nobility and Allan's awkward, timorous mediocrity. The contrast is palpable in the scene in which Allen comes closest to playing Bogart, the final scene of the film when he invokes the parting words of Rick (Bogart) to Ilsa (Ingrid Bergman) and then admits, "I've waited my whole life to say that." The risible distance of Allan Felix from Humphrey

Bogart in no way annuls the encomium to *Casablanca* in *Play It Again, Sam*. If everything could feel like *Casablanca*, Woody Allen's character might plea, how much the better for our lives. For life to feel like the movies in this case is to the greater good of life. To varying degrees and in varying ways, that is still possible in our time, and for that we should be grateful.

NOTES

CHAPTER 1

1   Woody Allen, "Whatever Works," *Commonweal*, April 15, 2010, http://common
wealmagazine.org/woody.

2   In a piece titled "Murder and Nihilism," Mike Santa Rita comments on the appli-
cability to prison life of the powerful depiction of nihilism in the novels of Dostoevsky: "not having a future, not having something to look forward to, breeds
nihilism in my opinion." http://www.explorehoward.com (April 21, 2009).

3   Friedrich Nietzsche, *The Portable Nietzsche*, trans. Walter Kaufmann (New York:
Viking Press, 1954), 129.

4   See Andrew Delbanco, *The Real American Dream: A Meditation on Hope* (Cambridge,
Mass.: Harvard University Press, 2000).

5   Nietzsche, *The Portable Nietzsche*, 129–30.

6   Friedrich Nietzsche, *Beyond Good and Evil*, trans. Walter Kaufmann (New York:
Vintage Books, 1966), #201.

7   Nietzsche, *Beyond Good and Evil*, #225.

8   Friedrich Nietzsche, *The Will to Power*, trans. Walter Kaufmann (New York: Vintage Books, 1967), #125.

9   Nietzsche, *Beyond Good and Evil*, #13.

10 Nietzsche, *The Will to Power*, #32.

11 Nietzsche, *The Will to Power*, #9.

12 Nietzsche, *The Will to Power*, #22.

13 Roger Shattuck, *Forbidden Knowledge: From Prometheus to Pornography* (New York:
St. Martin's Press, 1996), 227–99.

14 Shattuck, *Forbidden Knowledge*, 280.

15   Nietzsche, *The Will to Power*, #2.

16   Nietzsche, *The Will to Power*, #4.

17   Nietzsche, *The Will to Power*, #12.

18   Nietzsche, *The Will to Power*, #55.

19   Nietzsche, *The Will to Power*, #15.

20   Nietzsche, *The Will to Power*, #55.

21   See Peter Berkowitz, *Nietzsche: The Ethics of an Immoralist* (Cambridge, Mass.: Harvard University Press, 1995).

22   Alexis de Tocqueville, *Democracy in America*, trans. George Lawrence (New York: Anchor Books, 1969), author's preface to vol. 1.

23   See Nicholas Christopher, *Somewhere in the Night: Film Noir and the American City* (New York: Free Press, 1997); J. P. Telotte, *Voices in the Dark: The Narrative Patterns of Film Noir* (Urbana: University of Illinois Press, 1989).

24   Christopher, *Somewhere in the Night*, 20.

25   Telotte, *Voices in the Dark*, 17 and 86. Throughout this book, unless otherwise noted emphasis is in the original.

26   Telotte, *Voices in the Dark*, 87.

27   Telotte, *Voices in the Dark*, 220–22.

28   Friedrich Nietzsche, *The Genealogy of Morals*, trans. F. Golffing (New York: Anchor Books, 1956), 191.

29   John Rawls, Robert Nozick, Thomas Scanlon, Judith Jarvis Thomson, and Ronald Dworkin, "Assisted Suicide: The Philosopher's Brief," *New York Review of Books*, March 29, 1997, 41–47.

30   Cornel West, *Race Matters* (New York: Vintage Books, 1993), 17–31.

31   Tocqueville, *Democracy in America*, 11.

32   Tocqueville, *Democracy in America*, 336.

33   Tocqueville, *Democracy in America*, vol. 2, chap. 2.

34   Walker Percy, *Love in the Ruins* (New York: Ballantine, 1971), 191.

35   Walter Gilbert, 1986, quoted in Shattuck, *Forbidden Knowledge*, 178.

36   René Descartes, *Discourse on Method*, trans. Donald A. Cress (Indianapolis: Hackett, 1998), pt. 2, 11.

37   Mark Edmundson, *Nightmare on Main Street: Angels, Sadomasochism, and the Culture of the Gothic* (Cambridge, Mass.: Harvard University Press, 1997).

38   Roger Scruton, *Death-Devoted Heart: Sex and the Sacred in Wagner's Tristan and Isolde* (New York: Oxford University Press, 2003).

39   See M. A. Gillespie, *Nihilism before Nietzsche* (Chicago: University of Chicago Press, 1995).

40   René Descartes, *Meditations*, trans. Donald A. Cress (Indianapolis: Hackett, 1998), I.

41   Thomas Hobbes, *Leviathan*, ed. Edwin Curley (Indianapolis: Hackett, 1994), chap. 31.

CHAPTER 2

1　Jim Thompson, *The Getaway* (New York: Vintage Crime, 1958), 180.

2　William Peter Blatty, *The Exorcist* (New York: Harper & Row, 1971).

3　Walker Percy, *Lancelot* (New York: Farrar, Straus & Giroux, 1977), 53.

CHAPTER 3

1　Jacques Ellul, *The Technological Bluff* (Grand Rapids: Eerdmans, 1990), 351–52.

2　"Sam Mendes on 'Revolutionary Road,'" December 25, 2008. Interview recorded at http://www.javno.com/en/celebrities/clanak.php?id=218296.

3　Indeed, Mendes fails to grasp the irony of Yates' book, in which the author never takes the self-interpretation of the characters at face value. See Adelle Waldman, "Blaming the Burbs," *The New Republic Online*, December 22, 2008.

4　Wendell Berry, *Sex, Economy, Freedom, and Community* (New York: Pantheon Books, 1994), 143.

5　Berry, *Sex, Economy, Freedom, and Community*, 140.

6　Berry, *Sex, Economy, Freedom, and Community*, 125.

7　See Jeffrey Wells, "Romanian Masterpiece," *Hollywood Elsewhere*, October 23, 2007. http://www.hollywood-elsewhere.com/2007/10/roumanian_maste.php.

8　Paul O'Neill, "The Only Rebellion Around," *Life*, November 30, 1959.

9　René Girard, *I See Satan Fall Like Lightning* (Maryknoll, N.Y.: Orbis Books, 2001), 10–11.

10　Harry Stein, "What *Mad Men* Gets Wrong: The Fifties, a Decade of Forgotten Loyalty, Honor, and Patriotism," *City Journal* (2009). http://city-journal.org/2009/19_4_snd-the-fifties.html.

11　Berry, *Sex, Economy, Freedom, and Community*, 135–36.

12　Berry, *Sex, Economy, Freedom, and Community*, 122.

CHAPTER 4

1　James Edwards, *The Plain Sense of Things: The Fate of Religion in an Age of Normal Nihilism* (University Park: Pennsylvania State University Press, 1997), 46.

2　Edwards, *The Plain Sense of Things*, 52.

3　Edwards, *The Plain Sense of Things*, 227–38.

4　Geoffrey O'Brien, "Sein of the Times," *The New York Review of Books*, August 14. 1997.

CHAPTER 5

1　Ray Pride in *The Reeler*, December 26, 2006. http://www.thereeler.com.

2　Terry Eagleton, *Reason, Faith, and Revolution: Reflections on the God Debate* (New Haven: Yale University Press, 2010), 148.

3　As cited in "Loss of innocence: 'Forrest Gump' at 10," *The Boston Globe*, June 20,

2004.http://www.boston.com/ae/movies/articles/2004/06/20/loss_of_innocence_forrest_gump_at_10?pg=2.

4   Eagleton, *Reason, Faith, and Revolution*, 96.

5   Jean-Jacques Rousseau, *Discourse on the Origin of Inequality*, trans. Donald Cress (Indianapolis: Hackett, 1992), 70.

6   Scruton, *Death-Devoted Heart*, 7. Both in Britain and in the United States, Roger Scruton is a leading conservative voice. That his book is an unqualified celebration of the Wagnerian vision is surely a sign of the degree to which contemporary conservatives can be seduced by the romantic vision.

7   Camillle Paglia, *Sexual Personae* (New Haven: Yale University Press, 1990), 23.

8   Simon Schama, *Citizens: A Chronicle of the French Revolution* (New York: Vintage Books, 1990), 861.

9   Sheldon Wolin, *Tocqueville Between Two Worlds* (Princeton: Princeton University Press, 2001), 566.

10   Eagleton, *Reason, Faith, and Revolution*, 39.

11   P. D. James, *The Children of Men* (New York: Warner Books, 1992), 7.

12   James, *The Children of Men*, 11.

13   James, *The Children of Men*, 167.

14   Ray Pride in *The Reeler*, December 26, 2006. http://www.thereeler.com.

15   James, *The Children of Men*, 79.

16   James, *The Children of Men*, 15.

17   James, *The Children of Men*, 73.

18   Ralph Wood, "Rapidly Rises the Morning Tide: An Essay on P. D. James' *The Children of Men*," *Theology Today* 51 (1994): 277–88.

19   James, *The Children of Men*, 282.

CHAPTER 6

1   Andrew Delbanco, *The Death of Satan: How Americans Have Lost the Sense of Evil* (New York: The Noonday Press, 1996), 3.

2   The series consists of the following books by J. K. Rowling: *Harry Potter and the Sorcerer's Stone* (New York: Scholastic, 1998); *Harry Potter and the Chamber of Secrets* (New York: Scholastic, 2000); *Harry Potter and the Prisoner of Azkaban* (New York: Scholastic, 2001); *Harry Potter and the Goblet of Fire* (New York: Scholastic, 2001); *Harry Potter and the Order of the Phoenix* (New York: Scholastic, 2004); *Harry Potter and the Half-Blood Prince* (New York: Scholastic, 2006); *Harry Potter and the Deathly Hallows* (New York: Scholastic, 2007).

3   Rowling, *Sorcerer's Stone*, 291.

4   Hannah Arendt, *Eichmann in Jerusalem: A Report on the Banality of Evil* (New York: Viking Press, 1965).

5   Hannah Arendt, "Eichmann in Jerusalem: An Exchange of Letters between Gershom Scholem and Hannah Arendt," in *The Jew as Pariah*, ed. R. H. Fieldman (New York: Grove Press, 1978), 250–51.

6 Arendt, "Eichmann in Jerusalem," 250–51.

7 Arendt, "Eichmann in Jerusalem," 250–51.

8 Nicholas Christopher, *Somewhere in the Night: Film Noir and the American City* (New York: Free Press, 1997).

9 John Lawrence and Robert Jewett, *The Myth of the American Superhero* (Grand Rapids, Mich.: Eerdmans, 2002).

10 Delbanco, *The Death of Satan*, 231.

11 Nietzsche, *The Will to Power*, #15, #55.

12 Rowling, *Sorcerer's Stone*, 293.

13 Rowling, *Sorcerer's Stone*, 85.

14 Rowling, *Sorcerer's Stone*, 253.

15 Rowling, *Sorcerer's Stone*, 258.

16 Delbanco, *The Death of Satan*, 231.

17 Rowling, *Chamber of Secrets*, 319.

18 Rowling, *Chamber of Secrets*, 321.

19 Rowling, *Goblet of Fire*, 643.

20 Rowling, *Sorcerer's Stone*, 121.2

21 Rowling, *Prisoner of Azkaban*, 213.

22 Rowling, *Chamber of Secrets*, 332–33.

23 Rowling, *Goblet of Fire*, 211–12.

24 Rowling, *Prisoner of Azkaban*, 393.

25 Rowling, *Sorcerer's Stone*, 298.

26 Rowling, *Sorcerer's Stone*, 282–83.

27 Rowling, *Sorcerer's Stone*, 297.

28 Rowling, *Sorcerer's Stone*, 305.

29 Rowling, *Sorcerer's Stone*, 306.

30 Later versions, *Goblet of Fire*, directed by Mike Newell, *Order of the Phoenix, Half-Blood Prince*, and the two-part *Deathly Hallows*, have been better than Columbus' wooden efforts but inferior to Cuarón's film.

31 Rowling, *Prisoner of Azkaban*, 83.

32 Rowling, *Prisoner of Azkaban*, 384.

33 Alan Jacobs, "Harry Potter's Magic," *First Things* 99 (January 2000): 35–38.

34 Rowling, *Sorcerer's Stone*, 213.

35 Rowling, *Sorcerer's Stone*, 300.

36 Rowling, *Sorcerer's Stone*, 297.

37 Rowling, *Sorcerer's Stone*, 299.

38 Rowling, *Sorcerer's Stone*, 299.

39 Rowling, *Prisoner of Azkaban*, 427.

40   Rowling, *Deathly Hallows*, 328.

41   Rowling, *Half-Blood Prince*, 652.

42   Rowling, *Half-Blood Prince*, 502.

43   Rowling, *Half-Blood Prince*, 592.

44   Rowling, *Deathly Hallows*, 326.

CHAPTER 7

1   Edwards, *The Plain Sense of Things*, 46.

2   Percy, *Love in the Ruins*, 3.

3   Edmundson, *Nightmare on Main Street*, 61–67.

4   Edmundson, *Nightmare on Main Street*, 178.

5   Jeffrey Overstreet, "Dumping Out the Big Toybox," The *Image* Blog, December 18, 2009. http://imagejournal.org/page/blog/dumping-out-the-toybox.

6   David Hume, *Dialogues Concerning Natural Religion* in *Classics of Western Philosophy*, 4th ed., ed. Steven M. Cahn (Indianapolis: Hackett, 1997), 942.

7   See the discussion of Christopher Hitchens and Richard Dawkins in Eagleton, *Reason, Faith, and Revolution*. We will discuss this book in following sections.

8   Adrienne L. McLean, "Media Effects: Marshall McLuhan, Television Culture, and 'The X-Files,'" *Film Quarterly* 51, no. 4 (1982): 2–9.

9   Bernard Williams, *Truth and Truthfulness: An Essay in Genealogy* (Princeton: Princeton University Press, 2002), 1.

10   Simon Blackburn, *Truth: A Guide* (Oxford: Oxford University Press, 2005), xiv.

11   Dan Brown, *The Da Vinci Code* (New York: Doubleday, 2003), 1.

12   The text of his Terry Lectures at Yale, Eagleton's book merits attention both for its hilarious send-up of the pompous Ditchkens and for its less successful attempt to infuse revolutionary politics with the spirit of the gospel.

13   Eagleton, *Reason, Faith, and Revolution*, 6.

14   Eagleton, *Reason, Faith, and Revolution*, 27.

15   Eagleton, *Reason, Faith, and Revolution*, 16.

16   Eagleton, *Reason, Faith, and Revolution*, 166.

17   Eagleton, *Reason, Faith, and Revolution*, 93.

18   W. H. Auden, "At the End of the Quest, Victory," *The New York Times Book Review*, January 22, 1956.

19   For a balanced assessment of the film on its own terms and in relation to Tolkien's text, see Greg Wright, *Peter Jackson in Perspective: The Power behind Cinema's* The Lord of the Rings (Hollywood, Calif.: Jesus Books, 2004).

20   Auden, "At the End of the Quest, Victory."

21 Pope Benedict XVI, *Caritas in Veritate* (San Francisco: Ignatius Press, 2009), ch. 4, §51.

22 Benedict, *Caritas in Veritate*, ch. 4, §52.

CHAPTER 8

1 Max Horkheimer and Theodor Adorno, *Dialectic of Enlightenment: Cultural Memory in the Present* (Stanford, Calif.: Stanford University Press, 2007).

2 David Thomson, *The Whole Equation: A History of Hollywood* (New York: Vintage Books, 2006), 296.

3 Brian Godawa, *Hollywood Worldviews: Watching Films with Wisdom and Discernment* (Downers Grove, Ill.: InterVarsity, 2009).

4 John Lyden, *Film as Religion: Myths, Morals, and Rituals* (New York: New York University Press, 2003).

5 Thomson, *The Whole Equation*, 49.

6 Thomson, *The Whole Equation*, 98.

7 Thomson, *The Whole Equation*, 74.

8 Thomson, *The Whole Equation*, 157.

9 Walker Percy, *The Moviegoer* (New York: Alfred A. Knopf, 1961), 18.

10 Eagleton, *Faith, Reason, and Revolution*, 158–59.

11 Hannah Arendt, *Between Past and Future* (Cleveland: Meridian Books, 1961), 207.

12 Flannery O'Connor, "The Fiction Writer and His Country," in *Collected Works* (New York: Library of America Classics, 1988), 806.

13 *The Graham Greene Film Reader*, ed. David Parkinson (New York: Applause Books, 1995), 414.

14 Stanley Cavell, "The Thought of Movies," in *Themes Out of School: Effects and Causes* (Chicago: University of Chicago Press, 1983), 8.

15 Arendt, *Between Past and Future*, 211–12.

INDEX TO MOVIES AND
TELEVISION SHOWS

INDEX TO PEOPLE, BOOKS, AND SUBJECTS